Breakthrough

Breakthrough

Taking the Gospel Across Forbidden Borders

by
Rudi Lack
with June Dooney

GLIFA, Good Literature For All
3704–Krattigen, Switzerland

Breakthrough

Taking the Gospel Across Forbidden Borders

Copyright © 1999 by Rudi Lack

Cover design by
Bryce Wagner

Published by
GLIFA, Good Literature For All
3704–Krattigen, Switzerland.
Tel/Fax: 0041 33 654 74 76
E-mail: 100555.734@compuserve.com

Printed by
PICORP in Minsk, Russia.

ISBN 3-906589-04-8

*To all those who partnered with me
over the years in spreading the
Good News on every continent.*

Acknowledgments

WRITING a book is a team effort, and I would like to acknowledge the members of that work group.

First and foremost, there is June Dooney, who crafted and polished the manuscript. Special thanks also go to Laurel Ace, who took my written building blocks and not only put them together, but also knocked them further into shape. Godfrey Dooney, June's husband, made us comfortable as we worked long hours and days, providing a writer's haven for the team. Then there are editors and readers who made helpful suggestions before we went to print.

Many thanks to them all.

Krattigen,
May 1999

Contents

1

A Seed Planted

A gray army truck roared into the missionary compound. Dust belching from its tires, it screeched to a halt beside my van and disgorged a dozen gun-toting African soldiers, all dressed in camouflage-combat uniforms. Accompanying them were three communist Chinese. Dr. Durrie and I stared in disbelief. "Hands up!" roared a burly-faced African officer, brandishing his gun in my face. My arms shot up automatically.

"Don't even think of running away!" the tough-faced officer sneered. Nothing was further from my thoughts. My heart raced. My muscles, already tense from my long day's drive in this central African country of Zambia, trembled from the sudden surge of adrenaline. Dr. Durrie, who had been pushed roughly to my left, stood by helplessly. Slowly the reality of my predicament filtered through my befuddled brain. I must have been followed. Someone had reported me!

"Where are your papers?!" shouted the African commanding officer, pointing his gun at me. Too traumatized to speak, I pointed weakly in the direction of my white Volkswagen van. "Go, get them!" he snarled.

"Rudi, trust the Lord. I'm sure he'll get you out of this," I heard Dr. Durrie whisper behind me. I appreciated his attempts to comfort me. But I was in real trouble; so big, I did not know if even God could get me out of it. In my wallet was a document declaring my status as a permanent resident of Rhodesia.

In 1975 there were no diplomatic relations between Zambia

and Rhodesia. The borders between these two nations were tightly closed. In order to get into Zambia from Rhodesia, I had taken an obscure route via Botswana. Had the customs officer at the border on the Zambezi River where I had entered known I was a Rhodesian resident, he would never have let me in. I had only shown him my Swiss passport and that had no record of the months I had spent in Rhodesia. Evidence of my Rhodesian residence was in a separate document. It was the paper of residence that posed my danger. If the soldiers found it, they would be certain to accuse me of spying for Rhodesia. Given their mood, they would probably shoot first and ask questions later!

Somehow I managed to persuade my legs to move. My hands shook uncontrollably as I tried to fit the key into the lock. I finally managed to get it open, and still trembling I picked up my wallet from the van. The soldiers were watching my every move. There was no way I could discard the incriminating paper of residence. *Lord, please get me out of this hopeless predicament*, I desperately prayed.

"Get on board," the soldier in battle fatigue ordered. My heart still beating wildly, I climbed onto the rear of the open army truck. From the grit and dust, I surmised it had been used to cart shingle for the Tan–Zam railway project. Clearing aside the gravel, I sat down. My fate was sealed. African soldiers piled in behind me. A Chinese driver, in his ill-fitting Mao uniform, fired up the motor. But before we could take off, another truckload of African soldiers and Chinese officials came careening into the missionary compound. They screeched to a standstill beside us. One of the African soldiers yelled, "Wait! We need samples of everything this rascal has distributed!" The African beside me shoved me roughly off the truck. "Go and fetch them from your van!" I staggered slightly as my feet hit the ground, and gave an inward sigh of relief. Here was my chance to cover my tracks.

Going over to my van, I opened the back and began fumbling in one of the boxes of books I had stored there. I pretended to be searching for the samples the Chinese had demanded. In reality I opened my wallet and, keeping it hidden among the books, rummaged through its contents to find the incriminating Rhodesian residence paper. Grabbing the wanted samples, I shut the van door and turned back towards the truck. Behind me, safely buried under a pile of literature was the Rhodesian residence paper. I breathed a little easier. Now my wallet contained only my Swiss passport, and that had absolutely no trace of my stay in Rhodesia.

A soldier pushed me back onto the truck. Dr. Durrie stood watching. There was nothing he could do. I cast one last, longing glance at him as I climbed on board and collapsed on the truck floor. Two of the African soldiers, their guns at the ready, sat beside me. The other four stood clinging to the side, whilst the Chinese officials sat in the front. The truck shot forward, with the soldiers clutching the sides firmly. Where were we going? What would they do to me?

By now the sun had set. As we bumped along at a steady speed, the chilly night air swirled in the open truck, making me shiver. But it was more than physical cold; a dread chill of fear was settling into my bones. I felt nothing like a Rudolf....

* * * * *

Rudolf, shortened to Rudi, was the name my parents gave me. Both committed Christians, my father Hans Lack was the pastor of several Swiss evangelical churches. When I was born, the Second World War was at its height. Our hometown of Aarburg was situated in German-speaking Switzerland, only an hour's drive from the German border. There was a real possibility the Nazis would overrun us. Aware of the threat this posed to Bible-believing Christians, my parents did not give me a biblical name. Instead they called me Rudolf, which means "daring wolf". I am sure God directed their choice; for even from my earliest days, I demonstrated my love for adventure and daring.

We often had missionaries come and stay. As a young boy, I would sit enthralled, listening to their adventures in far-off countries with exotic-sounding names I could barely pronounce. I well remember one night when I was around five.

My parents had invited a missionary from Africa to come for

the evening meal. As the evening wore on, they somehow over-looked the fact they had a five-year-old in their midst. Everyone was so caught up in the suspense of the missionary's story that my bedtime came and went without anyone noticing. For my young mind, the excitement was almost unbearable. I was glued to the edge of my seat, nails dug into my palms as I tried to ima-gine what terrible thing would happen next. What an adventure! When I grew up, I too wanted to be a bold and daring missionary; one who would brave the wild lions of Africa, the whistling gales of the Antarctic, the blood-sucking leeches of the Amazon and take God's message of love to the peoples of the world.

"Rudi!" I jumped as my mother's voice intruded on my five-year-old imagination. "You should have been in bed hours ago!" All eyes in the room turned towards me. I groaned in dismay. Now I would never get to hear the end of the story. It was not fair!

Despite my protests, my mother insisted I go to bed. Perhaps she thought the story was not quite fitting for my youthful ears. I was marched along the hallway up the wooden stairs of our Swiss home and into my bedroom. My mother sighed as she looked at the building blocks and clothes scattered around the room. "We'll deal with this in the morning. Now put your pajamas on and into bed. I don't know how the time got away so quickly."

She tucked the duvet cover around me. I looked up at her with pleading eyes. Understanding my disappointment, she plonked her ample frame on the edge of my bed and tenderly tussled my crop of thick, dark brown hair. "Sorry, Rudi, but it's well past your bedtime. You know that." Even so, she still took time to offer her normal nightly prayer for me. Laying her hand gently on my shoulder, she shut her eyes. "God, I commit Rudi into your loving care. Look over him while he sleeps and help him to grow into a man of God, one who will take your message of love out to a lost and dying world. Amen." Leaning over she gave me a hug. Against my cheek, I could feel the smooth sides of her hair which was drawn back into a tightly knotted bun. I sensed her deep care for me and gave a sigh of resignation.

Turning out my bedside light, my mother softly tiptoed out

of the room, careful to avoid the scattered blocks, and returned to the dining room. I snuggled contented beneath my duvet. The faint murmur of voices in the dining room grew dimmer. Despite myself, my heavy lids were closing and within seconds I was in dreamland fording African rivers, fighting off lions with a long, poison-tipped spear and bravely talking to strange, dark-skinned people about God. The seed had been sown. One day I too would be a missionary. Then I would have my own stories to tell!

My childhood was fertile ground for such dreams. As a pastor's kid, I grew up in the church. Bible stories were as familiar to me as the worn furniture in my parent's home. Ours was not a well-to-do family. Often we could not afford butter on the table. In those post-war years, times were hard for Christians and non-Christians alike. But my parents demonstrated a reality of faith in God.

One Christmas when I was around seven, my heart was set on a yellow postal truck. In Switzerland, mail is always delivered in a yellow vehicle. An enterprising businessman had made a miniature wooden version for children. For weeks before Christmas, I prayed nightly that Jesus would let me have the dream four-wheeler as a present.

As was the custom in our Swiss German home, presents were laid at the foot of the tree during Christmas Eve. I spied a brightly wrapped oblong package with my name on it. I shook it. A heavy object moved inside. It had to be my yellow postal truck. I could not wait to begin playing with it. But I had a few agonizing hours to wait before our presents were opened. I fidgeted and only half listened when at 7pm my father began the ritual of Christmas by retelling the Bible narrative of Jesus' birth. All I could think of was my new yellow truck. Our time of carol singing seemed longer than usual and my father's prayer never ending. Finally it came time to open the gifts. I eagerly tore the wrapping off my oblong-shaped package. Disappointment flooded my heart when I looked inside the ripped paper. There instead of the yellow postal truck was a wooden, red fire engine.

"Isn't it great?" my father said, running the engine along our rug-covered, wooden floor. "Look, Rudi, it's off to put out a fire."

"And such a bright red color. Everyone can see it," my mother added. But their attempts to comfort me failed. I turned away pouting, refusing to play with the red fire engine, my child's faith shattered. I had prayed for weeks for a yellow postal truck. Had not my parents taught me God always hears and answers prayer? Why had he not answered mine?

My parents were as disappointed as I was. But on my dad's limited pastor's budget, such an expensive gift as a yellow postal truck was out of the question. This cheaper red fire engine was all they could afford. "Hans!" My mother suddenly turned to my father. "Remember, a few weeks ago a lady in the church gave us a package for Rudi and told us to put it away for Christmas. I had forgotten about it. Would you go and get it, please? Maybe it will distract Rudi for a while."

My dad went off and came back with another brightly wrapped package. "Here you are, Rudi." Neither my parents nor my older brother Hans nor my younger sister Esther knew what the package contained. They watched over my shoulder with curiosity. I opened my new gift. Peeling the paper off, I squealed with glee as I uncovered its contents. There was my shiny yellow postal truck.

Later, when my parents asked the giver of the gift how she had come to choose this particular present, she explained, "I was in the toy shop and had already selected a gift when I felt God tap me on the shoulder. *Buy the yellow postal truck for little Rudi.*" God had rewarded the simple faith of a young lad. From that moment on, I never had any doubt. I was convinced God cared about the things that mattered to me.

But I was no saint. I had a very bad temper. When things did not go my way, I flew into a fit of rage. I would bang doors, yell and scream. I was small for my age and my older brother Hans bigger than average, yet I still took him on. We often got into scraps and had some wrestling matches in a "to-the-death" style. I received many severe spankings from my father as a result of my tantrums. I would feel bad for a while and temporarily reform; but then someone would cross me or things would not go my way and I would flare up again.

One day when I was 12, my brother Hans and I were in our cellar, building a pushcart together. The white-painted, hewn stone room with its earthen floor served both as my father's work-shop and a garden shed. In the middle of our project, an argument broke out between us. Exerting his authority as the older brother, Hans pushed me aside. That only made me more irrational and wilder. I tried to grab the tool out of his hand.

"Give it to me," I demanded. Hans lifted it teasingly above his head, well out of my reach. My fury reached volcano pitch. I grabbed the nearest "instrument", a yellow-handled pair of garden pliers. "Give it to me or I'll kill you!" I barked, moving threateningly towards him. Although physically I was no match for him, Hans could see from my determined glare that this was no idle threat. I meant it. Staring at the pointed pliers that were only inches from his chest, he began to rapidly retreat.

I heard clattering feet as my mother came down the wooden stairs that led to the cellar from the kitchen, where she had been preparing our evening meal. She bustled into the room, wiping one hand on her apron and tucking a wayward strand of hair back into her immaculate bun with the other. She stopped dead in her tracks when she saw me with the pliers pointed at my brother. Like Hans, she too knew I meant business. The two of them quickly backed out the cellar and banged the door in my face. The key was turned in the lock.

I dropped the pliers and tried wrenching the heavy, wooden door. But it was no use. It was firmly shut. I kicked at it, screaming. Then realizing I was a prisoner of my own making, without a window even for escape, I sank to my knees on the cold, earthen floor and burst into tears. Gradually my temper abated and my loud sobs turned into cries of self-pity. "Rudi,..." my mother called in a voice of concern, from behind the closed cellar door. "Are you all right?"

"No," I sulked. How could I be okay in such a predicament? A mixture of emotions overcame me. I knew I was wrong. Why had I lost control? I loved my brother. I did not really want to kill him. I wanted to say, "I'm sorry." But I could not.

"Rudi, I'm sorry I teased you," Hans' repentant plea came through the door. "Will you forgive me?"

I longed to say, "Yes, I forgive you, Hans," and to tell him I really appreciated him as my big brother. Instead, I yelled out,

"No! I won't forgive you! Go away!"

By now my father had joined my mother and brother. They all tried pleading with me behind the locked door. I did not answer them. I retreated to the corner of the cellar by dad's workbench and sat on the wood-chip covered floor, sulking. By now a good half-hour had passed. I knew God was not pleased with the way I was acting. I really did want to do the right thing. I had heard enough of my father's sermons to know I needed to turn from my pride and selfishness. If I fully gave my life over to Jesus, I knew things would change. Yet I found that hard to do. Part of me still wanted to be in charge and run my own life. Why did I have to be so pigheaded?

I had struggled with my explosive stubbornness all my young life. Now down here in the pits of my cellar prison, I realized it was crunch time. The chips were literally down. Was I prepared to give in and let God take full control of my life, or was I going to continue going my own way and possibly have worse consequences to face in the future? Maybe next time I would not just threaten my brother. Perhaps my temper would so take hold of me that I would go through with the dastardly deed and actually kill him. I shuddered at the thought.

My mind was made up. I would give my life over to Jesus. "Dad, I'm ready to say I'm sorry," I said meekly through the cellar door. There was an audible sigh from my parents, who no doubt had been praying quietly during my hour-long vigil. They opened the door for me. Head down, not daring to look anyone in the eye, I silently followed my dad up the cellar steps to his book-lined study. There, I knelt by his wooden wicker chair and prayed, "Lord, I ask you to forgive me for my bad temper. Please come and take over my life." It was a simple request, but one made in deep sincerity. Quietness settled on me. At the same time, a deep assurance entered my young heart. I knew without a shadow of a doubt what my future would be. The dreams I had harbored as a kid were not the wild imaginations of youth. God wanted me to be a missionary.

My confidence in this conviction remained unwavering as I entered my teenage years. My peers often misunderstood my intense devotion to God. My uncompromising stand cost me friends. But I did not care. I knew where I was going. From my conversion to Christ at the age of 12, my direction was set. I was determined nothing would alter it.

When I was 14, our class teacher gave us a weekly assignment. "Each Monday morning starting next week, all of you are to give a 20-minute talk in front of the whole class. You are free to choose your own subject. It will be an exercise in elocution and delivery as well as content."

We all took the assignment seriously. Each Monday as a different student waxed eloquently for 20 minutes on their selected topic, from cars and sports to other predictable teenage subjects, I pondered on what I should talk about. Only one subject really interested me: missions. Since my decision to follow Jesus two years earlier, I had shared my faith with many of my classmates, but I had never talked to them as an entire group. Now, I decided, was my chance.

I spent hours in preparation. I even played a color documentary film on Africa to supplement my talk. I also prayed fervently for God to give me the right words. Even so, when my turn finally came and I stood up to speak, my knees were knocking. Fifteen youthful pairs of eyes were trained upon my slim, 14-year-old figure. There were a few bored snickers from the cynics in the class. I could almost read their minds. "Ten guesses what Rudi Lack will speak on—religion!" Undeterred, I plunged in.

"God wants to use us to change the world," I challenged them. "But first you need to make a personal commitment to him." You could have heard a pin drop. My classmates were knocked sideways by my bold words. Even my most cynical peers had nothing to say. Such an outspoken religious talk had never before been given.

The negative response came days later when I was barraged with snide remarks and forced to duck paper balls thrown at me with cruise-missile accuracy. It was my first experience in suffering for Christ. But rather than diminishing my faith, this opposition only made me more determined to follow God's call and serve him.

God, however, was not the only love of my life. I also had a passion for chemistry. I did not excel in sports and struggled with subjects such as French and algebra. I quite enjoyed geography, history and natural science, but chemistry was a subject where I excelled. Chemistry lessons were my favorite, so much so that I spent most of my free time mixing chemicals, packing them into metal tubes and lighting the fuse. I performed my experiments in our front garden. It gave me a tremendous buzz to see these contraptions fly off like rockets across our neighbor's garden and into the nearby field.

While I enjoyed chemistry, I had, however, never seriously considered it as a life career. I only had one direction in life. I was headed for the mission field. I was nearly 16 and nearing the end of my schooldays when my father called me into his study. Sitting down on the same wooden wicker chair where I had knelt four years earlier to make my commitment to Jesus, I glanced around at the well-thumbed theological books that lined my father's shelves. One day, I would be studying such books and unraveling their revelations about God and his ways.

"Rudi, there's something I want to talk to you about." The serious tone of my Dad's voice interrupted my thoughts and brought me to attention. Seated behind his large writing desk, my father looked at me intently through his soft, gray eyes. A little rotund around his midriff these days, he, like me, had been small and wiry in his youth. He was nearing his mid-forties and his once thick, brown hair was beginning to thin. I had always respected my father and now I looked at him earnestly. "We need to talk about your future." My father leaned over his desk and looked me straight in the eye.

"Yes," I responded eagerly.

My dad had been my biggest mentor in my Christian walk. He had kept me in line and set a high standard for me to follow. I was sure he was about to endorse my long-held ambition to be a missionary. His next words completely took the wind out of my sails. "You love chemistry. I suggest you pursue it as a career. I'm sure you could get an apprenticeship as a lab technician at Pluss-Staufer." This was a research company only five minutes' walk from our home. I looked at my father stunned, not knowing what to say.

"But Dad, you know I want to be a missionary," I started to object. My father cut me short. His argument was reasonable. As one who had gone through a world war and always struggled to make ends meet, he wanted his son to be financially secure. My older brother Hans was already doing well in his accountancy training. In those days too, it was unthinkable for a young person to go straight into full-time missionary work. "Prove yourself in a profession first. Then do your Bible training." I was disappointed, but recognized the good sense of his advice. Still somewhat reluctant, I agreed.

I graduated from high school at the end of the year and duly signed up for a three-year apprenticeship as a lab technician with Pluss-Staufer. These years proved to be an important training ground—a time of character-building and instillation of principles that would prove invaluable in the years to come.

By nature I am a broad-brush person, not overly concerned about detail. I am in too much of a hurry to get the job done and get on to my next project. As a lab technician, working with dangerous chemicals, I learned the importance of precision. In the world of chemistry, a sloppy attitude is unacceptable. We were handling volatile substances that, if misused, could prove fatal. One slip and it would be all over. I learned this lesson the hard way.

I was into the first year of my apprenticeship and had been assigned the task of making a tranquilizing formula. The process took several days of boiling, cooling, measuring and mixing different chemicals. In the course of making the tranquilizer, an extremely toxic gas, phosgen, was released.

The white-painted, steel cylinder containing this poisonous gas had a black human skull on the side—a sign to all in the industry that this was an extremely potent substance. Even a small amount released into the atmosphere could prove fatal. After inhaling it, the person could be dead within minutes. It could also seep out under the lab doors and kill others. All lab technicians were supposed to wear a protective mask. But the mask was awkward to work with, so nobody bothered. A glass-corked bottle of ammonia liquid sat next to the unused mask on the shelf. If the phosgen was mistakenly released, a whiff of ammonia was our only hope. Even though I, like the others, did not bother to wear the gas mask, I was well aware of the danger.

My work required total concentration. I treated the white, steel cylinder and its various connecting tubes and glass containers with great respect.

One particular day, dressed as usual in my carefully laundered lab uniform, I took the wrench and proceeded very carefully to turn the release valve that allowed the phosgen to escape from the white cylinder into the glass tubing. There was nothing visible to see. Nevertheless I did not avert my eyes, even for a moment. Within seconds the gas would reach the liquid in the triangular glass container at the end of the tubing. As soon as bubbles started appearing in the liquid, my task was to measure it.

Right on cue, first one, then more bubbles began surfacing. Everything was functioning in order. I moved closer to peer at the measuring scale. There was a precise amount of gas I needed to let through. Then suddenly I smelt what every chemical technician dreads—a foul-smelling fume like rotting hay. The deadly phosgen was escaping.

Oh no! One of the tubes securing the glass valve must have sprung a leak. Fatal white clouds swirled around me. My pulse started racing. Instinctively I grabbed the ammonia bottle, jerked off the glass stopper, held the neck to my nose and sniffed. I then shoved the gas mask over my head.

The race for life was on. Had the ammonia's life-saving antidote·done its work? Had the hydrochloric acid, already formed in my lungs, been neutralized? After about a minute, my pulse slowed. I felt my heart pumping normally again and let out a sigh of relief. The ammonia had done its job.

I turned the wrench to stop the flow of phosgen, which until then had been escaping unrestrained into the lab, and collapsed onto a high lab stool, my head in my hands, as the full force of what had happened hit me. I could be dead. I could only thank God that a potentially fatal accident had been averted. But I had learned my lesson well. From then on I meticulously checked and rechecked my instruments. And no matter how awkward, I made every effort to wear the cumbersome gas mask as a precaution.

2

Follow That Man

THERE were many times during my three-year lab technician apprenticeship when work seemed anything but exciting. We had to write lengthy reports of everything we did. I found this tedious and boring. I also had to take orders from others, which I did not find easy. By nature I was a loner. In line with my name Rudolf, there were times when I wanted to break out and get on with my true life's calling as a missionary.

Instead, I knuckled under and learned my trade well. So much so that over the next two years, slowly, but imperceptibly, the sharpness of my missionary call dulled. I became deeply engrossed in my chemistry work and would often spend my evening hours working on company experiments.

I was still involved in church youth work and still active in my faith. But the mission call that had so absorbed my young life was gradually diminishing. I was no longer as outspoken about my faith. I was enjoying the security of a good job and found satisfaction in seeing my bank balance grow. Without realizing it, my focus in life was changing. I started to talk about settling down to a career as a chemical researcher. In the third year of my apprenticeship, however, God intervened dramatically to change my life direction and bring me back on course.

As a family, visitors were a way of life. When we had guests, mom would serve one of her specialty dishes of home-grown vegetables, French fries and steak, followed by a delicious dessert of apple pie topped with cream: a welcome change from our normal fare of hash browns and sausages. If nothing else, I enjoyed visitors because their presence provided a change of diet.

But one visitor came offering us a spiritual diet of his own. Adolf Schnegelsberg was a successful German businessman from my mother's home region of Stuttgart. I was 20 years old and my spiritual life probably at its lowest. I was still faithfully attending church and reading my Bible, but my commitment to God had lost its cutting edge. Adolf, who was with us for two weeks, breezed in like a gust of fresh air. We spent hours as a family sitting and talking around the dining table. A wiry, energetic man in his mid-forties, this German had a zeal and enthusiasm for Jesus that I had not seen before. His zest recharged my flagging spiritual life.

I listened enthralled as he told of the open-air meetings he held every Saturday in a local park at Stuttgart. He had led so many to the Lord, I felt convicted of my own feeble efforts to share my faith with my fellow workers at Pluss-Staufer. I had not led one of them to the Lord. They often used coarse language in my presence and told rough jokes, but I had been too timid to say anything. Now, as Adolf told of his bold exploits for the Lord, I felt ashamed. I wanted to be like him. I wanted to return to the fiery zeal I had displayed as a 14-year-old unabashedly declaring my faith before my class. Why had I turned so inward and lost my daring?

"The reason," Adolf explained when I confessed my failure to him one evening, "is that you've not yet been filled with the Holy Spirit, Rudi." I was offended. I did not say anything to Adolf, but I felt hurt when he suggested I was missing some spiritual dimension in my life. I had been raised in church. I had heard my dad preach from the Bible every Sunday. We had regular devotions as a family and I had my own personal "quiet time" with God. I knew the Bible inside out. I was sure I knew all there was to know about the Holy Spirit.

While our denomination was not "pentecostal" in its beliefs, my mother had had a personal encounter with the Holy Spirit and would sometimes relate a vision or prophecy she had received. She even occasionally spoke out in an unknown language—the "tongues" of Acts 2 that Adolf talked about. My father tolerated these expressions of the Holy Spirit, but he never pushed them or insisted, as Adolf did, that this was something everyone needed to experience.

A few days prior to his departure, Adolf invited my younger sister Esther and me to a January youth camp that his church was running in South Germany. "We can give you further instruction about the Holy Spirit and pray for you," he said. Again I felt offended. I was satisfied as I was. I did not need the Holy Spirit—at least not in the way Adolf talked about. Yet his bold, revolutionary faith had inspired me. I desperately wanted to be free from the cloak of timidity I had drawn around myself in recent years. I wanted to get out on the streets and into the parks as he was doing. My appetite had been whetted.

I struggled over whether or not to attend the January camp. A part of me wanted to go; another part resisted. I tussled with my decision for several days. Finally, the night before Adolf left, I made up my mind. "We'll look forward to seeing you there, Rudi," Adolf smiled when I told him the next morning. Although we had never spoken about it, he was no doubt aware of the inner battle I had gone through.

Our church youth leader also decided to attend. The camp was held in a Black Forest-style chalet set in the forest, not far from Stuttgart. As my sister Esther, the youth leader and I entered the building, we were confronted with 70 boisterous German youths, mostly from Adolf's pentecostal church. They already knew one another. I felt uncomfortable and dreadfully out of place.

The meeting that night was different from anything I had ever experienced. It was the first time I had seen anyone raise their hands. We seldom clapped hands in our church. Here nearly every song, led by a pedal-stomping pianist and several guitarists, was accompanied by vigorous clapping. At our home, we only had a pump organ. It seemed strange, almost irreverent. By the second or third day, however, their contagious excitement began to melt my icy resistance. As with Adolf, I was drawn by their love and dedication to God. It salted my thirst. I wanted what they had.

What was more difficult to digest was the teaching. I had

always been taught that we received the Spirit when we were converted. Here the leaders were telling us there was more. After one of the sessions, I challenged a camp leader about this. "I believe if we love God and are following him, we already have the Holy Spirit."

"Yes, you are born again by the Spirit and have him in measure, Rudi. But being filled with the Holy Spirit is different," the camp leader explained. He flipped through his Bible to Acts 8. "Here, it says Philip went to a city in Samaria and many were converted through his preaching. They were only filled with the Holy Spirit later when the apostles Peter and John came from Jerusalem and laid hands on them."

"Wasn't that because they were reaching beyond the Jews to the Samaritans?" I asked.

"You have a point, Rudi. But look here in Acts 19 when Paul met the Ephesians. Paul asks these believers if they had received the Spirit when they believed. If we automatically receive the fullness of the Spirit when we are converted, Rudi, why did Paul ask that question?"

I did not have an answer, but when I got back to my room, I looked up the passage in my Bible and read it again in context. Verses five and six made it even clearer. The Ephesians had only received John's baptism. Paul baptized them again in the name of Jesus. After that, he placed his hands on them. The Spirit fell on them and they spoke in tongues and prophesied.

My treasured theological position was being rattled. As a Bible-believing Christian, I could not deny what the Scriptures said. Yet I wanted to be absolutely sure. Our church youth leader and I had long discussions often well into the night. I also spent time over the next few days trudging alone through the snow-laden woods that surrounded the retreat center. *God, show me. I want everything you've got for me, but I must know the truth. Is this baptism in the spirit of you?*

My answer came Wednesday night. The evening meeting had been set aside for what the leaders called a "waiting" or "tarrying" time, an opportunity when anyone who so desired could be prayed for to receive the fullness of the Spirit. First, they gave us some teaching. As I listened, I realized I had thrashed out most of the points for myself and pretty much come to the same conclusion. The "baptism in the spirit" is a valid experience for today. Although it may be experienced at the same time, it is an experience distinct from conversion. It is not something limited to the early church and only valid prior to the completion of Scripture—as some teach—but is available to any born-again Christian. One of the evidences a person has received the Holy Spirit is their ability to speak in an unknown tongue, in the same manner the disciples did on the day of Pentecost.

"If the early church needed empowering with the Spirit in order to witness, how much more do we need it today?" the speaker asked. He had a point. But it was his concluding remarks that finally persuaded me. "Turn to 1 Corinthians 15," he instructed. There was an obedient rustle of paper throughout the meeting hall. "Now look at verse six. How many believers did Jesus appear to at one time after his resurrection?" We chorused our response.

"Five hundred."

"All those 500 heard his instructions to go to Jerusalem and wait. But turn with me to Acts 2:15." There was a further turning of paper. "How many were actually there in the upper room on the day of Pentecost?" Fewer voices responded. "A hundred and twenty."

"Have you worked out the percentage of 120 into 500?" he asked. I had not. I am sure no one else in the room had either. "Only 25 percent!" he said dramatically, lifting his Bible and pointing at the passage. "Only 25 percent of those who were instructed to wait for the Holy Spirit were obedient. Are you prepared to be among the minority 25 percent who will wait for him?"

His question hit me like a thunderbolt. Was I going to be among the 25 percent or the 75 percent? Was I prepared to wait? *Yes*, I determined. I would wait through the night if God required it. Fortunately my vigil was not that long. At the end of the meeting, those who wanted to be filled with the Spirit remained behind while the others left. I knelt by my seat. The leaders slowly circulated amongst the scattered "tarriers", laying their hands on them to receive the Spirit. When they prayed for me, a bubble of joy burst within me. My hands shot above my head. And, as if empowered by another force, I began speaking in a language I had never learned.

My experience that night revolutionized my Christian walk. The church youth leader and Esther had similar experiences. We returned home charged with spiritual electricity, our lives renewed and reactivated. I spent long hours alone in my room praying and reading my Bible. Before, this had been a necessary chore. Now it was a delight. There were no more night chemistry experiments at the Pluss-Staufer lab. Time was too precious for that. Instead, I spent the evening hours digging into the Scriptures.

My former timidity was replaced by a new boldness. I no longer accepted the bad jokes and dirty language of my fellow workers, and while I did not see any mass conversions, they did respect my stand. For the remainder of my two years as a chemistry researcher, my workmates kept their ill-fitting humor for when I was not around.

The year of my infilling with the Holy Spirit was also a year of great sadness. Around June, my mother, now 55, took ill and was confined to bed. She had experienced varying health and neither my youngest sister Judith nor Esther nor myself took her illness very seriously. Dad was away preaching at the time and by now my older brother Hans was living in the next town with his wife and two children and pursuing a successful accounting career. After several days though, mom still had not improved. Early one evening, I went to check on her. She spluttered and coughed as I came into the room, gave a deep gurgling gasp followed by a sigh and collapsed back onto the pillow. It did not sound good so I decided to phone the doctor right away and ask him to come over.

After ringing the doctor, I went back to check on her. She was lying quietly and seemed to have fallen asleep, so I left her and went into my room to pray for her. A short while later the doctor arrived. I ushered him up to my mother's room. She was still lying motionless on the bed. The doctor went over to examine her. I turned to leave. I had only taken two steps when the doctor called me back. "Mr. Lack! I'm sorry to inform you. But your mother is dead!"

It was a terrible shock. She had had a massive heart attack. We alerted my father immediately. Canceling his preaching engagement, he returned straight home and, half an hour later, collapsed ashen faced through the door. He lay sobbing on the floor. We all looked on stunned. Not a man to display his emotions, we did not know how to handle my father's distraught pain and overwhelming grief. The whole family staggered through the next few days in unbelief as we prepared for my mother's funeral, and as each of us in our own way sought to come to terms with her unexpected departure.

I had been very close to my mother. She was an outgoing, dynamic pivot around which our whole household turned. Many times in the weeks following, I pined to hear her laughter and see her bustling active presence. It took many months for me to get over her death. Several years later, my father met and married a lovely Christian lady, Marianne. Ten years younger than dad, Marianne was quieter and more staid than my own mother was, and while she was never able to replace her, Marianne and I had a good relationship. With a wife again at the helm, the Lack family settled back into a contented routine.

Following the completion of my three-year apprenticeship at Pluss-Staufer, the company asked me to stay on for a further two years as a chemistry researcher. As soon as this was completed, I headed for London, England, and spent the next two years training at the Assemblies of God, Kenley Bible College. I then returned to Switzerland and became an assistant pastor in the group of evangelical free churches my father directed.

At last, I was fully involved in the Lord's work. But still I was not satisfied. My cherished dream was to be a missionary and fulfill Jesus' command to reach the whole world. I did not want to remain buried in Switzerland all my life, working with a single denomination. My ambition was to travel the world for God and to minister predominantly with young people. But how could I do this? Where should I start? I did not know of any missionary organization that would allow me the freedom to fulfill this dream. After two years in pastoral work, my frustration had reached fever pitch. I felt hemmed in and confined and started seriously scanning the horizon for other ministry opportunities. Nothing suitable surfaced, but I decided anyway to take the plunge and resign as my father's co-pastor.

January, seven years after I had received the experience of the Spirit that had so revolutionized my life, I was back at the same youth camp in the Black Forest retreat. Although I had not yet tendered my resignation, I had definitely made up my mind to give up my pastoral duties.

One night prior to the evening session, a German camp leader Fred and I were praying together by his bed. We were focused on the evening's activities. My particular concern was for the dozen teenagers I had brought with me. Many of them, like me, were resisting the teaching that we needed a deeper encounter with the Holy Spirit following conversion. My special concern was for 19-year-old Roli Sauser. A fun-loving, amiable young man, he was halfway through his training as an electrician. His family had been in the church for years, and he himself had been a faithful member of our youth group. But he had not yet been filled with the Spirit and was in danger of making the same mistake I had, in allowing his faith to be tempered into lukewarmness by his unbelieving workmates.

I was deeply engrossed in my prayers for Roli and the others when Fred interrupted me. "Rudi! God's giving me a vision for you. I see it in my mind's eye as clearly as if it was a painting on the wall." He began to describe it. As the revelation unfolded, his voice rose in excitement at what he was seeing. "There's a man standing next to you, Rudi. You don't know him, but he's going to play an important role in your future. Something else too, and this is really important. You are not to resign from your assistant pastoral position too soon. You will not need to run around looking for this man. God will bring him across your path. He will lead you into your future ministry. You are going to have a ministry that will go beyond the borders of Switzerland."

My spirit leapt at his final words: "beyond the borders of Switzerland". I got up off my knees and sitting on Fred's bed pondered on what I had just heard. I had never had such a direct prophecy given to me. I did not know Fred well, but I had confidence that what he had seen was from God. Fred touched me lightly on my shoulder. "Rudi, what I want to say now is not prophetic but I believe it's also a message from Jesus. It's a word of caution." I gave him my full attention.

"Yes! What?"

"Don't be impatient. It could be a year or even two before you meet this man."

My heart sank. I was ready to break free now. I did not know if I could wait another year, let alone two. But I was sure God was speaking through Fred. In obedience to his instructions, I did not turn in my resignation. Instead, even though somewhat reluctantly, I threw myself back into the pastorate.

Life became busier than ever. Added to my church duties, I started running a ten-lesson correspondence-cum-witnessing course. Before long, I had 500 students on my books. Of the many completed papers that came across my desk, one that moved my heart most was from Rosemary. Born without arms and a single leg, she had written her answers by tapping the keys with her one good foot. To complete her witnessing assignment she sat on the street corner in her wheel chair, tracts poked between her toes, for any passerby to take. Rosemary's determination against great odds inspired me to keep going.

Dad remained senior pastor of our three evangelical free churches and two satellite branches, but increasingly entrusted me with more responsibility. I now had my own official church study: a converted guestroom in our home in Aarburg. It had the same book-lined shelves that my father had, although not as many. From the small shuttered window over my large timbered desk, which was normally cluttered with my sermon notes and other papers, I looked out on an apple and pear orchard and over a road to the green hills beyond. Our house was situated on the edge of town, right next to our main church.

The following year my younger sister Esther married and moved with her new husband to Germany. They had met seven years earlier at our memorable Black Forest youth camp. That left my dad and my stepmother Marianne at home. My socialite 18-year-old sister Judith was frequently out and more often than not my father was away preaching in Germany.

The usual flow of evangelists, preachers, missionaries and other visitors through our home continued. They not only came from Switzerland and Germany, but also from around the world. Someone who visited several times was the American evangelist Willard Cantelon. One spring morning I received a letter from Willard. I picked it out from the others that had arrived on my desk and, opening it, quickly scanned its contents. He wrote of an American friend, an evangelist, whom he wanted us to meet. His friend Loren Cunningham had just moved to Switzerland. He was heading up an organization called Youth With A Mission. "The Lord's really blessing Loren's youth program. You need to meet him," he wrote.

I read the letter with interest, especially when Willard explained how Loren's dream was to reach the world through young people and towards that end he was setting up a School of Evangelism, or SOE for short, at Chateau D'Oex—a town about three hours' drive from Aarburg, on the French-speaking side of Switzerland. Loren's vision seemed to parallel my own unfulfilled dream. As I folded the letter and put it back in its envelope, a fleeting thought crossed my mind. Was Loren Cunningham *the man* I had been waiting for, the one who would lead me into my future ministry? It had been 18 months since the Black Forest retreat when Fred had prophesied about this man. So far no one had turned up.

I meant to follow up Willard Cantelon's letter, but I got caught up in the day's activities and it remained buried and semi-forgotten under a pile of other urgent mail. A few weeks later, my father and I were in his study discussing who we should have as guest speaker at our special Whit Sunday week-end conference. It was an occasion when our five churches combined together. We had tossed around several names, but none seemed suitable. Suddenly I remembered Willard's letter. "Dad, I've thought of someone who might fit the bill. His name is Loren Cunningham." I dashed to my study and pulled Willard's letter out from under the pile of papers. My dad scanned its contents. His midriff had expanded even further in recent times. His almost white hair made him look much older than his 53 years. But he still did not wear reading glasses and was as active in ministry as ever. Dad finished the letter and handed it back to me. "Willard certainly gives him an excellent recommendation. Phone him. See if he will come."

Loren Cunningham seemed more than happy to accept our invitation. So he was announced as our Whit Sunday guest speaker. It was arranged that Loren, along with six SOE students, would arrive Saturday afternoon. The first meeting started that night. At about 3pm, I was studying at my bedroom desk when I heard a vehicle approaching. I hastened downstairs and out through our front door, which opened on to the street, just in time to see a battered, faded blue van pull up. Looking closer, I realized it was actually an old, mobile bread bus. The back doors opened and a half-dozen young men and women clambered out. Inside, shelves that had once been stacked with bread were now being used as seating. A gentleman, whom I guessed to be Loren, got down from the front passenger seat.

I moved forward to greet him. "I'm Cam Wilson," the American-accented man said, shaking my outstretched hand. Seeing my quizzical expression, he went on to explain, "Loren's sorry, but he can't make it. He slipped a disc this morning and is lying flat on his back in Chateau D'Oex unable to move." Cam was the school's visiting lecturer for the following week. Loren had sent him as his substitute. "I'm sorry," Cam apologized, obviously embarrassed by the unexpected turn of events, "I hope this doesn't put you out."

"Not at all," I assured him. "We're grateful you can come." But I was disappointed.

I had been looking forward to meeting Loren. Cam preached an excellent message that night on missions. As I stood next to him, in my interpreter's position, I could tell from my father's nods of approval that he was more than happy with our substitute speaker. We were in for a good weekend. Cam would preach again Sunday afternoon.

After the meeting, as we were crowded into our living room having a late evening drink, Cam turned to me, "Rudi, is it all right if I phone Loren? I have a strong impression he should be here. Maybe his back has improved enough for him to travel."

"Of course." I directed him to the phone in the office. A few minutes later, Cam returned to the room with the announcement: "Loren's back isn't any better, but he's decided to come. We will need to send a student back in the blue bus to collect him. He is still unable to sit, so he will have to lie on one of the bread shelves."

I thought of the three-hour journey Loren would be taking from Chateau D'Oex stretched out on the shelf. He would be traveling over some steep, winding mountain passes. I marveled at the caliber of a man who with a slipped disc was prepared to suffer such a trip to preach one sermon at an unknown church. It made me even more curious to meet this Loren.

He arrived in the bread bus early Sunday afternoon just in time for the service. I watched as a well-built, dark-haired man gingerly let himself down from the van and walked stiffly towards us. Helping him was a vibrant, blond, shorthaired lady who I later learned was Loren's wife Darlene. After all the build up, I felt like saying, "Dr. Livingstone, I presume", but I restrained myself. Seeing how much he was suffering, I did not think he would appreciate my attempt at humor. "I can only lie down flat on the floor or stand," he told us. "I'll remain standing at the back of the church until it's my time to preach. Then you call me forward."

We had a time of worship. Some of the SOE students gave testimonies. Finally it was Loren's turn. I took my place in the front as his interpreter while he made his way from the back of the church, shuffling really, more than walking, down the long aisle. Easing his way up the few steps to the lectern, he held on with both hands and steadied himself.

A sense of anticipation settled on the congregation as they watched and waited. Seeing the awkwardness with which Loren moved and after Cam's dynamic sermon, I could sense them questioning, "Who have we got here?"

The moment Loren opened his mouth to speak, however, any cynicism evaporated. He spoke with a vibrancy and passion that I had never heard before. He shared his dreams of seeing young people marching like a mighty army across the world with the Gospel, reaching out into every corner of the globe, even those remote spots where no missionary had visited.

His talk was not merely visionary. He shared from his own experiences: inspiring stories of witnessing in Moscow's Red Square in communist Russia and taking teams of raw recruit YWAMers, as Youth With A Mission folks were known, on evangelistic outreaches into the Caribbean islands. They lived by faith, trusting God for all their provision. "No one gets a salary in YWAM," (pronounced why wham) Loren explained. That included himself as the founder and director.

I was impressed and deeply stirred. I had never met anyone who had so clearly expressed my own dream of reaching the whole world for Jesus. By the end of his message, I was ready to sign up. Surely this was *the man* Fred had prophesied about, the one who would lead me into my future ministry. The Lord put his seal on my conviction in a very special way. Halfway through his preaching, Loren's limbs began to ease. By the time he finished, he was waving his arms and moving around with all the vigor of a perfectly healthy person. Every sign of stiffness had vanished. God had supernaturally healed him.

That night Loren and his wife Darlene, or Dar as Loren called her, joined our family for dinner. "I'm so thrilled I've finally got to meet the Lack family," he enthused as he prodded a fork into the generous portion of roast meat Marianne had served him. "Willard Cantelon spoke so highly of you. I've been trying to get in touch for months. I believe my slipped disc was Satan's last attempt to prevent us meeting." I chewed silently on Loren's words, wondering if there was more to this resistance from the enemy than even he realized.

Our dinner conversation was an enthralling continuation of his sermon. Loren enlarged on his plans to have young people encircling the globe for Jesus. I hung on every word, which to me was even more palatable than the treat of green peas on my plate. Towards the end of the meal, Loren suddenly turned to me, "Rudi! We're just getting YWAM off the ground here in Europe. Why don't you come and join us?"

I knew from his message there would be no salary. Although he had a big vision and up to 5,000 young people joining annually on short-term summer outreaches, as yet there were only a dozen full-time staff worldwide. Apart from Loren and Dar, there was no one on staff in Europe. But that did not deter me. My heart was already there. From my father's noncommittal reaction, I could see he was not so convinced. If I joined YWAM, he would be without a co-pastor. Perhaps sensing my father's reservation, Loren back-pedaled slightly, "I don't want to do the Lord's work. If this is of God, he'll show you, Rudi."

But God already had. In Loren, I had found *my man*. While it took a few more months to convince my father, others I respected in the church, including my stepmother, had given me the green light. Finally dad gave me his approval. I tendered my resignation, and in September 1969 I joined up as the first full-time European staff member in YWAM.

I was set on a course of action that would lead me on an exciting pilgrimage around the world, across borders and into foreign nations. Had the officials in many of these countries discovered what I was really doing, I would no doubt have had the words PERSONA NON GRATA—an unwanted person—stamped on my passport.

3

Lessons in Intercession

I spent my first few months with YWAM traveling alone throughout Europe recruiting new members. Because I had only heard
Loren speak a few times, I mainly talked from my own understanding of missions, using a series of slides that I had put
together. It was a lonely time. I was thankful for a two-week break
over Christmas, which I spent visiting my sister Esther and her
German husband in Berlin and then back home with family in
Aarburg.

After three months of living out of a suitcase, it was good to
be back home in familiar surroundings and sleep in my own bed.
But as I sat alone at my bedroom desk studying and looking out
across the now denuded fruit trees to the snow-covered hills, I
realized I would never settle in the family house again. I would be
back for visits and family would always remain close. But I had
now teamed up with another family, YWAM. I was eager to get to
know its other members.

This opportunity would come in two weeks when I enrolled in
YWAM's School of Evangelism. This was an eight-month course.
It was a necessary prerequisite for anyone wanting to join YWAM
as staff. Even though I had had two years of Bible college training, and been in the ministry for almost four, I was not exempt.
The course entailed three months of lectures followed by a
two-month field trip to the Middle East and concluded with a
three-month evangelistic outreach. The SOE was being held in
a three-story hotel which YWAM had recently rented on the

outskirts of the Swiss city of Lausanne.

After two weeks of idleness, catching up with friends and family as well as entertaining the usual flow of visitors, I was anxious to get going. As it was, I was forced to delay my departure a week. Dad was running a special series of meetings and wanted my assistance. I arrived feeling like a late starter and spent my first days catching up by tape on Loren's first week of lectures.

There were 30 students in the SOE. At 27, I was the oldest. Others, such as Joe Portale, Don and Deyon Stephens, David and Carol Boyd, and Al Akimoff, all Americans, had also spent several years at Bible college. I learned, over the lunch table, that Al was of Russian descent. I listened, fascinated, as he told me how his father, also a committed Christian, had emigrated with a whole community just prior to the communist takeover in the Soviet Union. They had been warned to flee through the prophecies of a teenage boy. In Al, I sensed a kindred spirit. Just over 1.5 meters tall, I could see he was no small fry when it came to spiritual enthusiasm. I determined to pursue our friendship further.

Another person who caught my attention during my first days at the SOE was a dark-haired schoolteacher, Reona Peterson, from the South Pacific nation of New Zealand. While I did not feel any romantic attraction towards her, I sensed an immediate spiritual bonding. Apart from Reona and myself, the other students were North American. The teaching was in English so I was grateful for my two years spent in England. This was the second school Loren and Dar had conducted in Europe; but as time would prove, it would yield the more significant crop of future leaders. Right then in 1970, we were just a bunch of young, and some not so young, men and women eager to learn more of God's ways. Although I had missed Loren's first week of teaching, I was grateful to be there for his second.

The winter Lausanne sun filtered its weakened rays through the classroom windows. I sat riveted as Loren explained his vision for YWAM. As he spoke, I felt the same stirring I had experienced that memorable Sunday service when he had preached at my home church in Aarburg. Loren explained that as a young man working with the Assemblies of God in California, God had called him to work with not just one, but every Christian denomination. It meant breaking new ground but he had taken the risk and together with Dar had founded YWAM.

While alone in prayer, God had shown him a powerful picture of waves pounding the seacoast. As one wave retracted, another took its place, each wave penetrating further inland. The images were screened like a movie on the white wall of a guestroom where he was staying. As he watched the images unravel, the waves turned into armies of young people marching across the nations, invading even the remotest corner of the world. "There's not one area of this globe that can't be reached for Christ," Loren declared. "God has called us to take the Gospel to every creature, to disciple all the nations."

I thought of the few of us who currently represented YWAM in Europe. I was the only full-time European staff member. During the last few months I had been traveling, I had not met anyone who had heard about us. Even in the United States, where YWAM had been operating for over ten years, there was still only a handful of full-time staff. Yet as Loren talked, it was as though these armies of young people were already marching. I determined I would be one leading the pack.

"There are different types of missionaries," Loren explained to us. "Some are like the forerunners or trackers. They are the scouts who break new ground. They don't usually stay long, but prepare the way for others to follow." My heart raced as he explained how these forerunners go in where no one else has been, slashing the initial track through the thick, tangled under-growth of the jungle. Loren shared how this was often dangerous, lonely work but absolutely essential. The tracker (or trailblazer, as they have come to be known in YWAM circles) makes way for the next group of missionaries, the pioneers. Last to arrive are the settlers. They widen the tracks into roads—maybe even pave them—and make them accessible for everyone else to follow. I knew instantly where I would fit. I was not one to follow others. *Lord, I'm going to be a tracker or trailblazer, one who goes in first,* I silently vowed.

I was disappointed to learn that the following week we were

having a lady speak to us on prayer. I pictured the praying women in our church—usually quiet, conservatively attired and, like my mother, their long hair pulled back into a bun. I guessed this Joy Dawson, a New Zealander, would fit the same mold. I was not prepared for the bomb blast that was about to hit us.

Joy Dawson, as I discovered from our first lecture, was anything but conservative. Smartly dressed, with the latest hairdo, she burst upon us like a tornado straight from God. She spoke with authority and conviction of a woman who was not giving us just good ideas on how to hear from God and pray, but who spoke from personal experience. Joy, I quickly realized, was a lady who meant business with the Almighty. She was not to be taken lightly.

Everything Joy did had a divine element to it—even going out for a meal. Saturday, at the conclusion of our week, we had free time. Early evening, I was chatting with Joy and Reona—who knew Joy from New Zealand—in the hotel entrance, which also served as our common room. We were discussing the teaching Joy had given us about correctly discerning Jesus' voice. I was feeling hungry, so made the suggestion to go and eat. "Why don't we take my car and go for a cheese fondue?"[1]

"Great idea, Rudi!" Joy responded in her usual forthright manner.

There were only three of us and my red Saab could easily take five. Two students were sitting talking in the far corner of the common room. "I'll see if they want to come too." I started moving in their direction when Joy put out her hand to stop me.

"Let's not presume here, Rudi." She looked at me with her piercing eyes. "We need to seek the Lord in detail. We want his highest for this evening." She shut her eyes and bowed her head. I was taken aback. I had never considered consulting God for something as unimportant as this. After a few minutes, Joy looked up and shook her head. "No! It's only to be the three of us."

We had a good night and as a trio shared from our hearts. Had the others joined us, the conversation could easily have taken a more trivial direction. Above anything else, that "fondue

[1] This dish, created by Swiss mountain dairy farmers, is eaten with bread on long forks dipped into a central pot of specially blended melted cheeses.

evening" reiterated the importance of the teaching Joy had been emphasizing all week: the need to seek God in detail. It was a principle I would come to rely on heavily in the future.

It was during Joy's two weeks with us that God broke through in another crucial area of my life: the grip of finance. For the Swiss, money is a national bondage. Every child is literally born with a Swiss bank account. The parents' bank manager opens it on their behalf and even deposits the initial amount. Having worked for five years as a lab technician and a further two and a half years as my father's pastoral assistant, I had built up a healthy bank account. This was my nest egg. Even though I was now part of a mission where everyone lived by faith and trusted God for their provisions, it was a comfort to know that I had that private source of supply.

Loren had talked to us earlier of the need to give up our rights and hold everything with an open palm. His message of sacrificial living greatly inspired me and I eagerly took down scads of notes. But it was during Joy's second week with us that Loren's message was put to the test. Loren and Dar had decided to purchase the hotel we were renting here in Lausanne. It was crunch time. Youth With A Mission had limited funds. One morning at the conclusion of one of Joy's lectures, Loren presented a challenge to us. "Will you as students believe with us for the finance to be released? Ask the Lord to show you what he wants you to give."

Nearly all the students responded quickly to his appeal. I too was stirred. I thought of my healthy bank account with its several thousand Swiss francs. *How much do you want me to give, Father?* The lesson I had learned from Joy through our fondue evening was fresh in my mind. A few figures ran through my head. Would I give a hundred francs or five? Then as clear as if he had been standing right in front of me, the Lord spoke to my heart. *Empty your bank account and empty your pockets.* The command was clear and simple. But my obedience was not.

It was one thing to be enthralled by Loren's stories of faith and hear of God's provision. It was quite another thing to be in the hot seat myself. I had no doubt the Lord had spoken. Both Loren and Joy had challenged us on how he loves a cheerful giver. But I felt far from cheerful and I entered into one of the biggest internal battles I had ever faced.

If I give away all my money, how would I live? Who will provide for me? I argued. *I will provide*, the response came back. I knew from Scripture that that was true. Christ promised that if we seek his kingdom first, he will provide for all our needs. *All my money?* I questioned. *Isn't that being irresponsible?* The Spirit reminded me of the church in Acts 2. The early Christians had sold houses and given material provisions to the poor. For every objection I raised, God brought to my mind a Scripture that refuted it.

Finally, after battling for a couple of days, I gave in. I went to the bank and withdrew every cent in my account. I placed all the money I possessed in an envelope and handed it to Loren. "Thanks, Rudi," he smiled as he accepted the envelope. He did not say very much, but I knew he understood. What I had given was more than a generous gift towards the payment of the hotel. It was evidence that a strong bondage had been broken—one that not only held me back but also my whole Swiss nation. I felt strangely free. I had no money and no assurance of receiving any. But I had been obedient to God. Now I no longer had a bank account to rely on. It was up to him to provide for my needs.

That weekend Joy Dawson, Dave and Carol Boyd and myself had planned a trip into the classy French town of Chamonix, a tourist resort that sits at the foot of the highest mountain in Europe, Mont Blanc. Chamonix was an expensive place and I was going there without a cent in my pocket. How would Jesus meet my need? The day would prove a foretaste of the way ahead.

Not only did God provide, in this case through Joy's generosity (she paid for everything), but he also demonstrated to me that day that when he supplies it is with overflowing abundance. We took the expensive cable car journey up to the top of the mountain, something I would have hesitated doing had I been relying on my own resources. We also dined on wonderful French cuisine at one of the mountain restaurants. Within a few short weeks, God would provide thousands of francs through unexpected and unsolicited gifts. My bank account would be healthier than it had ever been.

The fourth week of our school only impacted and confirmed what we had heard from both Loren and Joy. Our speaker was Brother Andrew from Holland, the founder and director of a ministry called Open Doors. I had not heard of Open Doors or Brother Andrew, but I was immediately impressed by his quiet, determined manner. From his external appearance, it would have been easy to dismiss him as a mild-mannered, soft-spoken Dutch man. As soon as he began to share details of his ministry, however, all 30 of us were on the edge of our seats. This was very different from anything I had been taught at Bible college.

Brother Andrew was definitely one of the "trailblazers" Loren had referred to. He used the term "brother" to hide his true identity. This was because for the last 15 years, he had been smuggling Bibles in behind the Iron Curtain into the so-called closed countries of communist Eastern Europe. "There are no closed doors," Brother Andrew said, pounding his fist on the wooden lecture stand and startling us with his sudden outburst. "Not even those behind the Iron Curtain are closed to the Gospel."

He told how he had gone into Moscow with no contacts, just the conviction that God had Bibles for him to deliver. He attended the only open Baptist church there. Afterwards, as the congregation was thinning out, a sad-looking man came over and talked with him. In the course of their conversation, the man made the comment, "I have come 3,000 kilometers from Siberia to Moscow because I believe the Lord told me I would get a Bible here. But there are no more Bibles here than in Siberia. I've come 3,000 kilometers for nothing." With that Brother Andrew reached into his pocket and pulled out a Bible, giving it to the man. "I've come 3,000 kilometers from the West to give this to you."

"Dare for God," he challenged us. "You can go anywhere if you are willing to go and never come back." There was a stunned silence as we each reflected on the implication of his words. It was one thing to hear his stories. It was another to think of going ourselves. "Be prepared to go to those places where you won't get red carpet treatment," Brother Andrew continued. I could almost feel some students drawing back. This was going too far. But for me, it was rekindling my childhood dreams of fighting off wild natives in Africa. I did not want to be just an ordinary missionary staying within the comforts of the safety zone. Like Brother Andrew, I wanted to be out taking risks for God, willing to face danger and going where no one else dared.

We had had four weeks of lectures. Coming up was our first chance as a student body to put into practice some of the principles we had been learning. A group of us were going on a weekend outreach to Grenoble in France—hardly the nail-biting, behind the Iron Curtain stuff Brother Andrew had inspired us with. But at least it was a start. It would be my first YWAM outreach, and I was looking forward to it.

Friday afternoon, following the final morning lecture by Brother Andrew, we headed for Grenoble in a convoy of vans. It was a two-hour journey from Lausanne and ten of us, including my Kiwi friend Reona and the Russian American Al Akimoff, traveled in the same faded blue bread bus that had transported an immobilized Loren to our Aarburg church last Whit Sunday. The wide shelves, designed to display bread, were spread with mattresses and served as our seating. Our luggage was stacked underneath on the bottom bread shelf. I have to admit I have ridden in more comfortable conditions, but none of us complained. What was a little discomfort when we had opportunity to share the Gospel with lost souls?

It was a full weekend. Not a moment was lost. Friday night, we launched our outreach with an open-air meeting in the streets of Grenoble. We sang with gusto, accompanied by a couple of guitarists, preached our hearts out and testified to the greatness of God. A few passersby stopped briefly and listened. But most of the shoppers hastened their pace as they came in our direction. Some totally ignored us. Others gave us a wide berth and deliberately walked on the other side of the road.

Undeterred, we were out on the streets again the next day, distributing tracts and seeking meaningful encounters with people. A few politely took our literature. Many blatantly refused. Later, we found many of our discarded pamphlets either thrown in trash bins or cast unread on the ground. We could only hope that for the few who had kept and read them, the printed message had hit home.

We also spent time on Grenoble's university campus. We

spoke to students in the cafeteria and even went from room to room in the student hostels, knocking on doors and engaging in lengthy, often intellectual debates which went nowhere. Despite our zeal, the students remained largely unimpressed by our efforts to persuade them of spiritual truth. Most treated us with disdain. Although they did not necessarily verbalize it, their message was clear: "Come on, you guys, get serious. Start living in the real world." Nobody indicated any serious interest and we left the campus disheartened, our evangelistic zeal deflated.

Sunday morning, we dispersed among different churches in Grenoble. We sang, shared testimonies and some of us preached enthusiastically on the revelatory truth we had received from school. The Sunday congregation gave us the usual dutiful attention, and people chatted politely with us afterwards. But there was no outward sign at any of the services that our words had had any life-changing impact. We returned Sunday afternoon, wearied from our weekend's frantic activity. We had talked with many people and done everything we knew to effectively communicate the Gospel, but nothing dramatic had happened. Where were those exciting, Spirit-led encounters Brother Andrew, Joy and even Loren had talked about?

"We didn't quite hit the mark, did we?" Reona commented as we traveled back. Her words echoed my own unspoken thoughts. "Where did we go wrong?" I asked. "We certainly put everything into it." Others began to join in the conversation. It was apparent everyone shared the same sense of letdown. As far as we could tell, nobody had shown any positive response to all our efforts.

"Well, at least the seed has been sown," Al encouraged.

"Yes, I agree, but...," Reona said slowly.

"But what?" I asked.

"I don't think we prayed enough," she said. "We put in all the practical preparation, but we were so busy to get away and so anxious to get out that we did not really intercede."

There was an embarrassed silence. We all knew Reona was right. We had briefly committed our activities to the Lord before launching onto the streets and into the university, but we had not really prayed; at least not in the way Joy had instructed. We had not even thought of coming in aggressive attack against spiritual forces that were seeking to hinder our efforts, or blind the minds of those we were trying to reach. I was reminded of Joy's words: "If you're going to see any significant move of God, it must be birthed in prayer." How could we have been so impressed by her teaching, and yet so slow to put it into practice?

I knew Reona had often joined in a prayer group with Joy back in their home city of Auckland, New Zealand. She had shared how exciting those times had been. "Why don't we start praying together on a regular basis in the evenings?" I suggested. "You could lead us, Reona. You know something about the kind of intercession Joy taught us." A few faces lit up. "I'd be a starter," Al volunteered. When we shared our idea with the other students, some showed interest. Loren's wife Dar got really excited. "I think that's great. I might not always make it because of my other commitments. But I'll join you when I can."

So it was agreed. We would start a voluntary prayer time in the evenings for anyone who wanted to join us. We decided to meet in the lecture room. None of us realized, as we gathered for our first evening get-together, just how crucial these prayer meetings would be in preparing us for our future role in the mission. In the group were Don and Deyon Stephens, David and Carol Boyd, Reona, Al, Dar, Joe Portale and myself. Apart from Reona, we were complete novices in this type of intercession.

Reona outlined the procedure. Her instructions closely followed what Joy had taught us. First, we would wait in silence for God to reveal any sin in our lives. "If it's a private sin between you and God, then confess it silently," Reona suggested. "But if it was done in public, and others are aware of it, it's good to confess it out loud."

We knelt by our chairs waiting. Gradually one, then another, began to confess his or her sins. Some admitted their prayerlessness, others their lack of concern for the unsaved. Someone asked forgiveness for his selfishness and lack of consideration for others. Living as we were in community, this was a major issue. *You need to confess your selfishness too*, the Lord convicted me. He reminded me how at lunchtime that day I had grabbed the last apple on the plate. It seemed such a small thing. But even as I had taken it, I knew I was being greedy.

Admitting my sin to God was one thing. Exposing my true heart condition before others was another matter. *What will the others think of me?* I struggled for a few moments, then blurted out, "Forgive me, God, for my selfishness. I'm sorry for being greedy and taking that last apple at the table." Strangely, instead of feeling alienated, my confession seemed to draw me even closer to the others in the room.

It was taking time for everyone to speak out his or her sins, and I was beginning to get restless. When were we going to get down to actually pray? I had spent many hours on my knees before God in years past, but I had never gone through such lengthy preparation before. "Can't we just get on with it?" I protested. "There are so many needs to pray for. Do we really need such a drawn out process of heart preparation?" There were a few nods of agreement. Don backed me up.

"I think Rudi's right." But Reona stuck to her guns.

"That's fine if you just want to pray for things. But if you want to really hear from God and learn what is on his heart, then we need to really prepare ourselves. That's the difference between meaningful intercession and just praying for things."

We had to agree with her. In her teaching, Joy had really emphasized our need to deal with sin if we were going to hear accurately from God. She had likened it to tuning in to a radio. Unconfessed sin is the static that hinders our clear communication with God. As she pointed out from Psalm 66:18, *when we cherish known sin in our heart, the Lord will not listen.*

Finally everyone had spoken out his or her confessions. We then stood up and, in line with James 4, declared our authority over Satan. In Jesus' name, we defied any attempts he might make to interrupt our meeting or put wrong thoughts in our mind. James promises that if we resist the devil, he has to flee from us. While we can clean out the "rooms" of our lives by confessing our sins, and so erect a barrier against Satan's invasion, that is only half the job. As pointed out in Luke 11:24-26,[2] we also

---

[2] *When the unclean spirit has gone out of a man, he passes through waterless places seeking rest; and finding none he says, "I will return to my house from which I came." And when he comes he finds it swept and put in order. Then he goes and brings seven other spirits more evil than himself, and they enter and dwell there; and the last state of that man becomes worse than the first* (RSV).

need to take a positive stand by inviting the Holy Spirit to take over us. This was a principle Joy had also emphasized in her teaching: "You need to seek the fullness of the Spirit and give him control of your prayer time."

"Now let's take time to worship God and be filled with the Spirit," Reona suggested. Some lifted their hands as we focused in prayer on God's majesty. "Come fill us with your presence," someone prayed. "Yes, fill us," everyone else agreed. Someone started softly singing a chorus. The rest of us joined in. A beautiful, quiet peace descended. Jesus' presence was so real. It was as though we had tiptoed into his throne room. I almost expected to open my eyes and see him standing in all his glory before me. Earlier I had been anxious to rush on into prayer. Now I wanted to linger, basking in the warmth of that glorious presence. But Reona sensed it was time to move on.

"All right. Now, let's spend time listening for what God has to say to us," she said quietly, careful not to disturb the beautiful atmosphere. "Then we'll share together what he is showing us." A blanket of silence wrapped around us, and we waited expectantly for the Father to show us his agenda for the night. I knelt by my wooden lecture chair. Almost immediately a Scripture verse popped into my mind. But then I was bombarded by doubt. How could I know this was from God? What if I shared this verse and it was different from everybody else's revelation?

I consoled myself with the thought that even the great prophet Samuel did not get it right the first time. When God had spoken to him as a young boy, he had mistaken his voice for Eli. I was certainly a novice in this kind of intercession. All of us were on a learning curve. I continued to wait, but no other thoughts came to mind. Sitting on my chair, I looked up the verse in my Bible. By now some of the others were also on their seats looking up Scripture. In obedience to Reona's instructions, no one spoke. Finally she broke into the silence. "Let's all share what we're getting."

One by one, we spoke out the topics for prayer we felt God had given us. For some it was an individual, for others it was a country or event. Then as we focused on these various items, I was amazed how our unconnected revelations dovetailed together. As each of us spoke out what had come to mind—a Scripture verse, an impression or a vision—these jigsaw pieces fell into place to create a clear picture of God's agenda for us in intercession.

Night after night, we followed a similar pattern. Sometimes it was more obvious what was on the Lord's heart. Other times we needed to return to him to check it out. But always as we took the time to spiritually prepare ourselves and then wait and listen, we were astounded at the detailed way Christ revealed his mind to us. From time to time, other students joined in. Occasionally there were only two or three of us. But as we continued to meet regularly, our confidence and ability to hear Jesus' voice grew and we had a growing assurance that our intercessions were having an effect.

One evening we felt to pray for one of the students, Dave. He had been struggling with the course and talked of quitting. We were still interceding for him at about 1am when I had a strong urge to go to his room and speak to him. I struggled with the idea. *Father, I can't go up and wake a guy up after midnight, and tell him he's running away from God.* Yet I felt God was speaking to me, and I did not want to disobey. So, without saying anything to the others, I slipped away from the group and quietly made my way up the stone stairs. Reaching the landing, I headed for Dave's room and gently opened the door. My heart was pounding. I was beginning to have second thoughts. "Dave!" I whispered. Fortunately Dave had a room of his own, so I did not have to worry about disturbing a sleeping companion.

There was no response. I moved across the room, closer to the bed, and tried again. "Dave! Dave!" I heard a gentle snoring. I suddenly got cold feet. I decided I had made a mistake, and turning back I started tiptoeing towards the door. I was halfway across the room when I jumped in fright. A loud jarring ringing had erupted behind me. Startled, I turned to see where the noise was coming from. It took a few moments for me to realize the ringing was the alarm clock on Dave's bedside table.

Transfixed, I watched in the dim light as Dave's hand slid from beneath the bedclothes and groped in the direction of the alarm. Banging down the clock's knob, he turned it off. He pushed back the covers, pulled himself into a sitting position and then let out a muffled gasp. In the eerie moonlight, he must have seen my silhouetted figure. He turned on his bedside light. "Rudi Lack! What are you doing here?" he stammered with a mixture of surprise and annoyance. Unknown to any of us, Dave had deliberately set the alarm so he could wake up early and slip away from the school, unnoticed. Now, thanks to our prayer vigil, I had exposed his escape plan. Still in shock, but greatly encouraged by the precision of my God-inspired visit, I perched myself on the edge of Dave's bed, and using every argument I could, I sought to convince him to stay. I tried to show him he was about to make the biggest mistake of his life. Dave seemed to listen.

Finally, confident my words had got through, I left him and returned to the others who were still praying in the classroom downstairs.

When I woke up the next morning, I was disappointed to discover that my confidence had been misplaced. Despite my pleadings, Dave had slipped away from the hotel, just before dawn. None of us ever saw him again. Neither did I ever discover what happened to him. While I felt discouraged, I also realized we each have a free will. Even though Christ may direct us to pray for someone, they still have the ability to resist even his most urgent pleadings. I could only hope that Dave would recognize God's personal love for him, that he would see the evidence of this in the fact that someone cared enough to come and speak with him in the middle of the night. Hopefully sometime in the future, Dave would face up to, and deal with, the problems which were so deeply troubling him. Such experiences encouraged us to persist in intercession.

4

When the Going Gets Tough

As the three-month SOE lecture phase progressed, we continued to meet every night in the classroom downstairs. Kneeling on the wooden floor, leaning on hard-backed chairs, as with our prayers for Dave, we would often continue well into the night. We had become so engrossed in prayer that two or three hours could pass without us realizing it.

Around midnight, a few heads would often start nodding and our numbers thinned as some headed for bed. God's presence was so real and his revelations to us so inspiring, that I did not want to stop. I had never realized prayer was so exciting. Reona felt the same way. Often just the two of us would be left praying. Sometimes we continued into the early hours of the morning. I should have been exhausted and unable to concentrate during the next day's lectures. Instead I found myself refreshed and spiritually alert. It brought home the truth of God's promise in Isaiah 40:31: *Those who wait on the Lord will renew their strength; they shall rise up with wings like eagles.*

Our times of intercession generally followed the same pattern. We would begin by repenting from any unconfessed sin, then take an aggressive stand against any spiritual forces that might disrupt. We would spend time in praise and worship and being refilled with the Holy Spirit. Then we would wait with expectancy for God to show us his prayer agenda for the night.

We were not spiritual giants, just a bunch of normal Bible school students, with all the usual hang-ups and fears. We did, however, have one thing that marked us out; we meant business with God. As night after night we asked in simple faith for him to lead us in our intercessions, we were thrilled at the details he revealed to us. Increasingly, we found ourselves focusing on communist countries. There were times when we felt directed to pray for nations I had barely heard of before. One such country was communist Albania, which boasted that it was the only true atheistic nation in the world.

I well remember the first time God directed us to pray for Albania. We began our session by interceding for an unsaved person we had met on one of our outreaches. As we exhausted our prayers for him, we waited for God to show us the next item on his agenda. Into my mind came the nation of Albania. We had never prayed for that country before and I wanted to make sure I had heard from God. Instead of speaking out what I was sensing, I said, "I think I know the country we are to pray for next, but I'd like someone else to confirm it."

We leaned over our chairs in concentration. A few throats cleared. Nobody said anything. The minutes seemed to stretch into hours. I shifted uneasily on my knees. *Was I doing the right thing?* Doubts invaded my mind, ramming me sideways. *You're making a fool of yourself! Nobody's going to come up with such an obscure country.* I could speak up and save face, but I kept quiet. If I was hearing from God, surely I could trust him to give the same revelation to someone else.

Finally Loren's wife Dar looked up, her eyes sparkling. "Is it Albania?" A broad smile not only creased my face but also Reona's.

"That's the nation the Lord gave me too," she said excitedly. How thankful I was that I had held my tongue. The fact that three of us had received the same nation greatly bolstered the group's faith. We started praying in earnest for this demonically bound country. From then on, it took high priority in our intercessions.

One night while we were in prayer, Reona described a picture she was seeing of a Albanian lady with a scarf on her head. "God is showing me she's one of the few secret believers who have held out against the prevailing spirit of atheism," she said. We started to pray specifically for this scarf-headed

Mediterranean woman. In other prayer times, we continued to plead for God's protection on her. One evening, Reona told us how she believed God was directing her to visit Albania. It seemed impossible. But as night after night we continued to pray, Reona's conviction grew. She sensed God was giving her specific instructions. For instance she was to travel there by road.

It would be about a year later that Reona along with a friend would join a tour group, fly into the neighboring nation of Yugoslavia and then, just as the Lord had indicated, take a bus and travel by road into Albania. There, while languishing sick in her hotel room, she would meet the very Albanian woman she had seen in her vision. The lady was a hotel maid, and Reona would have the opportunity to give her a Gospel. This action would lead to her arrest. She would be threatened with execution by a firing squad but be miraculously set free.[3] For those of us in the prayer group, the most significant aspect of her trip was that while in Albania, she only encountered one believer—the scarf-headed woman Jesus had shown her in her vision and whom we had been regularly interceding for.

While God had focused Reona on Albania, I was directed towards the country of Bulgaria. It was Brother Andrew who had first alerted me to the needs of Bulgaria. Bordered on the south by Greece, on the west by Yugoslavia, on the east by the Black Sea and on the north by the Danube River, this five-million-strong Balkan nation was one of many that had been taken over by communism.

During both the First and Second World Wars, Bulgarians had strongly opposed the Soviet Union and sided with the Germans. In 1944, perhaps in retaliation, the Russians had marched into Bulgaria, planted their flag and declared it a Soviet state. Now, 26 years later, it had been nicknamed Little Russia and was ruled by one of the fiercest communist regimes. As Brother Andrew had explained to us, Bulgaria, like Albania, was a nation totally opposed to the Gospel. The Church had been cruelly persecuted and many believers imprisoned for their faith. Very few Christians possessed a Bible and it was extremely difficult for anyone in that nation to obtain one.

[3] A full account of Reona's experience is recorded in her book, *Tomorrow We Die.*

The more the Holy Spirit stirred us to pray for this seemingly God-forsaken nation, the deeper my compassion for these spiritually destitute brothers and sisters in Christ grew. I thought of the wealth of practical Christian teaching I was receiving in the SOE and the vast range of teaching books I had in my study back home. It seemed criminal that so many of these Bulgarian Christians did not even own one Bible. Brother Andrew had told us how he had visited Bulgaria a couple of times and clandestinely taken Scriptures in for the Christians. A desire was being awakened in me to follow in Brother Andrew's footsteps. But how could I do it?

Like many of the other students, I was uncertain where my future lay. I was committed to YWAM as full-time staff, but I had no specific idea what I would do when our eight-month course was finished. Towards the end of our three-month lecture phase, a visiting teacher challenged me about working with my own people. I realized there were deep spiritual needs in Switzerland and I seriously brought his suggestion before God. But, despite my willingness to keep working in home territory, I did not sense this was my mission field. I recalled my childhood dreams of working as a missionary in Africa. Surely God had something more exciting for me than working with a people who had been exposed to Christian truth for centuries. My desire was to be a trailblazer, one who tracked down untrodden territory for Christ. I asked God to show me where. But to date, he had not given me any clear direction.

Our three-month lecture phase was fast drawing to a close. Our attention was on our upcoming two-month field trip. During a weekend back home, I told our church about the SOE's planned field trip. We would be traveling from Switzerland through Italy, Yugoslavia, Greece and then by boat to Israel, and then back via Turkey and Greece to Switzerland.

After the service, Roli Sauser approached me, his eyes shining. Since his baptism in the Spirit at the Stuttgart youth camp two years earlier, his Christian life had been revitalized. Now 21, he was an electrician in training. "Rudi, I was so stirred about what you shared regarding the field trip. Do you think I could join you?" I shook my head.

"I don't think so, Roli. It's only for SOE students."

"I'm sure I can get two months' unpaid leave from work. I'd be willing to pay my own way." I did not like to dampen his enthusiasm.

"I'll ask," I promised. In my heart, though, I did not hold out much hope. When I returned to Lausanne and put Roli's request to Loren, I was surprised by his response.

"I don't see any problem, Rudi. It's not our usual policy. But I guess we can make an exception." So it was arranged. Roli would join us. As he eagerly clambered aboard with the rest of us and we headed out from the hotel at Lausanne, I had no idea how important his inclusion on the team would prove to be.

We were traveling in a convoy of two vans and one bus, including the blue bread bus and Don Stephens' old, gray Ford van. Our vehicles had seen better days. But that did not worry us. After three months of sitting, writing at a desk and learning the theory, we could not wait to be out where the action was. We set out knowing our general route—from Switzerland to Israel and then back via Turkey and Greece. But we were flexible. There would be room for the unexpected. Just how unexpected, we were yet to find out. Accommodation was equally uncertain. We had tents and sleeping bags and planned to stay in campsites. But we would also bunk down in church halls—anywhere we could find suitable accommodation to house a group of 30 budding missionaries. Being the only non-English speaker, my young friend Roli stuck to me like glue.

Once we hit the road, it was difficult to keep up our prayer times. With each day's itinerary different and no regular routine, it was impossible to establish a set time. We were busy morning to dusk either traveling, setting up camp or listening to field lectures regarding the Christian heritage of the particular area we were visiting. At night, we would flop exhausted onto our airbeds, too weary to consider praying into the early hours of the morning as we had back in the hotel classroom. Having broken the pattern for prayer we had established, it was easy to coast and enjoy the new experiences.

By the end of our first week, we had already lost the cutting edge of the spiritual alertness we had gained through long hours of intercession. We failed to press into God for every detail as Joy had taught us. Instead of asking God for the exact route we should take or our precise itinerary for that day, we let circumstances guide us. As a result, we unwittingly closed down our line of communication with God. The reality of this hit me the second week. By now we had traveled from Switzerland through northern Italy and, skirting the Adriatic Sea, were driving through Yugoslavia. Loren met up with us in Belgrade.

We were heading south towards Turkey following the main highway E761. Loren was at the steering wheel of the green Volkswagen and I was in the front passenger seat. Two possible routes lay ahead of us. We could go directly south via Greece or take the road through Bulgaria. As we approached the sign that indicated the division in the highway, Loren turned to me. "Okay, Rudi, which route should we take?" He knew my passion for prayer and had also sat in on Joy's teaching about hearing God in detail. He expected me to be "prayed up" and in tune with the Spirit. I looked at him stunned. Like the rest of the students, I had just got in the van and driven. I had not given any consideration as to the exact route we should take.

Not wanting to appear unspiritual, I tried to bluff my answer. I knew that like me, Loren also had a burning desire to visit Bulgaria. "Let's go via Bulgaria," I suggested. Loren looked at me for a moment, considered my answer, then slowly shook his head. "No. I don't think so, Rudi." Unlike me, he had spent quality time with Jesus and was spiritually tuned in. He had discerned this was not God's time to take a bunch of novice students into such a hostile, anti-Christian country as Bulgaria. So instead of turning off, we kept going straight head.

A few kilometers down the road, we came across an accident that seemed further proof Loren had chosen the right route. We were first on the scene and able to help the victims. While unharmed, the occupants of both vehicles were badly shaken. We provided them with basic first aid, and before continuing our journey, we were able to pray with them and leave some tracts. Everyone else climbed back into the van exuberant at this "God-given" opportunity to witness. I sat back in my front passenger seat feeling deflated, not just because my dream of visiting Bulgaria had been squashed, but more because I had not only let Loren down, but the Lord himself. I resolved, no matter how difficult it might be, I would resume my prayer schedule.

After an exhausting day's travel, we finally reached our destination: a church youth camp in Katerini, on the outskirts of Athens. We wearily tumbled out of our two vans and bread bus. After a quick meal, everyone retired for an early night to their sleeping quarters in the wooden cabins. I was as tired as everyone else, but instead of heading for my cabin I sought out Reona. "We need to get back to our prayer routine," I said to her, explaining how I had blown it with Loren at the Bulgaria crossroads. Reona, her cotton floral dress crumpled from the long day's journey, and looking as ready for bed as the rest of us, nodded in agreement.

"You're right, Rudi. We've fallen into the old trap of prioritizing activity over prayer." I thought back to our Grenoble outreach experience. How had we so quickly forgotten?

We resolved from then on to pursue our times of intercession together, no matter how inconvenient it was. Our greatest problem was finding a secluded spot. But we managed. Sometimes we met in an open field near our campsite in full view of everyone. At other times, when we camped in church halls and were so crammed we had to clamber over one another's bedding to reach our own, we would gather in a small circle on someone's mattress and pray.

After two weeks in Athens, we loaded our vehicles onto a ship and, along with several hundred Eastern European Jews, headed for Haifa in Israel. Our destination for the night was Jerusalem. It was a long journey, but an exciting one. I was deeply moved by the passion of these Jewish immigrants as they headed for their new homeland, a land that had been denied to them for so many centuries. But I was also deeply saddened as I sought to talk to them. I quickly realized the idols of materialism, particularly the pursuit of financial success, dominated their thinking. The God who had rescued their forefathers from the tyrants of Egypt's Pharaoh had long since been cast aside. Some we spoke to did not even believe he existed.

As we were to discover during our week in Israel, many retained an outward show of their culture: the weekly Sabbath, Bar Mitzvah[4] and key annual festivals such as Passover or Purim. But like Israel in the Old Testament, most had discarded the true foundations of their heritage. Only a handful of orthodox, religious Jews we met during our two-day boat journey to Haifa retained any strong belief in God and held tenaciously to the traditions of the Torah: the first five books of the Old Testament. Some spoke of a coming Messiah, but no one we spoke with during the journey would accept the idea that this Messiah had already come and his name was Jesus. It made me realize witnessing to these Israelites was not going to be an easy task.

We arrived in Haifa around midday. It took us a further two hours to clear customs and then drive the vehicles off the ship. We still had another two hours' drive to Jerusalem. It was early evening by the time our dust-covered vehicles finally pulled up in front of the big, wooden doors of a Catholic monastery situated outside the old city walls. Built of soft, golden Jerusalem stone and surrounded by a high wall, whose entrance way was barred by heavy timber doors, it looked impressive but welcoming. Thirty travel-weary students piled out, along with Loren, Dar and our one extra recruit, my young Swiss friend Roli. The nuns welcomed us warmly. We eagerly sat down to a hearty meal of flat bread spread with typical Israeli delicacies such as olives, cucumbers and cottage cheese. Our mealtime conversation was muted. All anyone could think about was bed.

"How about having a time of intercession together?" I asked Don, Deyon and the other regular attendees of our intercession group. My suggestion went down like a lead balloon.

Rudi! You can't be serious. We're exhausted." Even Dar, who was always so eager to pray, poured cold water on my spiritual zeal.

"I don't think so tonight. Thanks, Rudi," she said brightly. Only Reona showed any enthusiasm. Like me, she had keenly felt the Lord's rebuke regarding our prayerlessness during the earlier part of the journey. We had both determined to retain our

[4] Introduction from boyhood to manhood.

prayer routine, no matter what the personal cost.

"But where are we going to meet, Rudi?" Reona asked. The monastery was packed with YWAMers. There was hardly a spare corner, let alone an empty room. Then I had an idea. Our team vehicles were parked outside the monastery walls, beside the main gate.

"Let's go and pray in the green van," I suggested.

"Okay," Reona agreed. After the meal, while everyone else headed off to unroll their sleeping bags, Reona and I slipped into the courtyard. A silvery moon was creeping over the Judean hills. We went out through the heavy, wooden entrance gates and climbed into the green VW van. Immediately, I felt my spirit soar. This was where God wanted us, not sleeping the night away, but interceding for the nations, regardless of how physically tired we felt.

I had a special desire to pray for the Jews we had attempted to witness to during our boat journey from Athens. Before long, we were caught up in intensive intercession for this nation of Israel. Yet despite my genuine concern for these chosen people, I was fighting off distracting thoughts. What if the nuns or someone else saw Reona and me sitting here in the dark, alone in a parked vehicle? What would they think? There was no romantic involvement between us. God had made that clear to me. We were just good friends, drawn together by our common love for prayer. I am sure our leaders Loren and Dar understood this, which is why they had never questioned the time we spent together. An outsider, however, could draw a totally different conclusion. I did not want to tarnish YWAM's reputation, especially as the nuns had been so generous in their hospitality. I felt torn. I had such a strong urge to pray and the van was the only place we had to meet. I finally decided my thoughts were Satan's tactics to distract me. Pushing them aside, I concentrated on our intercession.

Around midnight, there was loud clanging. Reona stopped praying and looked up. "What was that?"

"I think it's the wind banging those big, wooden entrance doors," I said. Thinking no more about it, we got back to prayer. We went on to intercede for Albania and the nation especially close to my heart, Bulgaria. Finally, in the early hours of the morning, aware that we had completed our prayer assignment, and by now so overcome by the weariness from the day's travel that we could hardly keep our eyes open, we clambered down from the van and headed towards the monastery gates. I had just one thought—the welcoming comfort of my sleeping bag.

When we left the monastery, the large, wooden entrance doors had been open. Now, they were closed. I was right. That clanging sound we had heard earlier had been the wind banging them shut. Reona reached out to push the door open. It did not move. She tried a second time. The door remained firmly shut. Again she tried, this time pressing her whole weight against the huge timber frame and pushing as hard as she could. It still refused to budge.

At that moment, the truth dawned on both of us. It was not the wind that had banged those entrance doors shut. It was the nuns locking up for the night. They had bolted the doors from the inside, not realizing there were two students praying in a van outside. Reona looked at me in panic. "Rudi! What are we going to do now?" I felt helpless. There was nothing I could do. My earlier concern flooded back. We were stuck outside the gates in a situation which, while totally innocent, was potentially very embarrassing. We could not both spend the night in the van. "Do something," Reona fumed. She too could see how awkward our situation was. "After all, it was your suggestion to pray in the van," she added angrily.

I could have argued that she had agreed with me that the van was a good place for prayer, but she was not in a mood to be reasoned with. I stayed quiet. But my thoughts were racing. *What could we do? Lord, help us!* I prayed in silent desperation. Suddenly I had a surge of faith—an absolute certainty that God would provide a way through the heavy, wooden door. I went boldly up to it and gave it a light push. The door swung open easily on its hinges and a greatly relieved Reona and I went through, closed it behind us and went our separate ways to bed. It was not until the next morning that the full extent of the miracle dawned on us. We learned the nuns had definitely locked the doors at midnight. There was no way anyone could have got in from the outside: no way that is, apart from the divine intervention of God.

Such clear evidence of God's working greatly encouraged our faith and inspired us to keep going in our intercessions. We continued to meet nightly. By the time we reached Beersheba, Don, Deyon, David, Carol, Al, Dar and Joe—all the original members of our prayer group in Lausanne—as well as others had started to join us. When there was nowhere else suitable to meet, up to 12 of us would cram into our largest vehicle, the blue bread bus, and there spend several hours interceding for whatever God laid on our hearts.

I well remember, when we were camped on the edge of the desert in Beersheba, staggering out of the van after a long session of prayer and standing in awe as I looked out over the beauty of soft, burnished golden sand dunes shimmering under the moonlight. In the darkness, their faint outlines rolled along the horizon, billowing out across the desert like waves on a vast ocean. I was reminded of Loren's waves of young people marching the globe. It was a sight I would have missed had I not been up late praying.

In the morning, the scene was very different. We were awakened early by sunlight penetrating the sides of our tents. As we opened the flaps and looked out, a golden sun was peeping over the horizon, casting its long shadow over those same rolling sand dunes. There was almost a harshness, yet equally awesome beauty to the scene. I marveled at the sheer magnificence of God's creation, and in my heart thanked him for allowing me to be a part of this adventure with him.

By mid-morning, the temperatures had soared and we as a student body were out visiting from door to door. Because it was forbidden by law to "recruit" for other religions in Israel, we had to be very careful. We could not share our faith openly with the Israelis. Instead of calling ourselves Christians, we introduced ourselves as followers of the Messiah. By taking this approach, we found a greater openness, and on a number of occasions people invited us into their homes. Even so, it was not easy to broach the subject of Jesus Christ. In the Jewish mind, Christians and the Church are strongly associated with the persecuting Crusaders. Despite this barrier, we did see some respond to our message.

Our efforts at "evangelizing" the Israelis did not go unnoticed. One day, while we were still in Beersheba, I was out on the street with a couple of others when an Israeli newspaper reporter approached us. "I understand there's a group of Mormons here," he said casually. I was on my guard instantly. Mormonism was banned in Israel. What had this guy heard about us?

"We're not Mormons," I hastened to assure him.

"Oh, no. What are you doing here in Beersheba then?" he asked with added interest. I tried to make light of our activities, explaining we were students on a practical field trip, visiting different Middle Eastern countries. But his journalistic curiosity had been aroused. He sniffed a story. "I'd like to write an article about you for our newspaper. Would you do an interview with me?" Such publicity was the last thing we needed!

"I'm not the leader of the group," I said, desperately trying to put him of.

"Could I meet with the leader?" he asked. I glanced over at Reona and noticed her dark-haired head was bowed in silent prayer.

"I'm not sure where he is right now," I said truthfully. Loren had gone with another group.

"Could I stick with you for a while then?"

"Do you mind?" I said, "We'd rather be alone. Really, we don't have anything of interest to tell you." Seeing he was not getting anywhere, the reporter eventually left.

The next day, however, he turned up at our campsite. He seemed friendly enough, but we were careful not to divulge the true nature of our activities. That night as we got down to serious prayer, the Lord revealed to us this was a trap of the enemy. Any publicity could severely backfire on us. The next day the reporter was back again, snooping around, asking questions. Having been warned through our intercessions, we were even more careful to avoid giving him any information that could incriminate us. We must have finally convinced him that we were indeed a bunch of students on tour, as we did not see him after that. But it had been a close call. It showed us yet again the importance of remaining tuned into the Spirit and of not relaxing in our intercession.

5

A Dream

My concern for Bulgaria intensified and in particular the country's need for Bibles. An idea was forming in my mind. Did God want me to be an answer to my own prayers and take Bibles into Bulgaria myself? We would be going back to Athens. Perhaps I could take a side trip on our return?

I did not want to presume or elevate myself above the other students. Some had already been objecting to our nightly prayer meetings, saying we were pulling apart from the rest of the group. There were no grounds for their complaints. Our meetings were open to everyone. I did not want to take the risk of my motives being misinterpreted, so I kept my thoughts to myself. The only person I shared them with was Reona.

The more I pondered the idea, however, the stronger my conviction grew. I was becoming so sure Jesus was telling me I should go into Bulgaria, and that it was to be during this field trip, that I began storing up both Romanian and Bulgarian Scriptures. I had actually started in Athens. Whenever I had a spare moment, I would ferret out a Christian bookshop and buy more Bibles. Through the generous gifts of friends back home, God had provided finance for such purchases.

While the other students did not know exactly what they contained, they got used to seeing me return to our camping quarters carrying yet another box of books. As my cartons were stacking up in the van, some began to object. Space was at a premium and my extra "luggage" was not appreciated. Nobody spoke to me directly. But their message of discontent was getting through. The last thing I wanted was to cause a rift among the student body. Together with Don, Deyon and Reona, I had been appointed one of the team leaders. As a YWAM staff member, I should be setting an example of discretion.

As we continued on from Beersheba through Tel Aviv and back north to Haifa, the murmuring increased. Some students began to openly voice their complaints: "Rudi is going over the top." "What do we need that literature for anyway?" Even the other team leaders were beginning to express their concern. But I was so certain I had a mandate from Christ that I did not want to give up. I felt I needed to prepare and wait for him to somehow open the door. So despite the growing opposition, I doggedly continued my ferreting expeditions for Bibles.

By the time we reached Haifa, this had become my major focus. A trip was planned for Mount Carmel. I would have loved to visit this biblical site where the great prophet Elijah had slain the Baal prophets. But my greater concern was to obtain more Bulgarian Bibles. So, foregoing the trip, I went off in search of a Christian bookstore. Even though I had not yet broached the subject with Loren, I was now convinced God wanted me to take Scriptures into Bulgaria. "What are you going to do with these?" the lady at the counter asked with interest, as she packaged up my order of Bulgarian and Romanian Bibles.

"I'm going to take them into Bulgaria," I said boldly. It was the first time I had voiced my aspirations to anyone besides Reona.

"Why Romanian too?" she asked.

"Once inside any communist nation, it's not so difficult to shift them between the different countries," I replied.

"I'll pray for you every day," she smiled. I left the store greatly encouraged by her response. But I also realized the time had come for me to seek further confirmation. I needed to know for certain that this was a task God was calling me to, and not just my bright idea.

One night, while in Istanbul, I confided in my young Swiss friend Roli. We were drinking coffee together at one of the outdoor cafes. During the trip, Roli and I had spent a lot of time together, and although five years my junior, I had come to appreciate him as a friend. "What do you think, Roli? Am I going off the deep end?" He ran his finger round his cup thoughtfully, but did not answer. I could see he did not share my enthusiasm.

"I don't know, Rudi," he finally answered, taking a sip of his black Turkish brew. "Why don't you ask Loren? Put it to him straight. If this is God's plan, he'll okay it." His words gave me hope.

"You're right, Roli. Loren hears from God. He'll know if I'm on track or not." I looked at Roli straight in the eyes. "If he does approve, will you come with me? I couldn't go alone." Roli wrinkled his forehead. It was one thing to encourage me. It was another to consider going himself.

"See what he says," he replied without committing himself. I did not try to press him further. My biggest and first hurdle was to get Loren's permission.

The next day I saw him standing alone, a short distance from the tents and took the opportunity to talk with him. I told him everything: my burden for Bulgaria, the Bibles I had already collected and my desire to take these into the Scripture-starved Church of this communist nation. I also shared about the murmuring of discontent that was filtering through from the others. Loren looked over my shoulder to the activity in the tents behind me. He did not comment. He had already had his ear to the ground and was no doubt well aware of the reaction to my "book stacking". From our prayer times together, he also knew of my burden for Bulgaria. But I do not think he realized until this moment, just how serious I was.

I knew Loren well enough to know that his silence did not indicate disinterest. He had taken in every word I had said. Now in his usual calm, unhurried manner, he was weighing them, considering every angle and possibly seeking the Lord in silent prayer for wisdom. I stood shifting uncomfortably from one foot to the other as I waited for his response. Would he dismiss my idea as a hair-brained scheme and squash it altogether?

At last Loren looked at me, "If you were to take Bibles into Bulgaria, do you have anybody to give them to?"

"Not really," I admitted sheepishly. Apart from the information I had gleaned from Brother Andrew and what I had personally researched, I had only limited understanding of the church behind this Iron Curtain nation. I had learned that not all who called themselves Christians (not even official church ministers) could be trusted. Many were informers—deliberate government implants sent in to spy on the true believers.

"What do you mean 'not really'?" Loren asked.

"Someone warned me about the head of a certain evangelical denomination in the capital Sofia," I replied. "I don't know his name, but he is evidently a government informer and cannot be trusted."

"I see," Loren said thoughtfully.

"God was able to lead Brother Andrew supernaturally to contacts. I'm sure he can do the same for me," I quickly added. Loren looked at me but did not comment.

"How many Bulgarian and Romanian Bibles do you already have, Rudi?" I did a quick mental count.

"Just under 200."

"And you feel you still need more?"

"Think about it, Loren. Two hundred Bibles in a country of five million where only a handful of Christians own a Bible, that's a mere drop in the bucket." He nodded. He could see my point.

"Where are you going to get these Scriptures in Turkey?" he queried.

"I've contacted the British Embassy. They were able to track down the Bible Society headquarters for me here in Istanbul," I replied. Loren raised his eyebrows, obviously impressed by my diligence.

"I've not contacted them, but I'm certain they'll have ample supplies."

"So how many more do you feel you need?"

Instantly the thought, *Ten Bulgarian and ten Romanian*, came to mind. That number seemed too small. I dismissed it as an instruction from the Lord. Instead, I answered, "At least ten more Romanian and fifty Bulgarian."

"Okay," Loren replied. What he did not tell me was, he was making this a test. If the Bible Society had that amount of Bibles in stock, he would take it as the sign of God's blessing on my mission.

That afternoon, I went off to the Bible Society headquarters, my heart singing. "How can I help?" the lady at the counter asked sweetly as I entered.

"I'll have fifty Bulgarian Bibles and ten Romanian, thank you," I said confidently.

"I'm sorry, sir, we don't have that many." My smile evaporated.

"Oh!" I recalled my impression of ten Bulgarian and ten Romanian. "How many do you have?" I asked in a more subdued tone.

"I'll go and check for you. Wait a moment." The assistant disappeared into a rear room. I stood tapping the counter, my faith ebbing away like water in a leaking container. *She'll find some extra out the back*, I tried to assure myself. After a few minutes, she returned. "We've just got ten Romanian and ten Bulgarian, sir." I looked at her stunned, my mouth ajar. It was the exact amount that had come to mind when Loren had asked me. "Do you still want them?" the lady asked, noting my dazed expression.

"Yes. Yes. I'll take all you've got."

Ten Romanian and ten Bulgarian! God had been speaking to me. How was I going to explain myself to Loren? I opened my wallet. As I pulled out all my notes, I suddenly realized how little it contained. Even if the society had 60 Bibles in stock, I could not have afforded them. I only had enough money in my wallet to pay for 20!

I decided to be up front with Loren. So I confessed my sin of presumption and explained how God had really told me to purchase 20, not 60. I was glad I was honest, especially when Loren explained how he had made the availability of the Bibles a test. Now that he could see God's hand in this venture, Loren gave me his blessing. "All right, Rudi, you may take your Bibles into Bulgaria. But you only have four days—no more. You can be our trailblazer and scout out the possibility of sending in future outreach teams." I was elated. I had permission to go. I had my Bibles and Don had generously offered us his Ford van. All I needed now was a partner to go with me and help with the driving. I went looking for my young Swiss friend. I found him in his tent.

"Loren has given me permission. Will you come with me?" Roli looked up from where he was perched on his air mattress and stared at me for a few moments. My heart missed a beat. If Roli would not come, who was I going to ask? Then a broad smile spread out over his face.

"All right, I'll come, Rudi. When do we leave?"

The next day, we traveled from Istanbul back to the church youth camp in Katerini, on the outskirts of Athens, where the Scottish evangelist Duncan Campbell was flying in to spend a week with us. We set our departure date for just over a week's time, following his visit. Duncan Campbell had been intimately involved with the revival in the Scottish islands of the Hebrides, and had been conducting a series of powerful revival meetings around the world. His time with us proved a real inspiration, just the sort of encouragement Roli and I needed as we prepared for our trip.

When the other students realized this was not just a "hair-brained Rudi Lack scheme", but a journey the leadership had not only officially endorsed but were excited about, more warmed to the idea of our going. For our operation to be successful, however, we needed the backing of the whole student body. As Brother Andrew had told us, the reason Open Door's smuggling trips behind the Iron Curtain were so successful was because people back home were praying specifically for God to make the seeing eyes of the customs officers blind. Without the rest of the students' concerted prayer support, we had far less chance of getting across the border undetected or finding suitable contacts to whom we could deliver our precious load. To this point of time, we did not have that support. There were still a few dissenting voices. Ideally we needed the entire field outreach interceding for us around the clock, for the full four days we would be away. I was finding it difficult to rally that kind of commitment.

Now that our proposed smuggling trip had been approved, it was dawning on me what I was really letting myself in for. Christians behind the Iron Curtain had been imprisoned for years for possessing a forbidden Bible or holding an illegal church service. Some had languished three or four years behind bars, just waiting for a trial. I was reminded of Brother Andrew's words, "God has told us to go. But he has not promised that we would come back." It was one thing to listen, enthralled by his stories, in the safety of a Lausanne classroom. Now that I was about to embark on this journey of faith myself, I was not so sure. I recognized I needed to do some serious praying.

The day prior to our departure, Reona agreed to spend a day in prayer and fasting with me. As we sat in the Ford that would be our transport the next day, we sought to cover every aspect of the trip in prayer. We specifically asked for safety on the road. Neither Roli nor I had any mechanical expertise. While we were grateful for Don's generosity in lending us his van, it had given us endless trouble on our way through Israel and Turkey. If it broke down or if we had an accident, particularly inside Bulgaria, it would be almost impossible to repair or find parts.

Reona and I also spent much time pleading for God to give us the right contacts. That was now my major concern. While I had all the Bibles I needed, I did not have any trustworthy person I could give them to. I had recently been given the name of a Pastor Uskatzow who lived in Sofia. But I did not know anything about him. All I had was his name and address. I also knew that I needed to avoid the director of a certain evangelical denomination: the one I had been warned was a government informer. As Reona and I prayed through on this issue, our spirits lifted and my confidence rose. Although I did not know how, I was sure that God would lead me to the right person.

We were midway through our day of prayer and fasting when Loren came over to the van and shared a Scripture with us. It was Matthew 7:15: *Beware of false prophets, who come to you in sheep's clothing, but inwardly are ferocious wolves.* It did not seem to make much sense. "How do you feel that applies, Loren?" I asked.

"I'm not sure. Maybe the Lord's trying to warn you to stay alert and not trust everyone you meet," he said.

This warning through Loren was confirmed later when, towards the end of our day of fasting, two Scripture references were strongly impressed upon Reona. The first was Revelation

12:12: *Rejoice then, O heaven and you that dwell therein! But woe to you, O earth and sea, for the devil has come down to you in great wrath, because he knows that his time is short!* The second was Jeremiah 46:27-28: *But fear not ... nor be dismayed ... for lo, I will save you from afar ... fear not ... for I am with you.* While I was encouraged by this promise of protection, I particularly noted the further warning of impending danger. I had no idea what form it might take, but it put me on my guard.

That night a young English-speaking couple in their late twenties arrived at our camp. Although not connected with YWAM, they had heard about us and asked if they could stay for a couple of days. They had been traveling through Europe, ministering. I was excited to learn they had been behind the Iron Curtain. "Where have you just come from?" I asked as the three of us sat down alone at one of the round tables in the dining room to a typical field trip meal of rice and fish. After my day of fasting, I was eager to dig in.

"Bulgaria. We've been visiting the Church there." My heart jumped. Food suddenly became unimportant. The timing of their visit was amazing. Surely they were God's answer to our prayers. They probably had reliable church contacts they could put me in touch with.

I put my fork and knife down and was about to tell them about Roli and my proposed trip the next day when something stopped me. I recalled the verse Loren had given us about watching out for wolves in sheep's clothing. It suddenly occurred to me that I knew nothing about this couple. They seemed friendly enough. I had no reason not to trust them. But it struck me they had been rather too open about their contact with the Church inside Bulgaria. I did not want to walk into a trap. While I had no tangible evidence to support my suspicions, I decided discretion was called for. I listened with interest as they chatted openly about their time in Bulgaria. But I did not say a word about our own plans to leave for that very nation the next day.

I wondered if I was being over sensitive, so after the meal I sought Loren out and privately shared my concern. "Could this couple be the 'wolves in sheep's clothing' that you warned us about earlier?" He looked thoughtful.

"They may, but then they may not. I'm not sure, Rudi." He bowed his head in silent prayer. Ialsoprayed.Was I being over dramatic? They were probably just a couple of exuberant Christians who were keen to share their experiences in a foreign country. But still that doubt remained. Loren looked up from his prayer. "You could be right, Rudi. I think it would be wise to say nothing."

As the couple went off to settle in one of the spare cabins on the campsite, Loren drew the student body aside and warned them against saying anything to the visiting couple about our planned trip the next day. His warning brought home to the students, as nothing else had, the reality of the risk Roli and I were taking. All lingering opposition immediately evaporated. This possibly "wolves-in-sheep's-clothing" couple proved to be the rallying point we needed to get everyone on board.

Earlier, when I mentioned the need for a round-the-clock prayer meeting, there were only a few takers. Now everyone caught our excitement and indicated their willingness to be involved. The entire field trip agreed to take up the battle in prayer. Each student volunteered to commit to a 24-hour prayer chain that would operate throughout the entire four days we would be away. There were even takers for those early morning "graveyard shifts". I praised God for the Scriptures he had laid on Loren's and Reona's hearts. Even though the reality of the battle still lay ahead, I was confident that now all the backup troops were in place. Victory was assured.

6

Border Crossing

I had hoped for an early night to be fresh for the long journey from Athens to the Bulgarian border. Roli and I would be traveling up some fairly tortuous mountain roads. With all the confusion caused by the presence of the "sheep-in-wolf's clothing" couple, it was 1am before I got to bed. I lay awake, restless, turning in my sleeping bag, thinking of all the drama of the previous day and the uncertainty of the journey still ahead. While I felt assured God was in control, it still concerned me that we did not have a recommended contact to whom we could deliver the Bibles.

I fell into a fitful sleep, dreaming of border guards seizing our cargo, of Roli and me being dragged off to prison and me boldly preaching to my captors. Even in the midst of persecution, I was determined to live up to my name "daring wolf". Despite my few hours of restless sleep, I woke early, just as the first few rays of sun filtered through the cabin window. I quickly dressed and made my way to a secluded spot on the beach just in front of our camp. Sitting there in the sand, I turned the pages of my Bible. It fell open at Psalm 45. As I read, verse four seemed to jump off the page: *Let your right hand display awesome deeds* or, as it was translated in my German Bible, *daring deeds*.

I sat looking out to sea, letting the full impact of the words soak in. Suddenly I heard footsteps and looked up to see Reona coming towards me. She too had awoken early to pray. She sat beside me and for several minutes we both sat without talking, drinking in the beautiful calm of that early morning beach scene. Nothing about our tranquil surroundings reflected the possible dangers Roli and I might encounter that very day.

Finally Reona broke the silence. "Rudi, I believe the Lord has given me some Scriptures for you during my 'quiet time'." She flicked through the pages of her Bible. "This was just part of my reading this morning. It's Psalm 112." She began at verse one, highlighting the sections of the psalm she sensed specifically applied. I shut my eyes and listened to the lilt of her Kiwi accent as she read: *Blessed is the man who fears the Lord, who finds great delight in his commandments.... Even in darkness light dawns on the upright.... Good will come to him who is generous and lends freely, who conducts his affairs with justice. Surely he will never be shaken.... He will have no fear of bad news; his heart is steadfast, trusting in the Lord.*

I opened my eyes. "That's tremendous, Reona." I looked up Psalm 112 in my own Bible and reread the verses for myself. I marveled afresh at how amazingly accurate and pinpointed God's word could be. *Good will comes to him who is generous and lends freely.* We planned to freely give away the Bibles without cost. *He will have no fear of bad news....* That was certainly a word of encouragement and tied in with my word from Psalm 45 about "daring deeds".

Reona interjected into my thoughts. "The other Scripture I got for you was Numbers 10:1." I turned to it in my Bible and read along with her. *So they set out from the mountain of the Lord and traveled for three days. The Ark of the Covenant of the Lord went before them during those three days to find them a place to rest. The cloud of the Lord was over them by day when they set out from the camp.* Three days, I mused to myself. Loren had given us four. Maybe we would have our task accomplished in three? Whatever, the message was clear. God had promised to go before us, protect us and bring us back safely. I was greatly encouraged.

By now it was nearing 7.30am. Our camp was beginning to stir into life. I had one preoccupation—getting the Ford loaded with our contraband goods. We had to take care to do this without letting the visiting couple know what we were doing. Their presence made the whole process much more complicated. We parked as far away from their cabin as possible and, with the help of the other students, managed to load up without either of them seeing or suspecting that anything unusual was taking place.

"Where are you going to hide these, Rudi?" one of the students asked, a box of Bibles in his hands. It was a question, that until this moment, I had not even considered. How were we going to conceal our precious load? Brother Andrew had told us how they had hidden their books behind car panels. Don's battered van did not have any inside paneling, so we could not use that method. There was no obvious place to protect them out of the sight of the prying eyes of a border guard.

"I know," Roli said, coming to my rescue. "Let's pack them into suitcases among our clothes and then scatter them with camping gear." I nodded with approval.

"Great idea, Roli. Let's do it."

With enthusiasm, someone began blowing up an air mattress. Another person found a big, rubber bathing ring which they inflated and threw into the back of the van along with a variety of camping equipment. What we hoped an unobservant eye would not see—packed in suitcases and hidden from sight under the blankets, rubber ring and in amongst a camping stove, cameras, magazines and food—were 200 Bibles. As an afterthought, someone threw in an old rusted iron that they had found on a nearby beach. Rusted and little more than a piece of junk, it was a creative touch that would later prove a significant part of the whole disguise.

While we worked loading the Ford, one of the mechanics gave the van a final check-up. Despite Reona and my prayers for safety in driving, I still felt nervous about taking this well-worn vehicle which had such a poor record of roadworthiness. But it was the vehicle God had provided. I had to trust that he would get us there and back without incident.

We had originally planned to be away early in the day, but packing and final preparations took longer than expected. It was late in the afternoon before the vehicle was loaded, and we were ready to depart. Everyone gathered to see us off. Fortunately the visiting couple had left earlier in the day, so there was no more need for secrecy. But Satan's last-minute attempts to disrupt our plans had truly been turned for good. It was wonderful to be leaving, knowing we had united prayer backing. "Go for it, guys!" Don shouted, banging the van and sending us, dust billowing, on our way.

The shouts of farewell fading behind us, I gripped the black steering wheel and, settling into the cracked vinyl seat, prepared myself for the 12-hour drive ahead. I did a quick mental check. Did we have everything? Wallet? I felt in my pocket. Yes. It only contained 100 dollars. My personal reserves had been exhausted in purchasing Bibles. A few students had pressed money into my hand before we left. I had also received a last-minute and unexpected gift from friends back home. Prior to our departure, Loren had discovered how little money we had and suggested that we borrow field trip funds. But I felt not to do this. We would trust God to supply.

I glanced over my shoulder into the back of the van and smiled at the strewn array of camping gear, even down to the rusty old iron. No one would suspect that hidden below the innocent array of outdoor equipment were 200 Bibles. I just hoped it would be a good enough disguise to fool the border guards. Roli and I chatted for a while and then traveled on in silence. Now that the excitement of the day was behind us and it was just the two of us, we continued in subdued reflection, both engrossed in our own thoughts. What would the next few days hold?

I knew if we were caught at the border, we would not only lose the Bibles, but all our gear including the van. As battered as it was, this would be a tragedy. It was not only Roli and my only means of transport, but it was a vital part of the fleet for the remaining weeks of our two-month field trip. It would also be used for the upcoming three-month outreach, a time when we as students embarked on our own mission outreach with no school staff directing us.

We made our way north from Athens through rolling countryside with its profusion of olive groves and wild flowers. To our right, the rich blue of the Mediterranean Sea was dotted with Greek islands. By late night, we had reached the high mountain ranges that we needed to cross before coming down into the wide valley that would bring us into Bulgaria. The van crawled up the steep incline. It was nearing midnight and, although sealed, the road at this point was narrow and gravelly. It took all my concentration to negotiate the sharp, hairpin bends. My late night and early morning rise, plus all the drama of the last two days, was beginning to take its toll. I found myself struggling to keep awake.

Roli was already fast asleep in the passenger seat beside me. I should have stopped earlier to let him take over the wheel, but I had been reluctant to wake him, so I had kept driving. Ideally, we should have stopped sooner and found somewhere to set up camp for the night. Now it was too late. Also, on these twisting roads, there was nowhere suitable to stop. We had been so late in getting away that we had already lost over half a day in travel time, so I pushed myself to keep going. As we turned a sharp bend, I had an excellent view of the moonlit cliffs dropping sharply away to my right. I was thankful that the Ford seemed to be standing up to this tough, mountainous climb. The last thing we wanted now was for it to break down.

I maneuvered yet another turn, and I looked again at the sheer face of those cliffs as they fell away so magnificently to be swallowed up into the pitch black of the gorge floor many hundreds of meters below. Not much chance of survival if a vehicle was to go over the bank. I shuddered at the thought and gripped the steering wheel even tighter as I sought to give full concentration to my driving.

Coming up was a particularly sharp corner. I held tightly to the steering as I approached the bend. Suddenly it seemed as if the wheel was torn from my hands. For a few seconds, the van tires spun madly out of control. "Oh no!" I screamed. I had visions of us crashing down the side of the gully, and Roli and me plunging to our deaths in the hellish black of the rugged gorge. Roli woke, startled.

"What? Where?"

Then, just as quickly as it had begun, the van righted itself, and we lurched forward safely round the bend.

"Wow! That was a close one, Rudi. What happened?" Roli was now wide awake.

"I don't know," I gasped. Even though the problem had clearly righted itself, my heart continued to pound. In my weariness, had I had a lapse of concentration? I was not aware that I had done anything wrong. It was as though the van had a mind of its own and had gone berserk. "It's almost as if the devil himself was trying to throw us off the road and put an end to our mission," I whispered.

"Praise the Lord for those back at the camp praying for us," Roli said quietly. "Their prayers were certainly answered that time." I nodded.

"Yes. How thankful I am we're not in this venture alone, Roli." I encouraged myself too about God's promise to bring us back safely.

Nevertheless we were both badly shaken by the incident. As soon as there was a safe spot to stop, I pulled over and we spent time thanking Jesus for his protection. We also took the extra precaution of taking regular turns at driving and increased our own individual prayer vigil. We did not want to give any further opportunity, be it by direct spiritual assault or through our own foolishness, for Satan to get a foothold on us. As Roli took the wheel and I settled into the passenger seat, I breathed another silent prayer of praise for those back at the camp who right now were awake interceding for us. What we would only learn later was how specifically they were being directed to pray.

Because of our delayed departure and limited time restraint of four days, we decided, despite our near accident, to continue driving through the night. While one slept, the other drove. By four in the morning, we had come down from the mountain pass into the gentle plains of the wide valley that formed the frontier between northern Greece and southern Bulgaria. We were now only a few kilometers from the border. We could have easily kept traveling straight across. Guards would be on duty right through the night. But from Joy Dawson's teaching, I had learned that it was essential to seek God in detail. I sensed it was important to ask him for the precise hour that we should cross. So instead of continuing, I pulled the van off the road and parked in a field, under a tree.

Roli was still fast asleep in the passenger seat. Rather than disturb him, I reached for my Bible and, quietly opening the van door, eased myself out. Sitting in the field, some distance from the van, I began to voice my prayers into the semi-darkness of the early morning sky. Dawn was still some way off. "Lord, I take authority over the enemy and any interference in my mind," I prayed. I wanted to make sure that I was really going to hear from God. Then I asked the Spirit to show me any unconfessed sin in my life. Nothing came to mind, so I continued declaring my total dependency upon him. Finally, having fully prepared myself, I asked my crucial question, "Lord, what time do you want us to cross the border?"

Our whole mission into Bulgaria could stand or fall on my hearing correctly from the Father on this matter. If we crossed the border out of God's timing with the wrong guard on duty, our precious load might be discovered, and we would be sent back even before we got in. Worse, our van would be confiscated along with the Bibles. With our limited funds, Roli and I had no way of getting back. This really was crunch time.

I would only discover later that, at this precise moment, hundreds of kilometers away at the camp near Athens, God was tapping Loren on the shoulder. Shaking him awake, he urged him to pray for us. Earlier, students on the prayer chain had also felt impressed to pray that we did not rush across the frontier, but wait for the Lord's perfect timing.

I repeated my request. "Show me the exact hour you want us to cross the border?" I waited in expectancy for him to answer. I did not have to wait long. Into my mind came the words, *in the sixth hour.* I opened my Bible and flicking through its pages came to the account of Jesus' death in Mark 15. In the semi-light, I scanned the page. There it was in verse 33: *In the sixth hour....* To me that meant one thing. We were to cross at six o'clock that morning—in just one hour's time. It did not dawn on me that the Jewish day begins at six o'clock and the sixth hour would have been midday. In my ignorance, God used this Scripture to give us his exact timing for our border crossing.

I returned to the van, woke Roli and shared my revelation. By now the first faint rays of dawn were appearing over the mountains behind us. Roli and I sat waiting in the van. We were hungry, having not even stopped to eat. We had just taken short snacks as we traveled. There were provisions in the van, but we were too nervous to eat. Both of us were dog tired. We had only dozed fitfully through the night in broken sleep as we each took his turn in the passenger seat. It was tempting to turn the ignition key, drive those few kilometers and get the crossing over and done with. But I knew we could not dare disobey God. He had given us six o'clock as our crossing hour, and even though I might never understand the full reason for his timing, I knew we must not move until that precise moment.

The final hour of waiting dragged by monotonously. I have never found waiting easy. I am a man of action. Just sitting there, with nothing to do, was one of the most difficult aspects of the trip so far. The burden of the silence seemed almost intolerable. I could not even concentrate in prayer, and with the tension of what could possibly lie ahead of us at the border, neither Roli nor I felt like talking.

The minutes ticked by slowly. I checked my watch for the umpteenth occasion: 5.55 am. I sighed in relief. At last it was time to go. I took a last glimpse around the rear of our van strewn with camping gear. Every inch of floor was covered. It was a mess, but at least genuine. I reached for the key and turned the engine on. The tired motor spluttered into action. At the same time, Roli pulled out our passports and held them at the ready. Stamped with the many entries and exits of our zigzagged field trip through Italy, Yugoslavia, Israel, Turkey and Greece, they added further to our guise as a couple of unshaven camping tourists.

Taking a deep breath, I put my foot on the accelerator and pulled from the field where we had parked, back out onto the road. The moment of reckoning had finally come. I glanced over at Roli. He was gazing out the window, looking amazingly unconcerned. Did he really understand what lay ahead of us at the border, and the consequences we faced if we got caught?

Adrenaline rushed through my veins like the water over Niagara Falls. My heart pounded with a mixture of fear and apprehension. Praying Brother Andrew's prayer furiously under my breath, I determinedly drove the few kilometers to the frontier. *God blind the eyes of the border guards.* I did everything I could to keep focused on the Lord, and reminded myself over and over of his promises of protection and assurance that everything was under his control. A small, wooden hut with its two zebra-painted posts on either side of the road came in sight. I slowed down. We had reached the Bulgarian border. I glanced at my watch. It was just six o'clock. By now the sun's orange glow streaked the sky.

I pulled up at the drab timber shed which served as the customs office. At that early hour in the morning, our beat-up gray Ford was the only vehicle in sight. A solitary, dark-olive uniformed guard emerged from the hut. Shoving his capped head through the open window, he spoke gruffly in heavily accented English, "Get out." He gave the gun around his belt a tap, emphasizing his authority. As if we would dream of disobeying!

Roli gave me my passport, and we followed the guard meekly up the few concrete steps that led into the wooden building. There, with the help of other uniformed officials, we completed all the necessary paperwork and changed some of our Greek drachmas into the local currency. All the time, the first guard stood behind us watching, waiting, not saying anything. Finally, when it was clear we were through, he turned and, pointing to the van, barked, "Now examination, van and baggage."

My nerves, which had settled slightly while we had been concentrating on the paperwork, tensed. I tried to act casual and gave the guard a friendly, disarming smile. These men were trained to detect anything amiss. Although seemingly disinterested in our paperwork, this guard had been watching Roli and me like a hawk, checking to make sure we were who we claimed: a couple of well-traveled, camping tourists.

I followed him back to where our gray heap was standing. Lagging behind, Roli pulled out from under his arm an English newspaper that he had taken from the van. Seating himself on the bottom step of the customs shed, he adjusted his spectacles and began reading. This was part of the cover we had already agreed upon. It was designed to put the guard off track from discerning our true purpose for entering this nation. I smiled as I looked back at Roli warming himself in the ever strengthening sun and nonchalantly reading his English newspaper. If the moment had not been so tense, I would have been tempted to laugh. Like me, Swiss German was Roli's native tongue. He could barely read a word of English!

For my part, I played the role of the innocent, friendly and ever co-operative tourist. I threw open both the side and back doors of the van for the guard as a deliberate ploy to show that we had nothing to hide. "Hmmm," the guard said, observing the mess inside the van. A shirt was dangling from the side of the window. The inflated rubber tire and air mattress, along with all the other camping gear and of course our suitcases full of Bibles, filled up most of the back. "You like to travel," he remarked dryly.

"Yes, we've been on the road quite a while," I responded in a tone that I hoped came across as relaxed and carefree.

But despite my friendly banter, it quickly became obvious that this border official was not about to be distracted from his primary duty of searching our van. I began to question my guidance. Had I really heard from God about crossing at six o'clock? With a well-trained eye, the guard sized up the interior. He looked closely at the van's sides but quickly assessed that, with the lack of panels, there was no way contraband goods could be hidden. He paused a moment looking at our disheveled camping equipment scattered on the floor. My heart missed the beat. Was he going to have me move the camping gear? Would he make me open our suitcases, and as a result discover its forbidden content? Pushing back his dark-olive cap, he scratched his head. It almost seemed as if he suspected something was not in order, but he did not know what. I stood behind him, saying nothing and hardly daring to breathe. Surely this guard could not be the one God meant us to have? I must have misheard.

Then suddenly an uncharacteristic smile crossed his face as he pointed to the rusty iron—the one a student had thrown in at the last minute for good measure. "Do you actually use that thing?" he asked incredulously. "No, we just found it on a beach in Greece. We thought it might come in handy," I replied. He turned back and, shaking his head with the quirk still on his face, handed me back our passports, now stamped with our entry permit into Bulgaria.

As I climbed back into the driver's seat, Roli casually folded up his newspaper and strolled back to the van. He looked like a disinterested tourist; but as he slid beside me into the passenger seat, I could see his hands shaking. He was as nervous as I was. Stepping back, our olive-green uniformed guard, his distinctive, red communist trimmings bordering his collar and sleeves, signaled us through.

"Come on, Rudi. Let's get away from here," Roli muttered under his breath.

I did not need any encouragement. I already had the van in gear, and my foot ready to hit the accelerator.

"Enjoy your trip," the guard, now all smiles, bid farewell. The van leapt forward. Within seconds, the border hut was a small dot behind us. A few kilometers further on, now well out of sight of any officials, I stopped the van. Releasing all the tension built up over the last couple of days, Roli and I let rip. We got out of the van, gleefully slapped each other on the back and then spent a good half-hour loudly praising God for getting us through, for blinding the eyes of the guards and for allowing us to bring in our illegal goods undetected. As we clambered back into the van, however, the reality of the task ahead hit me. We still had no idea who we could safely deliver our cargo to. I only had the single address of an unknown Pastor Uskatzow in Sofia. Although we knew nothing about him, he was our only lead. It was little to go on, but it was all we had.

7

Bulgarian Adventure

I had taken the precaution of writing Pastor Uskatzow's name on a separate piece of paper and hiding it safely in my wallet. In my hand was a slip of paper on which was written the name of a street where he resided. It was in Cyrillic script, so we could not even pronounce it. We had no map and no means of locating it. But at least we knew it was in Sofia. So with no other alternative to choose from, we headed for the capital, a five-hour drive away through the lush, green Bulgarian countryside. While Roli took over the wheel and sought to make as good time as possible over the badly repaired, potholed, asphalt roads, I sat back and as much as I could, in that tense uncertainty, enjoyed the passing countryside. We had the border crossing behind us, but our potential troubles were far from over. At any time, the secret police could pounce on us and uncover our secret load.

I noticed the harvest was underway. Even at this early hour, farmers were already hard at work in their fields. Through the nodding heads of grain, I could see their heads bobbing as they reaped the harvest with hand-held tools. Modern farm machines, I noted, were few and far between. It would take long hours of backbreaking labor before the crops were brought in. My heart went out to these poor, downtrodden men and women slaving under such antiquated conditions. *God, release them from the bondage of communism,* I prayed silently. How thankful I was, we had obeyed the Lord and, despite the risk, pushed through with our resolve to come to Bulgaria. While we could not help with physical provisions at this time, at least we had with us a good supply of spiritual nourishment. The urgency of our mission gripped me afresh. *Jesus help us to deliver our "bread" safely.*

We passed an occasional horse-drawn gypsy cart. Then there were wagons carrying families of gypsies, from elderly grandmothers to babies-in-arms, and each wearing colorful, traditional dress. The bells tied to the horses' harness made delightful rustic music. In any other setting, I would have been deeply struck by the simple beauty of such a sight. But right now, I was too acutely aware of the spiritual oppression upon this land to enjoy it. This was a nation where persecution reigned supreme not just for the Christians, but for the whole population. Despite communist claims of freedom, freedom as we knew it in the West was totally unknown, be it freedom of religion, speech or the press.

I gazed out the window, my heart filled with a variety of emotions from anger at the injustices I could see in the passing rural scene, to excitement at God's protection on the border, to apprehension at what still faced us. We had no road map. Neither Roli nor I could speak the local language, and I had no idea how to find the solitary address of my one contact, Pastor Uskatzow. Gradually the countryside flattened and, as we started to enter the outskirts of Sofia, the potholed, asphalt road turned into an uneven cobble-stoned surface which made driving even more difficult.

Carts gave way to foot traffic and horses to rusty 20- and 30-year-old cars. We were also surprised at the number of ambulances moving through the traffic. *Sofia must be a very accident-prone city*, I thought to myself, making a mental note to take extra care when I next had my turn at driving. It was only later we would discover that these ambulances were a cover for the secret police. When you really needed an ambulance, the real thing was in short supply.

I was also particularly struck by the numerous slogans plastering the walls and the many oversized billboards displayed on street corners. Although I could not decipher the writing, their communist message was clear. It made me realize afresh just how difficult it would be to maintain a simple faith in God under the bombardment of such atheistic ideology.

I took over the driving, and wondering what direction to steer the car, I claimed Proverbs 3:6: *In all your ways acknowledge him and he will make straight your paths.* "Lord, direct us," I prayed. In a city of two million, trying to locate the Cyrillic address on our piece of paper was like looking for a needle in a haystack. Suddenly I spotted a tourist hotel. Maybe someone there spoke German or English and could help us. But we needed to maintain our guard. So pretending we were tourists taking a rest break, rather than Bible couriers in search of a delivery drop-off, we sauntered into the hotel, ordered some refreshments and casually asked the waitress about a good tourist spot to visit. As an apparent afterthought, I asked if the hotel had a map. Smiling, the receptionist handed one over, no questions asked. Things were looking up!

Back in the van, Roli, reading from the map, acted as navigator, while I cautiously maneuvered the gray Ford up and down numerous narrow, rough-surfaced streets. At each corner, we stopped to check the signpost. Finally our patience paid off. Roli's map reading proved successful, and we located the street that matched the Cyrillic writing on our piece of paper. Rather than pulling up in front of the house, I took the precaution of parking a few streets away. We pulled off to the side and left the van semi-concealed under the overhanging branches of a tree along the banks of a river. Even so I felt uncomfortable about leaving it. This dilapidated vehicle could easily be broken into and its contents revealed. *Lord, set your angels guard over it,* I prayed under my breath as we made our way back to the street.

There was another reason why we did not want to leave the van where it could be obviously spotted and linked to us. We had no background on this pastor, and no idea what kind of situation we might be walking into. The last thing we wanted to do was create problems for the local Christians. If the authorities found a believer had been in contact with foreigners, they could be arrested. As we had already been warned, anyone could be a spy, even the head of a prominent evangelical denomination. He was a man we needed to stay clear of at all costs.

The intense mid-afternoon sun beat down on our heads as we

walked up the street looking for the exact number of the house. This proved almost as difficult as deciphering the scripted street name. Many of the homes did not have numbers, and those that did did not follow a logical order. After a frustrating search, we found ourselves standing in front of a worn-looking two-story house that resembled all the others on the street. It was set back in a small garden with the front door a mere five meters from the road. The garden was separated from the street by a low, wooden fence and gate.

The setting was a little too exposed for my liking. What if someone passing by on the street recognized from our voices that we were foreigners and reported the inhabitants of the house to the secret police? They could be put into prison and it would be our entire fault. But we had come this far, there was no backing down now. Feeling very apprehensive, I gingerly knocked on the door. We waited nervously. There was no response. Reaching out, I knocked again, a little more forcefully. This time we could hear someone moving inside the house. Suddenly a young lady, who I guessed to be around 20 years old, leaned over the balcony above us. "Hi," she said in English, obviously recognizing from our appearance that we were foreigners. "What do you want?"

I took a couple of steps back so I could see her better. "I'm looking for Uskatzow," I said. By now I was right at the gate, and I realized how vulnerable my position was. Anyone passing by on the street could overhear us. "He's my father and he's not here," the girl replied, seemingly unperturbed. "Can I help?"

I did not want to announce the true intention of our visit out here in the open for everyone to hear, so I just said, "Oh, we're just tourists and were given his name by someone." Then grabbing at straws, I added, "There doesn't happen to be a church service on tonight is there?" This was the only contact we had. If we let this opportunity slip through our fingers, we had nowhere else to turn.

"Yes. You're very welcome to attend," the girl shouted back, still leaning over the balcony. "I'll come down and give you the address." I was surprised at her openness. Where was all the secrecy that we had understood was so necessary in this anti-Christian nation?

The girl disappeared, and a few minutes later, appeared at the front door with a piece of paper with the church address neatly written upon it. I tried to read her expression. But could not discern anything. I felt slightly uneasy, and rather than give her more time to memorize our faces, I quickly thanked her. Turning on our heels, Roli and I left.

As we made the 15-minute walk back to the riverbank where the Ford was parked, we discussed our encounter with this girl. From our conversation, it would almost seem as if Christians could meet quite openly. At least she did not seem concerned about publicly informing us of the church service. Were the stories we had heard of communist oppression exaggerated or were we walking into a trap?

I looked at the piece of paper she had given to us and gave a start. The church name was the same evangelical denomination whose director we had been warned about. Should we attend the church service or not? As Roli and I discussed the pros and cons, we realized we did not have a choice. This was our only contact. We did not have anyone else to deliver our Bibles to. I thought of the students who were faithfully praying around the clock for us. I remembered the lady in the Christian bookshop in Haifa who had promised to pray. The last thing we wanted was to take our Bibles back across the border with us, so we decided to take the risk. Hopefully there would also be genuine believers in that congregation. We would just have to trust Jesus to lead us to them.

We filled in the remainder of the afternoon wandering through the marketplace in Sofia. We were particularly struck by the limited range and poor quality of goods that were available. Even the fruits and vegetables seemed tired and wilted. People shuffled their feet and walked with heads bowed. Communism claimed to bring freedom and prosperity for all. But from our observation, there was little evidence of this. Life went on; it seemed to be a dull and colorless existence.

The service was due to start at seven. Around six, giving ourselves what we considered plenty of time, we climbed back into the van and set out in search of the church building. The task proved more difficult than we anticipated. Roli poured over the map, and as before, we stopped at every street corner to check the Cyrillic writing on the signpost.

By seven, we seemed to be no nearer to our destination. By eight, when we still had not located it, I started to panic. The light was fading fast. Surely we had not come this far only to foul things up now. I sensed this was a direct attack from the enemy to prevent us from making contact with the Christians and offloading our supplies. We only had tonight. Tomorrow we had to start heading back. "Let's pray, Roli," I said. We lifted our voices in aggressive prayer, bound the enemy and asked God to clearly direct us.

By now a heavy blanket of darkness had fallen over the city. Only a few dim street lamps were available to light our way. Reading the Cyrillic-scripted street signs had been hard enough by day; by night it was almost impossible. We got out of the van and walked up and down the uneven mud streets, narrowly missing the deep ruts and holes created by the continual flow of carts. It struck me that they were not good advertising for social-ist propaganda. Even farm tracks in remote parts of Switzerland were better kept than these city roads!

Again and again, we stopped under the faint light of a street lamp and peered at the map. Greatly frustrated by our lack of progress, we would climb back into the van. Time was rapidly slipping away. By now we were well over an hour late for the service. Checking yet again and finding the street sign did not match, we stood together under the dim light and, almost beside ourselves, prayed for God to unravel this maze of streets and lead us to the right place. We had to find the Christians that night. We had already spent more than a day getting here. If we did not deliver the Bibles that night, we had no alternative but to take them back with us to Greece when we returned the next day. Surely the Lord had not brought us this far only to frustrate our efforts?

Finally, almost two hours after the starting time, we turned a corner. As we had done dozens of times already, we carefully checked the street sign to see if the lettering matched the address on our piece of paper. It looked identical. We checked again and could hardly believe it. We had found the street. As we had done earlier in the afternoon, we took the precaution of parking some distance away. We left it along the same meandering river—

although not the same spot—where we had parked it earlier in the day and took a ten-minute walk to the church. Its unpretentious brick building was tucked in between houses. But we could hear from muffled singing inside that we had found the right place. Roli and I opened the door, walked quietly inside and slid into a back, wooden pew. I could hardly believe that, although two hours late, we had actually made it.

I guessed around 200 people would have been crammed into that plain, small hall. The ladies, wearing typical Eastern European headscarves and embroidered dresses, were seated on one side. The men, as was their custom, were on the other. After a few minutes, I realized this was a prayer meeting rather than a teaching session. Different church members were praying out loud. I could not understand what they were saying, but my heart was deeply moved by their fervent devotion. I looked over to Roli and smiled. I could see he was equally impressed and drinking it all in.

We had found the building, but now we faced another challenge. How were we going to make contact with someone we could trust and to whom we could deliver the Bibles? Nobody knew us and as the service continued and then started to draw to a close, nobody had apparently even noticed us. *Stand up and announce that you're visitors from the West*, the thought came to me. It could help draw someone out from the woodwork. But it could also alert our presence to the wrong people. There may well be government informers in the church. *No!* I determined. God had brought us this far. I did not want to blow it now. I would trust him to lead us to the right person.

I looked around the wearied, wrinkled faces of the congregation. How long had it been since they had had solid teaching from the Scriptures? *These people need encouragement. Get up and give them a message*, the thought came to me. I hesitated. I did not want to push myself forward. *You'd better make a move now or it will be too late*, the inner voice persisted. *Just walk up to the front and say who you are.* The battle within was intense. Was I being unnecessarily cautious? Should I just walk boldly up front and announce who we were? *Don't be a coward. Go now!* the same voice persisted.

No! I responded firmly, suddenly recognizing where that voice was coming from. This was not the Holy Spirit. It was Satan trying to pressure me to do my own thing. God had called me to this mission. I needed to trust him to complete it. *I'm not going to push myself. If you want me to speak, Lord, you have someone ask me.* It seemed an unlikely request.

So far no one had acknowledged our presence or indicated that they had even noticed us. Then, just as things were winding up, the leader walked down the aisle. Coming up to me and speaking softly in broken English, he asked, "Who are you and where are you from?"

"We're believers from Switzerland," I whispered back.

"We can't allow you to speak, that's forbidden," he responded in hushed tones, "but you can bring greetings." I nodded.

"I understand. I'd be happy to do that." Following him back up the aisle, I turned and for the next 15 minutes had the joy of bringing "greetings" from the apostles Paul and Peter and other biblical leaders to this Scripture-starved congregation. How thankful I was that I had not pushed myself forward but waited for God to orchestrate my opportunity to preach.

The service over, people crowded around us. None of them could speak German or English so we could not communicate in words, but their facial expressions indicated their delight at our presence. That was encouragement in itself. Finally everyone left. Only the leader remained. Warmly shaking my hand, he thanked me profusely for my words. "What you shared was wonderful. I'm sorry you couldn't have more time, but we have to be careful," he added. "You understand."

"Perfectly!" I answered, grasping his hands and looking into his gentle, dark eyes.

I warmed to this man. His English was broken, but at least we could communicate. I was sure he was our contact. Before I told him our real reason for coming, I needed to make sure of one thing. I needed to know whether or not he was the head pastor of this denomination.

"Are you the director?" I asked politely, as if making an off-handed inquiry.

"Oh no!" he replied. "I'm an assistant pastor. The head is Pastor Uskatzow." My heart missed a beat.

"Pastor Uskatzow!" I repeated.

"Yes! Do you know him?" he asked.

"No. No," I said, stuttering slightly as the revelation dawned. Pastor Uskatzow was the government informer—the same man we had been told to avoid at all costs.

"He's out of town at the moment," the assistant pastor replied, unaware of the double flips my stomach was doing at that moment.

"We were given his address. But we didn't actually meet," I said. How easily Roli and I could have walked into a snare without realizing it. If Pastor Uskatzow had been at home when we called that afternoon, we would probably have given him the Bibles in all innocence, unaware that we were giving them to a government informer. I sent a silent prayer of thanks to all those praying and for the Holy Spirit's obvious intervention. But now I faced another dilemma. Could the man standing in front of me be trusted?

The Lord had not led us to anyone else. The rest of the congregation had left. He was our only remaining link with the church in Bulgaria. "What's the purpose of your visit?" the pastor asked. Here I realized was my lead. There was no point in beating around the bush; so grasping my courage with both hands, I leaned over and, whispering in his ear to make sure no unseen eavesdropper could hear, blurted out quietly, "We've brought in Bibles." His brow wrinkled slightly in semi-disbelief.

"Bibles?"

"Yes. We smuggled them across the border." The pastor swung his gaze from me to Roli, who nodded in affirmation.

"Bibles!" he repeated, a whole range of emotions, from delight to fear, flashing across his face. "How many?"

"One hundred Bulgarian and one hundred Romanian," I replied. He let out a soft whistle.

"I've spent 15 years in prison for the Gospel," he whispered with concern. "I'd be in for another 15 if I was caught with that many Bibles. We're going to have to be careful. Where are they?"

"In our van," I replied, "but we've parked it some distance away so no one could trace it to the church building." He looked relieved.

"That was wise."

"I don't have a vehicle, only a bicycle. I'll come with you and take you to a suitable place where I can store them." I nodded, thankful there was someone else now to make the decisions. "It's not safe to leave Bibles here," the pastor explained. "We have government informers in the church, some quite high up." He did not actually name Pastor Uskatzow, but I surmised that he was well aware of his bosses' activities.

"I know," I said, silently thanking the Lord yet again that he had led us to the right man. I breathed deeply as I realized how close Roli and I had been to walking into a trap. "It'll take us about ten minutes to drive there from where your van is parked," he said.

To cover our tracks, Roli lagged behind to make sure no one was following as the pastor and I went ahead. The feeble glow from the dim street lamps only provided a limited pool of light, so we mainly walked in the dark. But this was home territory for the pastor and he deftly led us in the direction of the river. Progress was faster now that we had a local guide. I recalled Roli and my frustrated search for the church a few hours earlier and praised God we did not have to maneuver these streets through the dark by ourselves.

We reached our van. The moon shimmered in its silvery reflection on the river as the pastor and I jumped in the front and Roli clambered into the back. He would need to transfer the Bibles from their present hiding place amongst our clothes in the suitcases into the cardboard boxes we had especially brought for the purpose. I was glad we had taken that precaution. Suitcases discovered to be from the West would be a dead giveaway to any snooping official that the Bulgarian Christians had had contact with foreigners. As I started up the van, my nerves were on edge. The next half-hour in which we would make the exchange was probably the most crucial in the whole operation.

I fought to concentrate on my driving as we wove our way through the dark streets across to an area of town Roli and I had not yet visited. In the meantime, Roli was scrambling in the back to get all the Bibles safely transferred into the cardboard boxes. We had just driven up to a set of traffic lights, and were sitting idling waiting to go over, when a policeman on a motorbike pulled up beside us. Obviously recognizing that ours was a foreign vehicle and possibly seeing some movement in the back, I could see him trying to peer through the windows into the van. *Oh no! Don't let us be caught red-handed with both the Bibles and a local pastor.* "Roli! Down! Hide! Quick!" I hissed through gritted teeth. Not understanding the exact nature of the danger, but sensing the urgency in my voice, Roli instantly slid under the air mattress covering the Scripture-littered floor.

The traffic lights changed. I stomped my foot on the accelerator and the van shot forward. I waited a few more seconds to see if the policeman would follow. But I had left him far behind. He had clearly not seen anything that had aroused his suspicion or caused him to take chase. Now that the danger was over, I called back to Roli, who was still hiding beneath the blankets.

"Okay. The coast is clear. But that was a close one. I was sure that policeman had seen something." I glanced at our Bulgarian passenger. I could see he was as nervous as we were. He, more than either Roli or I, understood the true nature of the danger we had just averted. As we continued to weave our way through the poorly lit streets, none of us spoke. The tenseness in the van was almost tangible. The only sound was Roli scrambling in the back as he worked to get the books packed into cardboard containers.

After about 15 minutes, we turned into a quiet, suburban street where the pastor signaled for me to stop. As I pulled up to the curb and turned off the motor, he pointed out a doorway about five houses up the road on the same side and said, "I'll go up there ahead and wait inside. Give me five minutes. Then follow with your delivery." We watched his outlined shape disappear inside the door, and then after waiting a few minutes, which seemed like an eternity, Roli and I each grabbed a box of Bibles and clambered out of the van. My heart was thumping as I half staggered over the uneven cobbled road with my heavy load.

In this part of town, the streets were fairly well lit. Right across from us was a small bar. I could see a number of soldier patrons clearly through the windows, it seemed we could not have picked a worse place. Reaching the doorway that the pastor had indicated, I pushed it open, and letting Roli through, quickly followed. The door banged behind us. Suddenly from the relative brightness of the street, we were plunged into pitch darkness.

We stood there for a few seconds adjusting our eyes to the dimness. Suddenly I heard the sound of footsteps approaching on the street outside. Still clutching my heavy box, I froze. Someone had seen us. We must have looked very suspicious, carrying two such large packages. The steps slowed as they neared the door. Then they came to a complete halt. In the faint glow from the street lamp creeping under the door, I could clearly make out the shadowy shape of a pair of boots.

I held my breath waiting. At any moment the door would fly open, revealing Roli and me standing there red-handed with our boxes of Bibles. My arms ached from both the tension and the extreme weight of the 100 Bibles I was carrying. Just when I thought I could stand it no longer and was about to drop the box, the steps moved away.

Breathing a little easier, now that the immediate danger seemed to have passed, we carefully inched our way through another rear door and out into an open courtyard. I expected to see the pastor waiting there for us. But as I looked around the towering, gray, concrete multi-story apartment blocks that lined the four sides of the courtyard, he was nowhere in sight. My adrenaline started to race. Where had he gone? Then suddenly I spotted him, standing in the shadows beside the far wall. We hurried across the courtyard, and at his silent signal Roli and I put our boxes down on the ground in front of him.

"Up there," he whispered, pointing to a window in the building behind us. "I'm going to hide the Bibles up in the loft." He bent down to pick up a box, then stopped. Straightening slightly, he cocked his ear and froze. He stood in this position for a few seconds, listening intently. "Quick!" he suddenly whispered, a sense of panic in his voice. "Go and hide in that outhouse." He pointed Roli and me in the direction of a small, wooden hut. "Go, go!" he urged, giving us a shove.

Roli and I made a mad dash for the small shed, and squeezing through the narrow door, shut it fast behind us. The smell inside was atrocious and there was scarcely room for the two of us to stand. But it was a hiding place. And that was all that mattered. We stood there, trying to calm our noisy breathing, our hearts racing. At any moment, I expected a soldier to throw open the door and shout, "Hands up!"

I caught my breath as I heard the unmistakable sounds of footsteps approaching the outhouse. Bubbles of sweat erupted on my forehead, and my hands grew slippery. I let out an involuntary gasp as the door swung open. To my great relief, it was only the pastor. "It's okay," he whispered, beckoning us out of our foul-smelling prison. "It was just a tenant crossing the courtyard on his way home from the late night shift. But I couldn't take the risk." I could understand his concern. If he was discovered with foreigners, especially Westerners delivering Scriptures, he would face a stiff prison sentence.

By this time all our nerves were on edge. It would be safer if Roli and I left. As much as we would have loved to help store the heavy boxes away, it was safer to let the pastor hide them himself. Besides, he knew his way around the loft and was less likely to stumble in the dark. "We'll go," I said, turning to the pastor. A look of relief crossed his face.

"Yes. That's best," he agreed. Tearing off a corner from one of the cartons, I quickly scribbled my address on it and handed it to him. "If everything works out okay, send me a postcard saying, 'The weather is fine in Bulgaria.'"

"Okay," he agreed. He grasped Roli and me each by the hand and looking directly into our eyes whispered, "Thank you so much for delivering the bread of life. Now go, and God be with you!"

Once back out on the street, I glanced quickly around for any sign that we might have been spotted. The soldiers were still in the bar drinking and, thankfully, totally oblivious to our clandestine activities only meters away. But the danger was still far from over. Roli and I needed to get away as quickly as we could so that even if we were apprehended, no suspicion would be cast on our Bulgarian friend.

Moving as quietly as possible down the near-empty street, we found the van still safely parked by the roadside where we had left it. As Roli got into the passenger seat and I reached to turn on the ignition, I silently prayed that this old heap would not make too much noise and attract unwanted attention, especially from the soldiers in the pub. As I turned the key, however, instead of the engine coming to life, it let out a sick-sounding whine. I tried again. Still no life. Oh no! I had visions of Roli and me stuck here in Sofia with one broken-down van and subjected to inquisitive communist police questions.

"Try pushing," I whispered urgently to Roli. He jumped out, and while he pushed from the rear and the van jerked loudly over the cobblestones, I tried the key once again. Relief! This time the engine gave a healthy spurt and came to life. "Quick. Jump in," I commanded Roli. We cluttered off noisily down the street. It was hardly a James Bond style exit, but thankfully the soldiers, totally unaware of our drama, kept on drinking.

I put my foot on the accelerator, anxious to get as far away as possible from the scene of our "crime". At that hour just after midnight, there was very little traffic around. We were clipping along at a steady speed when a uniformed figure stepped out from the side of the road, wildly swinging a red warning light. My heart sank. How could he know who we were? As far as I was aware, no one had seen us.

I pulled the van over. The policeman stuck his head through the window and, talking nineteen to the dozen, hurled a barrage of abuse at us. It was all in Bulgarian and, although I could tell he was angry, I could not make out a word of what he was saying. In frustration, he waved his hands around and then pointed to the speedometer. Suddenly it dawned on me what his concern was, and I breathed easier. He knew nothing of our clandestine Bible smuggling. We had been pulled over for speeding! Apologizing profusely, I pointed to our camping gear in the rear and, using mime, tried to explain we were a couple of tourists headed for the border. Clearly frustrated by the language barrier, the policeman finally gave up and let us go.

We drove off much more sedately. But all the pent-up stress and tension of the past few hours had taken its toll. By now I was totally exhausted. I handed over the wheel to Roli, clambered into the back of the van and sprawled out on the air mattress. Within moments I was asleep. Suddenly I was jerked awake by the crunch of gravel under the tires. The van came to a sudden standstill.

"What's up?" I said, sitting up startled out of heavy sleep. I could see Roli was about to climb out of the driver's seat.

"I can't keep going," he complained. "I'm so tired I can't think straight and nearly went off the road!" After the lack of sleep the night before, and the drama of the day, I realized we both need-ed to take a rest. There was no point in pushing ourselves unne-cessarily.

"Let's pull off the road and park," I suggested. I looked out the window and realized we must have been traveling for some time as we were well clear of the city and somewhere in the country.

We found a level spot in a nearby field to park. I was about to crawl back into my sleeping bag when I saw movement through the window. I froze and my heart raced. The figure moved closer to the van. In the moonlight, I saw it was a soldier. He was approaching us, his rifle at the ready. My heart sank like the Titanic. Even though we no longer had the Bibles, I had heard of people behind the Iron Curtain being arrested and held in prison without trial for years, just on the merest suspicion that they had committed some offense. My mind took flight as I imagined the very worst scenario. Almost by instinct, I reached up and turned on the inside light so our camping gear would be clearly visible. The soldier came right up to the window and after looking inside turned away, apparently satisfied. How I thanked God at that moment for our camping camouflage.

The soldier had disappeared into the darkness and I could breathe a little easier. But my sleep had been disturbed, and although I was still desperately tired, I only slept fitfully for the remainder of the night. I was acutely aware we were still in com-munist territory and not yet completely out of danger. So while I closed my eyes and tried to rest, my mind remained alert to the slightest unusual sound. At one stage near early morning, I heard the noise of a broken twig. I woke with a start. Glancing out the window, I saw yet another soldier creeping around. Why were they so suspicious of our old van?

Then it suddenly occurred to me who these soldiers were. We were nearer to the Yugoslavian border than I had realized. These men were not after us. They were merely guards on duty patrolling the frontier. But even with that understanding, I found it hard to relax. My nerves were on edge. I waited out the next few hours uneasily as I let Roli get some well-deserved rest and it was a reasonable time for us to cross into Yugoslavia.

Rather than draw attention to ourselves by returning across the same border to Greece and face possible questions about why our visit had been so brief, we decided to take another route back via Yugoslavia. That way we would encounter a different set of guards. The next morning as we drove the few kilometers to the border, I still had one unresolved question. What if, in the course of questioning where we had been and who we had visited inside the country, the guards asked us outright about whether or not we had taken in Scriptures? What would we say? It was unlikely. But it could happen. It was a question I had often pondered, but had not yet resolved. I had heard Brother Andrew on the subject, and could follow his example by giving a vague answer that we had left some literature in Bulgaria, without divulging its exact nature. But what if they asked specifically whether or not they were Bibles. As a Christian, I knew I could not tell a lie. All I could do was pray.

Lord! I prayed quietly under my breath. *Give us a smooth border crossing with no awkward questions asked. If we have absolutely no hassle, I'll also take it from you as a sign that the Bibles are safe and we've delivered them to the right person.* I was pretty certain our Bulgarian friend was genuine. But his working with a government informer such as Pastor Uskatzow still left that element of doubt. Roli and I had taken a certain risk in leaving them with him.

At seven o'clock, we pulled up at the border crossing into Yugoslavia and stopped behind a few other vehicles ahead of us. Soon a guard ambled over to us. "Passport, please." As I handed them over, my heart rate increased. Even though we now had nothing to hide, that sense of tension and fear was still there. The guard glanced at our Bulgarian entry stamps. Would he ask why our visit had been so short? I caught my breath. Looking at the passports, he nodded, and then strolling round to the back of the van, he opened the door and peered into the back. His eye caught the rusty old iron that we had deliberately placed in full view on top of the other camping gear. "That won't do you much good," he said jovially. He slammed the door, stamped our passports and handed them back to us. "Have a good journey," he said cheerily, waving us through. There had been no questions asked. The crossing could not have gone smoother. To me this was an answer to prayer; God`s confirmation that our mission had been a success.

We were not prepared, however, for the trouble we struck between Yugoslavia and Greece. The guards could not understand why we had only left Greece the day before and were now coming back, using a different route. Convinced we were carrying forbidden contraband, they made us strip the van completely while they searched it from top to bottom. It made me realize afresh the miracle of God's protection on both our entry and exit at the Bulgarian border.

Eight hours later, at around 3pm, our dust-covered van rolled into the base camp at Katerini, near Athens. We were exhausted, but exhilarated. The fuel tank was just on empty and we only had a few coins left in our pockets. God had honored our faith venture in every way. As Reona's Scripture had prophetically predicted, the whole trip had been accomplished in three days.

Everyone came flocking out to greet us, and we were swamped with questions. As we all crammed into the dining room—the largest in the camp—we began to fill them in on the details of our adventure. There were *ooohs* and *aaahs* as I shared about our near late-night mishap when our van had almost been thrown off the Greek mountain pass. "Why that was just when we were praying for God to specifically protect you from harm on the road," Don blurted out excitedly. Even Loren showed uncharacteristic emotion as he realized the significance of his early morning wake-up call to pray for us during our six o'clock Bulgarian border crossing. Others shared how they had prayed we would not rush across the border, but wait for God's specific timing.

Around the precise moment we had been stopped by the

policeman waving a red light, another group had felt strongly to pray about protection against speeding; perhaps they knew me too well! And then at exactly seven o'clock that morning, the very time we had crossed over into Yugoslavia, the burden had lifted from the prayer group and they had stopped praying. It amazed us to see how precisely God had coordinated their most intense prayers with our greatest moments of danger. It highlighted for me the importance of a principle I had learned in the Swiss army. For every soldier on the front line, there needs to be seven in the back-up team carrying supplies and caring for the wounded. Meanwhile, back at home base, fifteen more are involved in manufacturing weapons and keeping an eye on the overall progress of the battle. It was a principle I now realized also applied at a spiritual level. The success of our mission had not depended just on Roli and me. It was largely due to the students' faithful prayers at base camp as well as the financial support of those back home. But I was to find out all too soon that God had some other rather unexpected lessons to teach me yet.

Our trip into Bulgaria had been a mountain peak in our SOE field trip. It opened my eyes in a new way to God's greatness. In the classroom, Brother Andrew had taught us from his experiences. Now I had discovered the truth for myself: there are no uncrossable boundaries for God. The triumph of Bulgaria behind us, I was eager to search out fresh peaks on which I could set my sights. But as I quickly discovered, before we can climb a new mountain, we have to descend into the valley. Coming down from the dizzy heights of our Bulgarian adventure into the routine of team life took some adjusting.

This was especially hard as Loren had decided to take the whole group on a diversionary tour into Bulgaria instead of going directly north through Yugoslavia as originally planned. From the knowledge we had gained from our trail-blazing excursion of what roads to take and other pitfalls to avoid—such as how to handle the border guards—Loren felt it was time to expose the whole team to the reality of a hardened communist nation. But he also felt Roli and I should not go with them. Instead, with three others who had opted not to take the side trip, we would follow the original route through Yugoslavia. We would all meet together in three days in the Yugoslav capital city of Belgrade.

Everything within me yearned to join them. God had birthed in me a special love for this nation. I longed to go back just to revisit the land. It would be wonderful to renew contact with the pastor in Sofia. I longed to learn what had happened to the Bibles and to hear first hand the reaction of believers as they received their own copy. How had they felt when for the first time they scanned the pages of this precious book which had been denied them for so long? But it was not to be. If Roli or I were to join the team, it would arouse immediate suspicion from the border guards. They would want to know why we were returning so soon. Our presence could jeopardize everyone else's chances of getting in. So, as much as I longed to be a part of the team, I submitted without question to Loren's decision to exclude us.

Saturday morning, two days after our return from Bulgaria, we broke camp at Katerini, near the outskirts of Athens, our base for more than two weeks. It was an early start as we all had a long journey ahead. The small team I was leading was embarking on a 19-hour trip direct to Belgrade through Yugoslavia. The rest were taking their three-day detour intercession trip into Bulgaria. "See you in Belgrade, Rudi," Don shouted as he boarded the blue bread bus. "Yes. Have a wonderful time," I waved back. "We'll be praying for you." I sounded enthusiastic, but within a tug of war was in progress. I stood quietly watching as everyone clambered aboard the vehicles.

After the drama of the last few days, it seemed such a letdown. I loved the thrill of my first trail-blazing trip, of breaking new territory for God. But I also realized this was my time to be in the valley. It was time to experience the discipline of staying behind to pray as others went out. I watched with more than a tinge of envy as the two vehicles, crammed with my chattering friends, rolled out of the campsite and headed off in the direction of Bulgaria. They quickly disappeared out of sight. "Well, let's get this mess cleaned up," I sighed, turning to my four remaining companions. In their haste to get away, the team had left us to clear the rubbish, clean toilets and generally tidy up. We had a good hour's work in front of us. Then we needed to pack the old Ford and get going ourselves.

Nineteen hours later, after only brief breaks to eat, relieve ourselves, and change drivers, our battered but faithful van trundled into a campsite on the edge of Belgrade. It was 3am Sunday morning. We quickly pitched our tents, and not even bothering to wash, unrolled our sleeping bags, inflated our air mattresses and tumbled exhausted onto them.

The sun was well up before any of us had stirred. There was no pressure on us to do anything. It was tempting to take it as a rest day. But I was determined not to let the enemy of complacency overtake me. Stirring the others, I prodded them into life. "Come on, folks. It's Sunday. We need to get moving if we're going to get to church on time." There was little response to my sergeant major call for action.

"Church? Rudi, you've got to be joking." Roli moaned and pulled his pillow in resistance over his head. "Surely we can have a day off."

"It was a long day yesterday," the other four chorused. I felt tired too, but was determined not to give in to the desires of my flesh. So leaving the others snuggled in their sleeping bags, I went off in search of a local church. The campsite attendant helpfully located one for me from the phone book. I had no difficulty in following his instructions, and at 9.30, a good half-hour before the service started, I pulled up in the van before an unpretentious stone building. I walked in. A man whom I guessed to be in his mid-forties was at the back of the dark wood, paneled room, stacking up hymn-books. No one else had yet arrived. I held out my hand in introduction. "I'm Rudi Lack," I said, and briefly explained about our YWAM team and the purpose of our visit to Yugoslavia.

"So pleased to met you," the man responded in broken English, pumping my hand with unexpected vigor. "You're an answer to our prayers." I looked at him quizzically. "I'm the pastor here," he went on to explain. "We've been praying for several months that young people from the West would come and visit us." Then he added an unexpected footnote, "Will you preach to us this morning?" I was taken aback. I certainly had not expected this kind response. I had just come to attend church, not to give a message. How glad I was that I had had the strength to obey the Spirit's urging to attend church and not given way to my weariness and natural desire to linger in bed.

"It would be a privilege to preach," I responded with eager anticipation. Here was my first chance to tell about Roli and my experience of taking Bibles into Bulgaria. I would be really able to stir these people's faith. But, as I mounted the pulpit, the Lord spoke to me, *Rudi, you're not to say anything about your trip into Bulgaria.* Startled by this unexpected order, I quickly retorted, *Why Lord? It'll give my sermon so much more punch.* But even as I silently debated with God, desperately trying to justify my position, I knew the answer. Roli and I had been like heroes coming back from Bulgaria. It would be easy for me to exalt myself in front of this Belgrade congregation and I knew they would be impressed. But God was challenging my motive. He was the one that needed to be lifted up, not Rudi Lack.

I preached and it was fine, but not as powerfully as if I had shared about our Bible-smuggling excursion. The minister got up to give a final exhortation based on my message for evangelism. As I sat in the wooden pew half-listening to him, I pondered over what had just happened. Suddenly a thought occurred to me. What if the Lord wanted me never to tell this story? Would I be willing to hold it to myself forever? The Father was testing me at a new level. I was impacted afresh at how easy it is to fall into the sin of pride. While it is exhilarating to scale the mountain tops, that is not where the real test lies. Failure to pass the test of humility can disqualify us from conquering those peaks that are still ahead. I shuddered at the thought. Instinctively I knew our experience in Bulgaria was the mere initiation of God's future plans for my life. *Lord, don't ever let me be tempted to boost my own ego and so disqualify myself from completing your purposes in my life,* I prayed. *I want to scale every mountain and break through every obstacle that opposes the preaching of your Gospel.* It was an important lesson that would be vital for the future.

8

Crossing New Borders

Our field trip was fast drawing to a close. In less than a week, we would be returning to the hotel in Lausanne. Then the 30 of us would scatter in small evangelistic teams across Europe for our three-month summer outreach. I had several options open to me. I could join a team and go into Spain or France, or, as was my preference, I could freelance and travel between the different teams. I had pretty much decided on the latter course and made my plans accordingly.

I would initially connect with Don and Deyon, who were organizing a tent campaign in conjunction with a local church in Germany. From there, I would link up with Joe and his team in Paris in their personal coffee-bar evangelism. The remainder of my outreach, I would spend with Al in Spain. Under Franco's dictatorship, all overt evangelism was forbidden, so our emphasis here would be literature distribution. I was really looking forward to the variety of my outreach when I received an unexpected request to change course.

We were at the campsite in Belgrade where the others had met up with us. That evening, Loren approached me. "Let's go for a walk, Rudi." We wove our way in silence between the tent pegs, then took a path through some neighboring woodland. Once out of earshot of the camp, Loren came straight to the point. "Rudi, I've been thinking about your summer of service. I don't feel you should travel from team to team in Europe."

My heart sank like lead in a pool. Was Loren going to ask me to attach myself to one team? I had been so looking forward to the variation. I dreaded the thought of remaining stuck in one place for the full three months. But Loren was the leader. If that was what he wanted, I did not have a choice. I anticipated the worst. Loren's next words took me completely by surprise. "As a European, I believe you need more cross-cultural exposure. The Round-the-World team, led by Floyd McClung, is going to be in Kenya in about a week's time. I think you should join them."

I scuffed some broken twigs with my foot. In my heart, a mighty tussle was taking place. I really wanted to work with my SOE friends: Don, Joe, Al and the others. I had so looked forward to trying our evangelistic wings together in the various ventures we had planned. If I joined the Round-the-World team, I would be with people I did not know. Would I experience the same level of comradeship, hunger for spiritual truth and unreserved desire to seek God as I had found among my SOE compatriots? But an equally strong tug was my passion for adventure. Africa was an unknown continent. It offered new boundaries to cross, different cultures to penetrate and, most of all, the potential for adventure. Into my mind flooded memories of the exciting missionaries' stories I had heard as a young boy: tales of venturing into the uncharted bush in Africa, confronting untamed natives with spears and the danger of wild animals. In reality, I knew it was highly unlikely I would face any such danger. But the pull to explore new territories proved greater than my loyalty to old friends. Even before Loren and I turned back towards the Belgrade campsite, my internal war had been resolved. In my mind, I was already winging my way in the plane to Nairobi, Kenya.

Just two weeks later, my fare wonderfully provided for by my father's church in Switzerland, I landed in Nairobi. The Round-the-World Team had arrived a few days ahead of me. Comprised of two New Zealanders and eight Americans, they had already been on the road for six months. I had no need to be concerned about their enthusiasm. I soon discovered that rather than leading the pack, I was the one chasing to keep up.

Arriving at the airport around midday, I was met by my father's missionary friends, who took me to the guesthouse

where the Round-the-World Team was staying. The leader Floyd
McClung met me at the door. His lanky, two-meter frame towering over me by at least 16 centimeters, Floyd hastily picked up
my somewhat battered, gray suitcase and showed me to my
bunkroom sleeping quarters. "We need to get going straight
away," he said, turning to me. "The team is booked to minister at
a mid-week service that starts in 40 minutes. The others have
gone ahead."

The church service was only the hors-d'oeuvre. As soon as it
was over, we bundled into cars and headed off to a central city
park to take part in an open-air rally. "Could you speak at the
rally, Rudi?" Floyd asked as we drove through a maze of tooting
cars and bell-ringing bicycles. I looked through the window at the
unfamiliar sea of brown faces. I had barely had opportunity to
meet the team or the missionaries who were organizing our
program, let alone think about preaching. I was also having difficulty adjusting to the heat. It was now 7pm and the temperature
was around 30 degrees Celsius. But I was here to preach the
Gospel. I did not want to miss any opportunity. So disregarding
my personal discomfort, I readily agreed. "Yes, I'd love to speak,
Floyd." We started by singing some choruses that quickly drew a
crowd, and as I stood to speak, for the first time I felt at liberty to
tell about Roli and my smuggling excursion into Bulgaria.

From the open-air rally, we were then whisked off to the
national university where over 500 Kenyan students, mostly
non-Christian, crammed into a hall. The team sang, testified and
preached the Gospel. I scanned the audience of dark, shining
faces, each one drinking in Floyd's brief but punchy message. I
was impressed at his direct, sensitive presentation. Afterwards,
the students crowded around wanting to talk. A few were eager
just to practice their English. Others expressed genuine spiritual
interest and wanted to dig further into issues Floyd had raised in
his talk. Finally around midnight, exhausted but deeply satisfied,
I collapsed onto my bottom bunk. The warm balmy air, even at
that late hour, was hard to get used to, as was the chorus of
croaking frogs that floated through the open window. In the
distance, I could hear the squawk of an unidentifiable birdcall. It
was all very new and strange to me. It would take me some time

to adjust. But already in my first few hours since arriving in Africa, I was beginning to feel at home.

In the following days, I had a rapid introduction to African life. I quickly learned the hazards of failing to drink boiled water. Should anyone not follow this precaution, they were likely to be brought down with diarrhea or amoebic dysentery. This contagious virus could quickly spread to others and had the potential to wipe the team out of action for days. We were also instructed on how to identify a patch of long grass or dead leaves where a snake might lurk. The team had already discovered that, in the intense African heat and humidity, they could not maintain the same pace of life as back home and had adapted an African timetable: work in the cool of the morning and evening and rest during the heat of the day.

Even so, there was no slacking. Our few short months would pass all too quickly, and knowing this, Floyd, as leader, encouraged us to take every opportunity we could to evangelize. He also urged the missionaries who were organizing our program to seek out every opportunity they could for us to minister. This incorporated going into schools, colleges, universities—any kind of learning institute—and also visiting any church that would open its door to us, whether big or small. It did not matter what denomination it was or whether the school or college was government- or church-based; as a team, we were prepared to accept any invitation extended to us. Our only criterion: we must be free to share our Christian message.

My admiration of Floyd's leadership grew daily. Not only was he tall in stature, he was also broad in vision. No stone of opportunity was left unturned. When no other doors opened up, Floyd sent us out on the streets in personal evangelism, knocking on doors and distributing literature. I readily knuckled in under his leadership and looked forward with growing enthusiasm to my three months here in Kenya with this Round-the-World team.

About a week after I had arrived in Nairobi, I was relaxing, reading my Bible in the lounge at the guesthouse where we were living, when Floyd came in. It was early afternoon, rest time. No one else was around. "Like a cup, Rudi?" Floyd asked, filling up the electric jug.

"Tea with just a drop of milk for me, thanks." Putting my special brew on a small, cane table, Floyd pulled up a chair next to me.

"I'm glad I've caught you alone, Rudi. I've wanted to speak to you. I have an assignment that I think might interest you."

Assignment! As soon as he said that, I put my mug back on the cane table and leaned forward with interest. What was Floyd referring to? My mind flashed back to a conversation I had had with him a few days earlier. In the course of that, Floyd had explained to me how prior to coming to Kenya the Round-the-World team had been in India. There they had met up with Brother Andrew. When he learned the team's next stop was to be Africa, he had said to Floyd, "You must try and contact the communist Chinese working there."

"What did he mean?" I questioned. It was the first time I had heard there were communist Chinese working in Africa.

Floyd had explained how a few years previously around 30 emerging colonial African nations had appealed to Western nations for developmental aid. But the West had been reluctant. As a result, these nations had turned to Mainland China for help. Consequently, thousands of engineers and other skilled Chinese workers had in recent years been streaming into Africa, offering practical help by setting up irrigation schemes, agricultural projects and radio transmitters. At the same time, they had been propagating their own style of Marxist communism.

The largest of these Chinese development schemes was an extensive railway project in Tanzania, known as Tan–Zam. When finished, this would link the copper belt of Zambia with the port city of Dar-es-Salaam, a distance of some 1,500 kilometers. Literally thousands of Chinese were evidently working along this railway. Brother Andrew had challenged Floyd about this. "I believe God is giving your team an assignment. A Westerner cannot enter China, so God is sending the Chinese to us. You need to grasp this opportunity and take the Gospel to these communist Chinese workers."

It would not be an easy task. These Chinese were apparently cloistered together in closed communities and not allowed to mix with the general African population. Only Africans who worked directly with them had any contact, so access was almost impossible. But that was what stirred me. There was nothing I loved more than the challenge of a difficult assignment. Surely this was what Floyd had in mind?

"What's the assignment, Floyd?" I asked eagerly.

"A missionary from Uganda, one supported by your father's church in Switzerland, has invited us to send a team into Uganda. I was wondering if you would lead the team?" Floyd replied.

"Oh!" I tried not to show my disappointment. Uganda did not have the same appeal as reaching communist workers on the Tan–Zam railway, but at least it offered a fresh challenge. It was a new border to cross and would provide different opportunities for evangelism. So hiding my real feelings, I quickly responded in the affirmative. "I'd love to head up a team into Uganda, Floyd."

Four others were selected to join me: two American girls, Ramona and Natalie, an American fellow, Dan, and one New Zealander, Tom. As the new boy on the block, I felt hesitant at being chosen to lead, especially when at our first team meeting, Dan dropped some very pointed remarks about leadership responsibilities he had held in the past. A talented musician, Dan had been with the Round-the-World team from the beginning. He was clearly struggling with the fact Floyd had chosen me and not him. I deliberately ignored his comments. Our task was to evangelize, not focus on inter-personal tensions. I was confident that any freeze in our relationship would quickly thaw once we got involved in outreach and experienced the thrill of young Africans turning to Christ.

Within days of our decision to go, we were waiting to board a public bus that would transport us on our 12-hour journey west to Uganda. I watched dubiously as my gray suitcase was hoisted onto the bus roof and secured there by a rope, along with bamboo cages filled with hens, bunches of bananas and large bundles of cloth in which the Africans had stuffed their belongings. Inside, the bus was crammed with more baskets and vegetables. I squeezed between brightly clothed African women and sweating African men. Thankfully all five of us managed to find a seat, but on mine a spring had started to protrude through the worn vinyl covering. We waved our farewells through the partially opened, dirt-smeared window. "Remember to grasp every opportunity you can," Floyd encouraged as the bus started to pull away. We needed little urging. Our spirits were high. We were ready to take on Africa. Uganda, here we come! Our first chance to evangelize came even sooner than we had anticipated.

Leaving Nairobi's sprawling suburbs, the bus started on a steady climb. After about an hour, we rounded the top of the ridge. We gasped at the beauty of the awe-inspiring panoramic view of vast savanna grasslands stretched out before us, across an expansive rift valley. We descended into the valley and for the next few hours motored through meter-high, golden, waving grass. Occasionally I caught a glimpse of a gazelle as it bounded behind one of the clumps of trees that were scattered across the plains. I even sighted a lone giraffe. Across the other side of the rift valley, we made our way up through tea plantations. Here all we could see were the heads and chests of men and women as they worked with huge baskets on their backs in the sea of green. We crossed the equator at 3,000 meters and descended again, this time into lush, green tropical bush.

The temperatures had soared. In these hot, sticky conditions, the potpourri of vegetables, animals and sweaty human odors intensified. A welcome breeze flowed through the open window as our bus rattled at a steady pace along the roughly patched asphalt. Along the roadside, seemingly oblivious to the potential danger of the steady flow of traffic passing only meters away, raggedly dressed children played barefoot in the dirt. Just off the road, half-hidden by bush and banana trees, we could see wisps of blue gray smoke ascending from the simple, straw-thatched huts. Here the women were preparing their evening meal over open fires. My stomach started rumbling. The bus suspension was shot and as hard as I had tried, I had not been able to alleviate my discomfort from my seat's aggravating spring. It had been a fascinating journey, but very long and tiring. I was looking forward to a cool shower and relaxing in the missionary's home in Mbale. Here we would be spending our first few days. Mbale was only an hour east from the Kenyan border, which we would soon be crossing. It was not too much further.

Suddenly, without warning, the bus jerked vigorously and then came to an abrupt halt. I was jolted forward in my seat. The caged hens on the roof let out loud squawks of protest. The driver jumped down from his seat, rushed around to the front of the bus and lifted the hood. Out gushed clouds of hissing steam. The bus had overheated. *Bother!* The journey had been arduous enough without this happening. Surely the driver had enough sense to know he could not push a clapped-out vehicle as hard as he had been doing and get away with it. We could be stuck here for hours. I tumbled out of the bus with everyone else, feeling decidedly out of sorts. I was about to verbalize my annoyance when my attention was drawn to the group of curious African onlookers who had already gathered, seemingly from nowhere, around our broken-down bus. I recalled Floyd's final exhortation, "Grasp every opportunity you can get." Here, with this unscheduled stop, we had a ready-made audience.

"Quick, get your guitar," I ordered Dan. Within minutes, we had an open-air meeting in progress. The Africans, delighted by this impromptu concert, clapped in rhythm to our singing. The crowd quickly swelled as others, attracted by the music, gathered to see what was going on. I grabbed the chance to preach a short Gospel message. Kenyan schoolchildren learn English, so at least the educated among them would understand the drift of what I was saying. The team was already mingling among the crowd and beginning to engage in conversation when the driver signaled for us to board. The bus had cooled down enough for us to resume the journey. I took the hand of the dark-skinned teenager I had been chatting with. "Sorry. Got to go." He grasped my hand, reluctant for me to leave. In those few minutes, a genuine rapport had been established between us. As we boarded, some of our audience broke out in spontaneous clapping to express their thanks. The bus took off at speed down the road. I looked back at the now distant figures still waving to us. I had one regret. We did not have any literature to leave with them that would clarify and build on the brief message we had brought them.

The response to our impromptu roadside meeting would prove typical of the reception we would experience in Uganda. The nation was a field ripe for harvest. It would be a little while, however, before we would experience the fullness of that harvest for ourselves. There were some personal roadblocks that had to be dealt with first as well as spiritual barriers that needed to be removed.

After spending the first few days with the missionaries at the town of Mbale, we motored a further two hours inland, northwest to the town of Soroti, where we would spend the majority of our time in Uganda. To call Soroti a town is a misnomer. Really it was more an overgrown village. It had one main street centered on a dirt-trodden market square. From this hub, roads—more wide tracks—spread out at random, eventually petering out into the surrounding dense tropical bush. On either side of the road, partially eclipsed by encroaching bush and banana palms, stood modest two- and three-roomed wooden homes. Some of the more affluent were built of concrete, but all sported corrugated iron roofs.

Even the neat, cream-painted brick bungalow where we were staying and which had a Western-style lawn still had the same iron roof. The owners—a missionary couple—were on furlough, so our five-member team had the run of the whole house. Unlike the majority of homes in the area, we had the luxury of a spacious lounge, refrigerator and electric fans—a much-appreciated relief from the intense humidity. Like everyone else though, we still had to battle the flies by day and mosquitoes by night.

Dan and I shared a room. After our shaky start, we seemed to be getting along fine. There were still the few occasions when I sensed him reacting to my leadership, but I chose to ignore these and sought to concentrate instead on building positive bonds of friendship between us.

A stone's throw from the missionary's house was a modest, brick church. It seated around 100. The African pastor lived with his family in a house on the other side of the church. The pastor was accommodating a half-dozen Ugandans, African style, that is two in a bed. These were mainly lay people who had come to assist in our outreach. There were also a couple of full-time evangelists. Because the pastor's house was full to overflowing, one of the evangelists, Charles, was sharing the bedroom with our Kiwi teammate Tom.

Our time was limited; so heeding Floyd's instructions, I sought to grab every opportunity we could to spread the Good News. The first week, we spent our days knocking on doors and out on the roads evangelizing. We found people very willing to talk. Regardless of where they might be heading, the African men were willing to stop, sit under the shade of a tree and converse for hours. For them, time was not important. Each team member paired up with a Ugandan Christian who could interpret so communication was not a problem.

We did not lead anyone to the Lord during that first week, but we sowed a lot of seed. We also gave everyone we met an open invitation to attend the church service on Sunday. We had been asked to conduct both morning and evening services. I believed to see every bench full and people standing in the doorway.

Our most fruitful activity was in the marketplace. Since few homes had a refrigerator, shopping was a daily chore, particularly for the women. Shaded by makeshift, thatched shelters, the stallkeepers spread their wares out on brightly colored cloth on the dirt ground. It was a noisy, bustling scene. Women with a couple of youngsters in tow and a baby wrapped in cloth over their shoulder would haggle loudly over a few pennies as they sought to get the best price for their purchases: bananas, mangoes, bread food, vegetables and freshly caught river fish.

Amidst the racket and dirt, we set up our own stall and peddled our wares of low-cost Christian literature which we had managed to purchase, since our arrival, from the Bible Society. We charged a few pennies—a mere fraction of their real cost. But we sold them rather than gave them away as we realized people put more value on something they had paid for. As it was, we could hardly keep up with the demand. Some would buy two, three or even more books at a time. Books were expensive in Uganda. Even though the purchaser might not be sympathetic to the book's message, they knew they were getting a bargain and wanted to own one. We sought to talk with everyone who bought, and invited each to attend the Sunday services. We took the opportunity to invite everyone we spoke with to come to church. Many seemed genuinely interested.

Also that first week we visited government-run schools and preached the Gospel to a captive audience of students during their regular class sessions. By Saturday night, we were exhausted, but encouraged. We had sown a lot of seed during that first week and we fully expected to see the fruit of our labor in the numbers who would turn up for the next day's services. We wanted to be thoroughly prepared. As worship leader, Dan spent more time than usual selecting appropriate songs, while I gave much thought and prayer about the content of my message.

As a team, we also spent concerted effort interceding for both morning and evening services. Following our debacle in Grenoble, I had learned well the importance of being prepared through intercession. We had done our homework. Now it was up to God. Sunday morning, I dressed in my only pair of good trousers. Checking in the mirror to make sure my tie was straight and carefully combing my brown hair into place, I then led the team confidently next door to the old, brick church. There was hardly anyone there when we arrived. I glanced at my watch: 9.45. The service was due to start in 15 minutes. *You're operating on African time*, I reminded myself. *By ten, the church will be packed.* But by ten o'clock, only the front benches were filled, mainly with our team and the Ugandan co-workers. Only a smattering of Africans occupied the benches in the rest of the building. Still hopeful of a last-minute influx, I decided to wait a little longer for others to arrive. But when by ten past ten only a few more stragglers had drifted in, I realized with a sinking heart that, despite people's apparent interest, virtually none had taken up our invitation.

Perhaps more people will come to the evening service, I consoled myself as I commenced my well-prepared sermon to our minuscule congregation. But by evening, my confidence was further eroded. If anything, the attendance at the evening service was less than in the morning. I went to bed thoroughly discouraged. I had done everything I knew to do. We had grasped every opportunity we could to share the Gospel with these people. We had interceded passionately for them. Why had God not answered? Why had people not responded?

I lay in my bed staring into the darkness, my mind tussling with these unresolved questions. In the bed next to me Dan was snoring gently. Weary from the week's activities, he had dropped off to sleep almost before his head had hit the pillow. But as tired as I was, sleep eluded me. I tossed and turned until finally exhaustion overcame me. I fell into a fitful sleep and began to dream a horrible nightmare.

In my dream, I saw an African man bound in chains and being subjected to the most awful ritual of circumcision. Mobs of black men surrounded him, yelling and screaming. Frozen in horror at the sight, I watched as the ritual knife tore into the man's private parts. His face was filled with absolute terror. Blood gushed out from his jagged wound. I winced, feeling for him in his excruciating pain. I wanted to rush in and save him, but I could not. I was immobilized, unable to lift a finger. I continued to watch, helpless as the mob swooped in mercilessly and repeatedly cut into him. If ever there was a nightmare from the pit of hell, this was it. I woke drenched in perspiration, trembling in fright as the scenes replayed vividly in my mind.

I was only just coming to terms with the fact that what I had witnessed was not reality but a dream when, suddenly in the darkness, Dan, still asleep in the bed next to me, let out an explosive snort. It sounded more like the growl of a wild animal attacking than a noise a human would make. Already tense from my nightmare, this unexpected grunt scared me out of my wits. Catapulted awake, I sat bolt upright in my bed. Dan let out another equally frightening snort. Suddenly an uncanny fear gripped my stomach. A strange coldness entered the room. Even though it was a balmy tropical night, I found myself shivering involuntarily. The evil presence in the room was as real as if someone with sinister intent was actually standing over me.

Dan, who was still asleep, started moaning. He was breathing very heavily and mumbling incomprehensible gibberish. "Dan! Dan!" I called out to him. When he did not wake, I got up and shook him.

"What? Eh?" he groaned, only half awake. I turned on the bedside lamp. The brightness of the light jerked him into full consciousness. Startled, he sat up in bed his eyes wide open.

"What's the matter, Rudi? What's going on?"

"You were making the weirdest noises."

"I have had the most terrible nightmare," he groaned.

"Me too," I said. Suddenly I had a strong awareness that hoards of demons were surrounding us outside in the dark.

"Dan, I believe we are under spiritual attack," I said trembling. "We need to pray and take authority." I had heard reports of the supernatural power displayed by African witch doctors, but it was not until now that I had actually encountered such spiritual forces. Dan, his eyes wide as saucers, nodded.

"I think you're right, Rudi." I got up from my bed, paced our small room and began to pray with all the intensity I could muster. I spoke out scriptural promises of victory and declared the power we had in Christ. I claimed protection by the blood of Jesus and rebuked the evil forces with the same vigor as if we were fighting off a physical attacker. "Jesus, you have defeated the enemy. In your name, we declare he is under our feet." Yet, despite my bold sounding prayers, the fear and tension gripping my stomach did not budge.

Suddenly Dan broke into the prayer. "Rudi. I feel the Lord is convicting me of something I need to confess to you." I looked at him.

"What is it, Dan?"

"Right from the start I've resisted your leadership. If I am really honest, I have been jealous of you. I was disappointed Floyd didn't make me leader, especially as I've been on the team so much longer than you."

"Yes, I've been aware of your struggles, Dan, but I didn't want to say anything. I hoped that as we got into the outreach and our friendship grew, any difficulties between us would naturally dissolve."

"Will you forgive me for my wrong attitudes?" Dan asked, his voice breaking slightly.

"Sure," I responded. "But I need to ask your forgiveness too. I've also been in the wrong."

"Oh." Dan sounded surprised. "How?"

"The Scripture tells us when someone has something against

us, we are to leave our gift on the altar and first go and put things right with that person. I was aware things weren't right between us, but instead of facing up to it, I tried to ignore them. That was wrong. Will you forgive me?"[5]

"Of course." I sat on the bed beside him and gave his shoulder a squeeze. "I really appreciate you, buddy."

"Thanks. I want to let you know too that you're doing a great job in leading the team. From now on you have my complete support."

"I really appreciate that, Dan. It means a lot to me."

What an important lesson God was teaching us. I had anticipated that the thaw in our relationship would come through fervent evangelism. In reality, there is only one way strained relationships can be restored: through applying God's principle of confession and forgiveness. By our reconciliation, Dan and I had broken the foothold of entry Satan had established because of our wrong relationship.

Immediately after Dan and I had confessed our sins to one another, the tension in my stomach eased. The heaviness in the room dissipated. Our spirits started to rise in jubilation as we sensed this break in the satanic wall which only minutes before had seemed so impenetrable. Like victorious soldiers, we moved swiftly in to consolidate our victory and chase the enemy away from our territory. We prayed against every satanic stronghold in Soroti, for the enemy to be defeated in the surrounding villages and for God to show his victory throughout the whole of Uganda. We then started to pray for other oppressed nations such Albania, Cuba and China. It was the best time of intercession I had participated in since my sessions with Reona, Don and the others. Finally around 3am prayed out, but wonderfully at peace, we called it quits.

We had only just settled down to enjoy a few short hours of sleep when we were jolted into consciousness by a piercing female scream. Adrenaline charged through my veins. Dan and I reached for the lamp switch together. "What on earth was that?" he said tremulously.

[5] Matthew 5:22-24.

"It sounds as if one of the girls is being murdered," I said with equal nervousness. Dan and I grabbed our sweat suits and were about to dash to the girls' room next door when our door opened. An ashen-faced Ramona, her bathrobe hastily wrapped round her, barged through. A sleepy but equally shaken roommate, Natalie, followed. "What happened?" Dan and I chorused. Ramona did not respond. Instead, she collapsed onto my bed shaking uncontrollably.

"Were you attacked?" Dan asked in concern.

"Did someone break in?" I queried.

"Sort of," Ramona replied, gasping for breath. The three of us sat down beside her. Natalie gently put her hand on Ramona's shoulder. Gradually her breathing returned to normal and the story came out.

Ramona explained how she had been awakened from a deep sleep with the feeling of being pinned to her bed. "I felt someone had their hands around my neck," she shivered. "I couldn't move. It was the most dreadful sensation I've ever experienced."

"But there was no one there?" I questioned.

"Not physically," she replied. "But the spiritual power that was holding me down was real enough, I can tell you." Ramona went on to explain how she had tried to call out, but the pressure on her throat was so intense she could not utter a sound. "I thought I was going to choke to death," she said. "It was horrible."

Finally she was able to wrestle herself free. But then what she described as a bolt of lightning suddenly flashed through the room. "That's when I screamed."

"It sure was a blood-curdling yell," I commented wryly.

"It certainly sent shivers down my back," Dan agreed. "We thought you were being murdered." Ramona smiled weakly as she realized how her reaction must have effected us.

The intensity of the spiritual battle was greater than anything I had ever encountered before. Although Dan and I had experienced a measure of victory, it was very apparent that the devil was not giving up easily. We needed to get back into some more serious spiritual warfare. "I think we need to do some more praying," I suggested. The others readily agreed.

For the next hour and a half, the four of us continued to battle against the forces of darkness together. At one point Dan grabbed his Bible, opened it to Luke 10:17 and read the verse out loud: *The seventy-two returned with joy and said, "Lord, even the demons submit to us in your name." He [Jesus] replied, "I saw Satan fall like lightning from heaven. I have given you authority to trample on snakes and scorpions and to overcome all the power of the enemy; nothing will harm you.* Dan closed his Bible and looked at us intently, "I believe we need to claim that Scripture for ourselves. Jesus said nothing would harm us. Do we really believe it?"

We started to quote Scripture. "Nothing can harm us. Satan, you are a defeated foe." Faith began to rise in our hearts and our intercessions became increasingly defiant. We knew that the demonic forces were finally in retreat. But we also had a sense that they had not gone very far. They were still hovering outside. "Let's pray for the protection of those in the pastor's home," I urged. Finally around 4am we knew the battle had been won.

Despite my interrupted night, I woke a couple of hours later feeling surprisingly alert. My first thought was for those in the church house. Had they experienced any of the spiritual opposition we had? I decided to go and check. A rather bleary eyed Ugandan answered the door. "How did you sleep?" I asked.

"Not very well."

"Neither did we. We've been in spiritual warfare most of the night," I explained.

"We've been battling since early morning," the Ugandan answered. "It started at about 4am. In fact, some are still praying."

The resistance had been fierce; but as the next week was to prove, a spiritual breakthrough had been accomplished not only in Soroti but also in surrounding villages. Other parts of East Africa had been experiencing revival for about 40 years with intense times of prayer and repentance. Every denomination, especially the Anglican church, had been touched by the renewal with parishes growing in leaps and bounds and churches springing up in even the remotest villages. Now here in Soroti, we began to witness some of that renewal for ourselves.

In the following weeks, we saw hearts softened and many come to Christ. There were astounding scenes in outlying districts where whole families came together and smashed their clay beer pots. These red pots were the focus of community life, and the broken pot, a symbol of a new beginning. Whereas earlier, people we had spoken with had resisted our invitation to attend church, now they came flocking in our direction. We had Africans traipsing across our lawn, knocking on our front door and asking how they could be saved. There were times too when God supernaturally went ahead of us.

One day, Ramona was out visiting house to house. At one home, the woman eagerly ushered her in, almost as if she had been expecting her. Puzzled by her reaction, Ramona went into the humble abode. She sat listening in amazement as the woman explained her story. The previous night God had appeared to her in a dream and told her that the next day a Western lady would come and explain to her the way to get right with God. Ramona was that lady.

On another occasion, the church pastor and I were walking together along a narrow track when a Ugandan came towards us riding a bicycle. Because there was no room to pass, the cyclist stopped. The three of us struck up a conversation and, using the pastor as my interpreter, I seized the opportunity to explain to the man how through Jesus' death on the cross, he had opened the way for him to go to heaven. First, however, he needed to turn from his sin. He listened intently as the pastor translated my words. Then smiling, he replied in his native tongue. The pastor turned to me. "He says he believes you and wants to ask Jesus into his life." It seemed too easy. Had he really understood?

Several large drops on my bare arms warned of an impending tropical storm. "Let's go and talk inside the church," I suggested. The simple, brick building was only a short distance from where we were standing. Inside, sheltered from the darkened clouds that had already begun to release their heavy load, we continued our conversation. Almost deafened by the pelting rain on the tin roof, we huddled close on a wooden bench. In that more intimate setting, the cyclist readily unburdened his heart to us. Like so many of his fellow countrymen, he was addicted to beer and cigarettes. To maintain his habit, he had resorted to petty crime. He had also sinned immorally. Really his whole life was one of addiction. He operated in witchcraft and was troubled by tormenting spirits.

He looked at me with pleading eyes. "Can your Jesus free me?" The pastor interpreted his words.

"Tell him he can only be free if he is willing to confess his sins and turn his back on his old way of life." On hearing this, the man instantly fell on his knees sobbing and cried out what I realized was a genuine prayer of repentance. The pastor and I prayed for the man, and in the name of Jesus released him from the forces of evil that bound him.

As evidence he really meant business, he pulled a crumpled, half-used cigarette pack from his pocket. We went outside to the now clear sky, found a few dry twigs and lit a small fire. The converted cyclist eagerly threw the pack on the fire and smiled as it shriveled in the heat. Those flames enveloped more than a pack of smokes. They symbolized the dross of an old life that had been consumed and was now beginning to burn for Jesus. I watched a warm glow in my own heart as the Ugandan cycled off, a brand new Bible tucked proudly under his arm and a broad smile lighting his face.

A few days later, the pastor and I visited him in his home. He told us he had definitely quit smoking and, since the time we prayed with him, he had not had a drink of beer. It had been a chance encounter but, typical of the many we prayed for, this man was a piece of God-chosen fruit, ready to be picked. Further evidence that we had broken through the spiritual darkness in the area came the following Sunday. In contrast to the handful of faithful believers who had attended our first meetings, now, just as I had originally envisaged, the small church was now full and overflowing.

From this whole episode, I learned a key principle: feverish activity, no matter how sincere, and intense intercession, no matter how prolonged, are not enough. There are times when spiritual boundaries have to be crossed and evil barriers brought down before release can be experienced. It is the prayer of the fervent *righteous* man that accomplishes much.

It was only later that we would come to appreciate what a

critical time in God's calendar this was, not just for Soroti, but for the whole of Uganda. The dictator Idi Amin had only just toppled the previous government. His true colors had not yet been revealed. The nation was still to witness the full impact of his cruel Islamic rule, one in which all foreigners would be expelled and thousands of Ugandans brutally massacred.

We had not yet grasped the principle that God often pours out revival to prepare people for impending persecution. Right now, we were reveling in the thrill of experiencing that revival and seeing Ugandans, such as the cyclist and the lady Ramona had encountered, turn their lives over to Jesus Christ. As a team, we still had several more weeks to reap this harvest. We were eager to take full advantage of the breakthrough.

9

Call to the Chinese

THE revival continued unabated as we reached out beyond the township of Soroti into surrounding villages. The church building (and every village seemed to have one) was usually nothing more than a crude, open-framed structure comprised of a coarse, thatched roof propped up on roughly hewn poles. The moment Dan started strumming his guitar, barefoot, raggedly dressed youngsters came running. They stayed, happily twisting their black limbs around the poles, eyes in wide-open intrigue as we sang our songs and, with the help of our African interpreters, told personal stories of how God had moved in our lives. The villagers sat on the ground while hens scratched in the dirt around them. An occasional dog, cat or even a goat or pig meandered through the open congregation. Others hung back, eavesdropping from a less threatening distance in front of their huts. Almost every time we challenged our listeners to make Jesus Lord of their lives, some would respond. Then a door was opened to us we had never anticipated or thought possible.

One morning the telephone rang at the mission house. I picked up the hand piece and put it to my ear. "Lack!"

"Are you leader of the Youth With A Mission group?" a voice I did not recognize asked.

"Yes, that's me," I answered. *Who was this?* As if hearing my unspoken question, the caller immediately introduced himself.

"I'm a television producer with Uganda National TV." I was puzzled and a little nervous as to why a TV producer would be contacting me. "I understand you have a singing group. I would like to invite you to perform on our station." I gulped. Dan had proved his skill on the guitar and as a group our singing had some merit, but we were not professional.

"I, err.... Well, yes," I stumbled out an answer. I did not want to give him a false impression, but neither did I want to turn down such a unique opportunity. "We are a group of young people here in Uganda to share the Christian message, but we are not professional." In Africa in 1971, anyone from abroad was considered elite. On that basis alone, we were accepted.

A recording session was arranged. We decided not to try anything fancy but to put together a program along the same lines we had been presenting in the villages. The bright lights and cameras were more nerve racking than the open eyes of attentive African villagers, but we got through. The television producer seemed satisfied with our performance. We had only made one stipulation, that a contact address be screened at the end. This way people could write in for literature. While the producer assured me they would do this, I was aware that a higher authority might edit the address out and thus make our performance a less effective tool for evangelism.

The evening our program was due to be screened we were on the road between villages. We pulled over at a roadside cafe and, along with 50 Africans, watched it on black and white television. There were embarrassed giggles from the girls and pokes and snide remarks from the guys as we saw ourselves on screen for the first time. But despite the jokes, we all agreed that the presentation came over very well. The most comforting aspect for me was to see the address appear at the end of the program.

Our performance was screened a number of times over the following weeks. In fact, it proved so popular that people began humming our songs in the street. Our television appearance also opened other invitations to perform. But perhaps the most satisfying aspect was the mail response. Within days of it first being aired, letters began pouring in from people who had been deeply touched by the program. One businessman wrote:

I have just seen your TV program and felt compelled to write to you immediately. I am at my wits' end with worry and remorse over what I have done. I am a prominent businessman. Wealth, position and, to some extent, power is mine. But over the last few years, I have been increasingly unhappy and have felt that there was no purpose in life. I have had nothing to do with religion or the church since I was married. In your program tonight, I saw for the first time that there could be a solution to my misery. I have done all the bad things those happy people talked about, and worse.... In particular, I have behaved really badly towards one of my competitors, who still seems to be friendly towards me in spite of my actions. I can't bear to face my business associates because of what I have done.... Is it possible to help me by a visit? Please come after 6pm any day this week.

It was a thrill personally to follow up such correspondence as well as to send out appropriate literature. Our days were full and satisfying. New schools and villages kept opening to us as a result of our television exposure. We continued to conduct street rallies and sell our literature in the marketplace. Now that the spiritual resistance had been broken, we had more than enough to keep our team occupied for our final two weeks in Soroti.

For me personally, however, my heart was being stirred in a new direction. Ever since I heard about the Chinese communists working on the Tan–Zam railway project, I could not get them out of my mind and had been trying to figure out a way to reach them. The nation of Tanzania bordered on the south of Uganda. I discovered that one could take a three-hour bus ride from Soroti to the Ugandan capital of Kampala, and from there an hour-and-a-half plane flight to Dar-es-Salaam, the capital of Tanzania. I could be there in less than five hours. In my heart, a plan was brewing. I could leave the team in Soroti and go on a short fact-finding tour by myself into Tanzania. I was sure that Floyd would give me permission to go. After all, he had been the one who had encouraged us "to take every opportunity we could to evangelize"; and as Brother Andrew had said, this was a God-given opportunity. The Bamboo Curtain effectively kept us from going into China, but there was nothing to stop us from reaching out to the Chinese here in Africa.

I had not said anything to the rest of the team; but as the plan solidified in my heart, I became increasingly convinced God was speaking to me. However, I needed to be sure, so I decided to stay up one night after the others had gone to bed, and spend time asking God specifically if it was his will for me to make this fact-finding tour.

Shafts of moonlight pierced the latticed window, reflecting eerie crisscross patterns on the otherwise bare walls of the living room. In the semi-darkness, I knelt down by one of the mahogany dining chairs. A thin, straw mat was my only protection from the polished concrete floor. I could have chosen to sit on one of the more comfortable cane chairs, but I was already tired and did not want to fall asleep.

I spent time preparing my heart, checking my motives and asking God to show me any unconfessed sin in my life. Had I spoken harshly to anyone or been critical in any way? Immediately, I recalled an overly sharp remark I had made earlier that day to one of the team. The person had been slack in carrying out a duty, and I felt my retort was justified. Now under the conviction of the Holy Spirit, I recognized my attitude was wrong. I quickly repented, *Please forgive me, Lord.* I also made a mental note to ask for that person's forgiveness the next day. This was such an important question, I did not want anything to stop me hearing accurately from God.

I took a stand in the name of Jesus against any interference from the satanic forces. From our exposure to the high level of occult worship and witchcraft in Africa, and our own night drama, I had become aware as never before about the importance of exercising our authority over Satan. I also spent time quietly worshipping God and focusing my thoughts on his greatness and glory. I wanted to make sure I was absolutely in tune with him.

Having thoroughly prepared myself, I finally felt ready to ask my vital question. By now the full moon had moved higher in the sky and was projecting its soft, latticed reflections through the window onto the floor beside me. "Lord, do you want me to reach out to the Chinese in Tanzania?" I waited quietly for an answer, the silence disturbed only by the orchestra of Africa's night music: a 1,000-strong chorus of crickets interspersed by an occasional owl hoot. As the minutes ticked by, I continued to wait.

Then, clear and sharp, a Scripture reference came to mind:

Isaiah 52. I had no idea what it contained; so picking up my Bible from the dining table, I sat on the mahogany chair and flicked through the pages. As I came to Isaiah 52, the small, round glow of my flashlight immediately illuminated verse 7: *How beautiful upon the mountain are the feet of him who brings good news.* A little further on verses 11 and 12 jumped out of the page at me: *Depart, depart, go out hence.... But you will not leave in haste and you shall not go in flight for the Lord will go before you and the God of Israel will be your rear guard.* As I continued reading, I was also struck by the promise of verse 15: *For that which has not been told them they will see and that which they have not heard they shall understand.* I turned off the flashlight and sat in the darkness pondering what I had just read. God had answered my question. Of that, I was certain. I was to go to Tanzania. My only question now was: how was I going to break the news to the rest of my team?

By the time I emerged the next morning, Ramona was busy in the kitchen making coffee, pouring boiling water over newly ground beans. Charles, the Ugandan evangelist, had just returned from the market with a loaf of freshly baked bread. Its aroma mingled with the smell of the newly brewed coffee filling the dining room. Dan was already at the table, biting into a large piece of juicy, pink papaya from the well-laden fruit basket. I sat down and picked out a slice for myself. But I did not eat it. I was not hungry. I was too preoccupied with how I was going to break my news to the team.

Ramona joined us at the table. "Everything okay, Rudi?" she asked, noting my uneaten papaya slice. Even at this early hour, her light brown hair was immaculately teased with every strand in place. Dan reached out for another piece of papaya. "I must say, you seem rather subdued this morning, Rudi," he commented, munching into the fruit. With his healthy appetite, it amazed me how he retained his lithe figure. "Is there something on your mind?" By now Tom and Natalie had made their appearance.

"Well, I do have something I want to share with you all," I confessed. "I guess now is as good a time as any."

Placing my half-drunk cup of coffee on the table, I pushed

back on my chair. The clatter of utensils silenced. Breakfast was forgotten as all five pairs of eyes fixed their gaze on me. I decided to plunge right in. Starting from the beginning, I explained how stirred I had felt when I had first heard from Floyd about the Chinese communists in Africa, especially those working on the Tan–Zam railway project. I told them of my response to Brother Andrew's challenge to reach these Chinese and my thoughts of leaving the team in Soroti and making a fact-finding tour on my own into Dar-es-Salaam. I paused, watching for their response. All eyes remained glued on me. But no one said a word.

I went on to tell them about my prayer time the night before and how God had spoken so clearly through verses 7, 11 and 12 in Isaiah 52. At that, our Kiwi member Tom let out a low whistle. "Wow! Mate, I reckon God has really spoken to you." Dan nodded slowly.

"Yes. I think you are meant to go, Rudi. Don't worry about us. We'll be fine."

"We'll manage, no sweat," Natalie affirmed.

"And we'll be backing you all the way in prayer." Ramona added.

"Thanks for your support," I said, putting my now lukewarm mug of coffee to my lips. "I really appreciate it." Now I had shared my news and their reaction was so positive, a weight lifted from my shoulders and I breathed easier. While I had no doubt God had confirmed my plans, it meant a great deal to know the team was behind me.

The only dissenting voice was Charles, the Ugandan. "You realize, Rudi, that these Chinese are cloistered together in camps and not easy to get at," he warned. "One of my friends tried to give Swahili literature to a Chinese worker and almost lost his job over it." I nodded but did not comment.

"And what about contacts in Dar-es-Salaam. Do you know anyone there?"

"No, I don't," I admitted. "But then Roli and I didn't have any contacts when we took our Bibles into Bulgaria and look how God led us."

Despite Charles' more sobering assessment, my spirit was not dampened. Once I had phoned Floyd in Nairobi and got the okay from him, nothing could stop me. I had a green light. I was going for it.

Isaiah 52:12 said not to go out *in haste*, so I knew I was not to rush this trip. I therefore gave myself a week to prepare, and find out as much as I could about the Chinese situation in Tanzania. Here in Soroti, however, information was limited.

A few days after I had made my decision to go, the director of a missionary organization in Tanzania—a German named Fritz—came to visit. We had been expecting him for some time but that he had chosen to visit us now, just days before my proposed departure for Tanzania, seemed yet another divine confirmation.

I was out selling literature in the marketplace when Fritz arrived. By the time I returned, he was already sitting relaxing in one of our cane lounge chairs enjoying a cool fruit juice. Overhead, the metal roof creaked and groaned as it expanded under the sun's late morning rays. Dumping my carton of tracts on the table, I flipped on the overhead fan, which instantly stirred its welcome breeze. "Man, sure is a scorcher out there," I remarked, wiping the beads of sweat from my forehead and going over to greet him. Normally after coming in from the heat of the market, I took a rest, but not today. Now that Fritz was here, I did not want to waste a moment.

"Let me get a drink and I'll come and talk." I was eager to glean from him every bit of information I could about the Chinese. He was my very first, in fact, my only contact in Tanzania. Grabbing a bottle of Coke from the fridge, I pulled up a chair beside him and, after some brief preliminary chatter, steered the conversation around to the Chinese working in Tanzania. I was disappointed to find that he had limited local information about the situation in the capital. His organization was centered a few hundred kilometers west of Dar-es-Salaam. But he did have a broad understanding of the general position of the Chinese working in Africa and seemed willing to air his knowledge.

After about half an hour of non-stop questioning, Fritz turned to me. "Why the interest in the Chinese, Rudi?" I began to explain to him the purpose of my forthcoming visit to Tanzania. His eyebrows puckered. "Rudi, do you really know what you're undertaking?" he said, shaking his head. "What you're proposing is not only just difficult, it's almost impossible." He began to enumerate the nearly insurmountable barriers I would need to get over if I was going to successfully evangelize these communist Chinese. "First, the camps are scattered over many hundreds of kilometers in very isolated areas. Second, it's not only hard to get to them physically, but the government forbids it." Fritz counted off each point on his fingers. "Third, settlements are ringed with barbed wire. Fourth, foreigners to the area are closely scrutinized. Fifth, as part of their deal to receive foreign aid from the Chinese, the Tanzanian government promised not to allow any religious input into the camps."

Fritz paused, his right index finger resting on his left little finger as his voice took on an almost fatherly tone. "Rudi, with your white face, you would stand out a mile away if you tried to get into the camps. I'd be very surprised if you found any long-term missionary in Tanzania who would help you. No one would want to take the risk of losing their visas for the sake of evangelizing a few thousand Chinese. I doubt if even the local African Christians would have anything to do with it."

Fritz's comments brought me down from my spiritual high with a resounding thump, and over the next 24 hours, I soberly assessed the sheer impossibility of the mountain I was considering scaling. I squarely faced the potential pitfalls and dangers. I had to agree with him. This was not an easy mission. But as I assessed the risk, rather than weakening my resolve, it only made me more determined. Within me arose an even greater excitement than before. In my heart stirred the same cry of faith Caleb uttered when he and the rest of the Israelites stood at the edge of the Promised Land: *Lord, give me this mountain where the giants are.*

I had no doubts. The instructions in verses 7 and 11 of Isaiah 52 were precise. *How beautiful upon the mountain are the feet of him who brings good news,.... Depart, depart, go out hence.* I knew I had heard from God. If I were to back out now, like Jonah, I would be disobeying Christ's direct command to me. Obviously I would have to find more subtle methods than usual to get the message across to the communist Chinese. But because I was being sent as God's emissary, I was confident he would reveal his ways to disseminate his Word among these people. I was equally certain that he would have someone in Dar-es-Salaam who would help me. Exactly who and how I would locate that person, I had no idea.

A few days later, leaving the Soroti team in Dan's capable charge, I made the bus trip to the airport and there boarded a 20-seat twin engine, turboprop plane for Dar-es-Salaam. As the small plane circled the city and came in to land, my confidence remained high. I still did not have any Christian contacts in the city. But as he had done for Roli and me in Bulgaria, I was sure God had gone ahead to prepare the way.

Clutching my gray suitcase and a piece of paper on which Fritz had written the name of a cheap, downtown Christian hostel, I walked outside the airport into the sauna-like conditions of Dar-es-Salaam. How could people work in these temperatures? My thoughts flashed in sympathy to those thousands of Chinese sweating it out under the sun on the railway track. After only a few minutes in this intense heat, my shirt was already soaked with perspiration. I had intended taking a bus into town, but quickly abandoned that idea and decided instead to splurge my few precious shillings on a taxi.

I sat back, enjoying the welcome breeze coming through the open window of the beaten-up Morris as it rattled its way past tall, palm trees and dirt-streaked, white-plastered houses that lined the route into the city. The nearer we got to the center of the capital, the more densely concentrated the houses became. Conditions here were clearly more rundown than in Nairobi.

We pulled up outside a black, moss-covered concrete building about a block back from the sea. It was fronted with a tired, blue-painted sign on which was written in English, THE LUTHER HOUSE. It was not the Hilton, but it would be more suitable for my pocket than the outrageous fare the taxi driver was demanding from me. Before starting our journey, I had insisted that he put the meter on. I now realized it must have been rigged. "Ten shillings?" I questioned him again. "Ten shillings," he repeated, doggedly pointing to the meter. I had no way of proving that I, like so many other unsuspecting tourists, had been taken for a ride, so I reluctantly pulled out my wallet and counted out the unfamiliar currency. That would be the last taxi ride for me. From now on, my transport would be by local bus, regardless of the temperature. I climbed the few steps up the Luther House and checked myself in.

The next morning, having suffered a restless, sweaty night, I sat down for a community-style breakfast. I looked around at the handful of guests for someone to speak to. Maybe one of them could lead me to the local Christian who would be prepared to join hands in my venture of reaching out to the communist Chinese railway workers. I needed someone who was on fire for God and who had enough spiritual gumption to disobey the national law, which forbade anyone to evangelize those living in these barbed wire camps.

Among the mainly businessmen at the breakfast table, there was one lady. I struck up a conversation with her and discovered she was a missionary. We chatted about our mutual interest in reaching the lost. But heeding both Charles' and Fritz's words of caution, I hesitated to divulge the real reason for my visit to Dar-es-Salaam. I chose my words carefully. "Do you happen to know where there is a Christian bookshop?" I asked, in what seemed a God-inspired approach. Bookshops usually had a good knowledge of the local church scene. Maybe someone there could direct me to a lively church that would give me the support I needed.

"Yes, I was at a Christian bookshop just yesterday," my breakfast companion responded. "It's only a few minutes' walk from here." I scribbled down the name and street on my paper napkin. "You shouldn't have any difficulty finding it," she assured me.

She was right. The modest, one-room shop merged in with the rest in the block, but from the covers of the few books displayed in the window, along with the crosses and other Christian meorabilia, I knew I had found the right store. The words from my early morning reading of Psalm 37 came back to me: *Commit your way to the Lord; trust in him, and he will act.*

He will bring forth your vindication as the light and your right as the noonday sun.

Thank you, Lord, I prayed in silent gratitude. *Thank you for going ahead of me.*

As I walked through the door, a diminutive, gray-haired European lady behind the counter smiled at me sweetly. "Can I help you, sir?" she asked in soft, strongly foreign-accented English.

"Well, I'm hoping you can," I answered, returning her smile. No one else was in the store, which was to my advantage. Even so, now I was actually face to face with a local Christian here in Dar-es-Salaam, I was not sure where to begin. I shifted uneasily. "I'm Swiss German," I started. The lady's smile broadened.

"I'm from Sweden," she said, warmly shaking my hand. "Welcome to Tanzania." She seemed so open and friendly. I was sure this was the person God had set in my path to help me; so throwing caution to the wind, I ploughed right in.

I explained that I was with an organization called Youth With A Mission and that our aim was to release young people into world evangelism. "That sounds wonderful, young man," she said brightly.

"I only flew in last night. I don't know any local Christian and only have a few days here," I continued.

"Well, is there anyone I can introduce you to or any way I can help you in your mission?" she offered.

"I think you might," I said, leaning closer to her across the counter. Even though we were the only two in the store, I did not want the risk of any unwanted ears eavesdropping on our conversation. I lowered my voice a few decibels as I confided. "God's been laying a concern on my heart for the communist Chinese. I'm looking for someone who might...."

She did not let me finish my sentence. As soon as I mentioned *Chinese,* her face instantly darkened and her demeanor changed. From a charmingly helpful shop assistant, she was transformed into a paranoid freak. Waving her hands agitatedly, she began shooing me out of the shop like some unwanted stray dog. "No. No. No, you can't make contact with the Chinese. It's absolutely forbidden by law." I doggedly resisted her frantic attempts to get rid of me. She was my only Christian contact in Dar-es-Salaam. If this lady refused to give me a lead, I did not know who else I could turn to.

"Please...." I pleaded. "Can't you just give me the names of some local Christian people."

"Well, there's the Baptist church down the road," she said, calming down a little, and then, as I turned to leave, added offhandedly, "You could try Pastor Malya. He lives in Temeke near the community center. But," she added almost as an after-thought, "don't try him during the day. He's only at home in the evenings."

"Thank you very much," I said, making a mental note of his name as I stepped out from the relative comfort of the fan-cooled bookshop into the sweltering heat of the mid-morning sun. *Pastor Malya in Temeke. No point in trying him now if he wasn't home until evening. I may as well walk to the Baptist church down the road.*

My visit to the Baptist church drew a blank. The senior pastor was away and when I asked his African assistant a carefully phrased question about the Chinese railway project, he was noncommittal. "It's not our area of interest," he said curtly as we stood talking at his office door. He was equally unhelpful when I asked about contacts with anyone who could assist me. He did, however, give me directions about the right bus to the closest Chinese settlement.

Back out in the street, I glanced at my watch: 11am. *Where do I go now, Lord?* My only other lead was Pastor Malya in Temeke. But according to the bookshop lady, he would not be home this hour of the day. I decided therefore to take a bus and visit the Chinese settlement.

I found my way to the central bus station, and stood waiting for the right one to turn up. The terminal was a hive of activity. African women, balancing huge, open, woven baskets of fruit and vegetables on their heads, were hopping on and off buses. Some wore black Islamic veils; but unlike the fundamental Muslim women, their veils only covered their heads and not their faces. I even saw a scrawny goat being dragged on by its African owner. But although buses rolled in and out with regular monotony, I could not see any with the right number to take me to the Chinese camp. The midday sun beat mercilessly through the flimsy shelter and the heat radiated up from the black pitch pavement. I looked round for a seat, but there was none. By now my legs ached, my T-shirt dripped with perspiration and my frustration was growing by the minute. Had the Swedish shop assistant deliberately led me astray and given me the wrong bus number?

When the next bus pulled in, I turned to the African man standing next to me and pointed to it. "Where does this go?" He reeled off names I had never heard of. One, however, arrested my attention: Temeke! "Temeke?" I repeated. He nodded vigorously. Temeke was where Pastor Malya lived. But the shop assistant had said he would not be home until evening. It was still only early afternoon.

I had no idea how far away Temeke was. I did not know if it was a suburb of Dar-es-Salaam or a separate town. And when I arrived, how would I find this Pastor Malya? I did not even have the name of his church. The only clue the shop assistant had given me was that his house was next to the community center. I could be on a wild goose chase, yet I felt a strange urgency to board this bus. As I flopped into a seat towards the back, peace settled into my heart. I knew I had made the right move.

I looked around the half-empty bus. My attention was drawn to an African man sitting by himself in the front. *Go and sit with that man*, I felt the Lord prompt me. In obedience, I left my seat at the back and slipped into the aisle seat beside him. He glanced casually at me and then, as the bus lurched forward, reverted his gaze out the window to the passing scene of palm trees and the moss-stained plastered houses which gradually thinned out as we left behind the more built up area of Dar-es-Salaam. I noted the impressive multi-lens camera slung round the African's shoulder. *What great pictures I'd be able to record of Africa if I had equipment like that*, I thought with more than a tinge of envy. *Start a conversation with this man*, the Holy Spirit whispered in my heart. Using the camera as my starting point, I pointed to his camera and remarked, "Beautiful piece of equipment you've got there."

He looked at it admiringly. "Yes, it's a good camera all right," he responded in excellent English. "I'm a newspaper reporter, so it's pretty essential to my work."

Having broken the ice, conversation flowed easily. I learned that he had been raised hundreds of kilometers to the northwest of Dar-es-Salaam at the foot of the famous Mount Kilimanjaro. But he had readily traded life in his tribal homeland for a job in the capital. "It was such a wonderful opportunity, I leapt at the chance to move here. I haven't been back to my home village in years," he explained.

As a journalist, he might be able to give me some inside information about the communist Chinese working on the Tan–Zam railway project, so I raised the topic with him. "The Chinese? They are doing a great job," he enthused, "a real boom to the nation's economy." His political position so evidently expressed, I thought it wise to drop the subject of the Chinese. He might become curious about my interest and start asking awkward questions. I did not want a repeat encounter of the kind we had had with the reporter in Jerusalem, and my assignment here in Tanzania railroaded before it had even started. This African journalist was far less bombastic, but he was still a reporter; I therefore deliberately changed the subject. Besides, I had a more pressing matter on my mind. I was concerned I might miss my stop.

We had been travelling for nearly half an hour; and while we were still in Dar-es-Salaam, I judged by the increase of vegetation between homes that we were in the outer suburbs. I had no idea where I should get off. "This is my first visit to Temeke," I explained to my traveling companion. "Would you be able to show me where to get off?"

"No problem," he said obligingly. "I'm getting off there myself."

"Thank you," I said gratefully.

A few minutes later, dust swirling, the bus squealed to a halt and the reporter and I dismounted. The bus pulled away, leaving both of us covered with a fine layer of dust. Carefully brushing it off his camera, the reporter turned to me. "Where do you need to go in Temeke?"

"I'm here to visit someone I've never met," I replied, feeling decidedly awkward. "His name is Pastor Malya."

"Malya? That's interesting." My African companion mused half to himself and half to me. "I used to know someone by that name. We grew up as kids in the same tribal village in Kilimanjaro. In fact, we were best friends. I wonder if he's related? Where does this Pastor Malya live?"

Feeling even more foolish, I confessed, "I don't know. I was told his house is next to the community center."

"That's the community center there," the reporter said pointing to a building on the other side of the road. "Look, you can see the church about 100 meters further on."

"That must be Malya's house, right next to it," I said, thankful to have found it so easily. "I really appreciate your help." I reached out my hand in farewell. Now I had found Malya's place, I was anxious to get going. But I was not about to brush off my new friend so easily.

"I'd like to come and meet this man for myself," he answered. "Is it alright if I come with you?"

"Well, yes of course," I replied. I could hardly say anything else. Without this man's assistance, I would probably not have found my way here anyway. But how could I talk with the pastor about such a sensitive issue as evangelizing the Chinese with a pro-communist newspaper reporter present? I did not have a choice. The journalist was already striding towards the house. *Oh well, it's unlikely Malya will be at home anyway this early in the afternoon*, I consoled myself as I followed him down the narrow, sandy track that led to the steeple, white-plastered church.

Just before the church, we turned left up a path that led to the house. I knocked on the unpainted wooden door, which was shaded by a fruit-laden papaya tree, and waited. There was no reply. I knocked again. Then, trying to disguise my relief, I turned to the newspaper reporter. "Looks like he's not at home. Don't worry. I'll fill in the time and come back later this evening." We had started retracing our steps, and were already halfway back down the path when I heard the door squeak behind us. I turned to see an African, whom I guessed to be in his mid-thirties, framed in the doorway. Rubbing his eyes and obviously awakened from his mid-afternoon nap, he looked surprised, almost shocked, as he saw us. Staring intently at the newspaper reporter, he asked, "Are you looking for someone?"

"Yes. We are looking for Pastor Malya," the reporter replied.

"I'm Pastor Malya," the African responded. "Please come in."

More than a little stunned by his ready invitation, we stepped over the threshold into a simple but comfortably furnished living room. At his directing, we sank with gratitude into wooden armchairs. The skimpy foam cushioning offered little relief to my weary joints, but above a fan swirled its welcome breeze onto our sweaty, dust-covered faces. Pastor Malya disappeared into a small, adjoining kitchen and returned minutes later with two large, plastic 'glasses' of iced water. I gulped mine down gratefully.

Sitting himself on a seat opposite, he looked at us quizzically. "What's the purpose of your visit?" he asked politely. Unable to divulge the true nature of my mission, I instead talked in general terms, explaining about YWAM, how we were an international missionary organization, had teams in Kenya and Uganda and were interested in coming to Tanzania.

"We'd certainly be willing to assist in any way we can," Pastor Malya said. But although he seemed genuinely interested, it was clear I did not have his full attention. Even as he was talking to me, his eyes kept diverting to the newspaper man. Suddenly turning to him, he blurted out, "Don't I know you?"

"I think you may," the reporter answered, giving his name. "I'm pretty sure we grew up in the same village."

The pastor's eyes lit up in immediate recognition. "Of course, of course. I thought you looked familiar when I saw you at the door. Why, I haven't seen you in years." Standing up, they warmly embraced and then sitting back lapsed into their vernacular tongue. I sat as an uncomprehending eavesdropper, but I could tell, from their excited tones and animated hand movements, that they were probably reminiscing over childhood memories and chatting about mutual friends.

Switching back to English, Pastor Malya excused his rudeness and explained how they had been close buddies as children, but had each gone their separate ways and until now had totally lost contact with one another. He clearly recognized this as a God-given opportunity and, switching between his native tongue and English so that I could also participate, he began to share the

Gospel with his long-lost friend. Enthralled as I was by this remarkable boyhood reunion, when one then two hours had passed, I started to get agitated. I too was here on an assignment from God. Was I going to get a chance to share with the pastor by myself? Outside the sun was already beginning to sink. As much as I rejoiced in this chance to witness to a lost soul, I did not want my own mission jeopardized.

As I observed Malya uncompromisingly present the Gospel to his liberal-minded friend, I could see he was a man of vigor and faith. Of the few Christians I had so far met here in Tanzania, he was the only person who had the spiritual zeal and vision necessary to buy into my project of reaching the Chinese. The longer I listened to him debate the claims of Christ, the more convinced I became that this was the man God had prepared to be my Tanzanian co-worker. Just how prepared, I was yet to find out.

As if by divine cue, the reporter, who until this point had been totally engrossed in the conversation, glanced at his watch. "Six o'clock. Goodness, I didn't realize it was that late. I must get going." He rose abruptly from his chair and headed towards the door. "I've got business I must attend to." Pastor Malya got up to see him off. I sat alone in the semi-darkness as they chattered their farewells outside. Delicious smells of cooked banana wafted through from the kitchen where Malya's wife was preparing the evening meal. I suddenly realized how hungry I was. With all the activity of the day, I had not eaten since breakfast. Overriding these natural pangs of hunger, however, was an even more urgent desire: my need to reveal my vision for the Chinese.

By now the African night had dropped its curtain of darkness. Malya returned, switched on the light, and sitting down in the thin, foam-cushioned chair opposite, looked me squarely in the eyes and came straight to the point. "Now that we're finally alone, Mr. Lack, let's talk. What's the real reason for your visit?" I warmed instantly to his straightforward, no-nonsense manner. He was my type of person.

"Call me, Rudi," I said.

"Simon," he responded, extending his hand in renewed welcome. "So Rudi, why have you really come?" I opened my mouth to speak. But before I had a chance, Simon continued, "You may have noticed my reaction when I opened the door to you this afternoon."

"Well, yes, I must admit I did," I replied. "I thought it was probably because we were complete strangers and you weren't expecting us."

"That's true. I wasn't but in another way I was," he answered mysteriously. My curiosity aroused, I leaned forward. "What do you mean?"

"Two nights ago," he went on to explain, "I had a dream in which I saw my news reporter friend, coming to my house with a white man, someone I had never met. That white man, I now realize, was you." I stared at him in semi-disbelief, barely comprehending what I had heard.

"You saw me in a dream? Two nights ago?" I repeated.

"That's right," he answered matter-of-factly. "So I know God has brought you here, but why? What's the real purpose of your visit, Rudi?"

Greatly bolstered by this divine confirmation, I set all hesitancy aside and, fully opening my heart, shared in detail with Simon the flow of events that had led me to this incredible encounter. I told him of my conversation with Floyd and my initial reaction to Brother Andrew's call to evangelize the Chinese workers in Africa. I shared of my growing yearning to accept this challenge but with a targeted focus on the Tan–Zam railway project. I told him about the specific direction I had received from Isaiah 52 and of my journey of faith here to Dar-es-Salaam despite the fact I had no local contact. I shared how I had gone to the Christian bookshop and the Swedish lady's fearful reaction when I had mentioned the Chinese. I explained how she had given me his name, but stressed that I should only come in the evening because he was not home in the afternoon. "She's right," Simon interjected. "I'm seldom home during the day. Today was a rare exception. But how did you get to meet my boyhood friend?"

"I'd planned to visit a Chinese camp; but when no bus came, I decided to take the bus to Temeke instead," I explained. "That's when the Spirit directed me to move from my seat at the back and go and sit next to your news reporter friend."

It was now Simon's turn to open his eyes in amazement. He

shook his head slowly. "That's incredible! Our church has been praying for months about ways to reach the Chinese. Your coming is a direct answer to our prayers." We both sat momentarily in stunned silence as we reflected on the intricate weaving of events that had brought us together. Behind us, dishes clattered as Simon's wife laid the table for supper.

Rising to his feet, Simon beckoned me to the plain, wooden table. "Come eat with us, Rudi," he said, pulling out a stool for me to sit on. Steam mingled with the delicious aroma of cooked bananas that wafted from one of the two large bowls in the center of the table. The other was piled full of fluffy white rice. I dug hungrily into the ample portion that Simon's wife piled onto my plate. Our dinner conversation centered on one topic: how we could effectively evangelize the forbidden community of Chinese without raising suspicion.

"We can't employ the usual methods," Simon said, resting his knife and fork on the side of his plate.

"I've thought about that," I nodded, accepting another generous spoonful from Simon's wife.

"The authorities are watching us like hawks," Simon added. "Whatever method of evangelism we use, we have got to be very careful not to draw attention to ourselves."

"So, open-air meetings or literature distribution is out?" Simon put his utensils firmly down on his empty plate as if to emphasize his point.

"Absolutely." A possible strategy was beginning to form in my mind. "I wonder...?" I said, my final portion of rice suspended temporarily in mid-air. "I wonder if there may just be a way we could use literature."

"Impossible," Simon quickly countered. "They would pick it up immediately."

"I don't know," I said, explaining to him about Brother Andrew's Open Door ministry and how they had produced a Gospel imitation of Chairman Mao's little red book. "Maybe we could do an African version," I said.

"Mmmm...that could work," Simon said with interest. "That could just be our answer."

Shortly after the meal, some missionaries came for the

evening. I noticed Simon stayed quiet about reaching the Chinese, so I took my cue from him. I had no idea where these missionaries stood regarding evangelizing the Chinese, but, like Simon, realized the wisdom in remaining silent. The missionaries offered to drive me back to the Luther Guest House, so we did not have a chance to talk further that night. But I was not too concerned. Simon had already arranged to meet with me the following day and take me to a Chinese camp.

As I stood with him the next day in front of the crudely built wooden huts that made up the Chinese compound, my desire to reach them with the Gospel was fanned with fresh urgency. It was a barbed wire prison: one that not only kept the Chinese in, but also effectively kept the African and foreigner out. Over the next few days as Simon and I continued to meet together, we worked through the practicalities of our strategy. The dream of reaching the Chinese was fast becoming a realistic possibility. It was only a matter of time before they would have the opportunity to hear God's personal message of love for them. I resolved to make that time as short as possible.

By the end of my week in Dar-es-Salaam, my friendship with Simon had cemented. We had also reached some definite decisions. I would return to Europe, recruit more people to come to Africa on a short-term mission outreach and also contact Brother Andrew about printing a Chinese Gospel version of the little red book for Africa. Our newly recruited team would then be responsible for bringing that literature into Tanzania. On his part, Simon would encourage his church to continue to pray and look for ways to get the Gospel portions into Chinese hands.

"You have my 100 percent support," Simon encouraged me as we exchanged final farewells at the Dar-es-Salaam airport. "You supply the literature and I'll take full responsibility to see that it gets into the right hands," he promised.

"I'll certainly do everything I can," I assured him. We hugged like brothers. I was reluctant to leave. It had been an exhilarating, fulfilling few days and I was going to miss Simon Malya's company.

As the plane took off, I strained to see the last glimpse of the sprawling coastal capital of Dar-es-Salaam before it disappeared under the clouds. My heart was still there, particularly with those thousands of communist Chinese railway workers. I reclined in my seat reflecting on Simon's confident commitment to me. We would need thousands of pieces of literature to reach the Chinese. The cost would be enormous and I had absolutely no financial backing. Neither did I know anybody in Africa who could print the material. It was not going to be an easy task. But God's stamp was so clearly on this venture that despite the overwhelming odds, I felt quietly assured. He would work out the details.

10

Faith Rewarded

I had one more week with the team in Soroti before we reunited with Floyd McClung's group for my final week of summer outreach in Africa. We met together at a mission compound in the town of Kisumu where we were booked to run a youth camp for 300 young Africans. Situated on Lake Victoria, the compound belonged to the same missionary organization we had associated with in Nairobi and Soroti. The 20-acre enclosure was set in attractive, wooded bush land with the 20 or more brick bungalows scattered between the trees. It was a pleasant change to the crowded, fly-ridden conditions we had experienced in Uganda. The cooler climate, too, was a welcome relief from the sweltering heat of Soroti or the even more sauna-like temperatures I had experienced in Dar-es-Salaam.

All 11 of us were staying in the guesthouse. It had been six weeks since we had been together; so our first couple of hours was a boisterous reunion of laughter and animated conversation as we each vied to share our various experiences. Floyd McClung's Kenyan team had an amazing variety of opportunities presented to them. They had spoken in universities, schools and even been invited to teach at a Bible college. They had visited a number of towns and cities throughout Kenya and preached in large, prestigious churches as well as to remote village congregations. Like us, they found the same ready response to their message. We told of our spiritual battle and the breakthrough and consequent revival we had experienced in Soroti. There was rapt attention as I shared about my trip to Dar-es-Salaam, my encounter with Simon Malya and our plans to reach the Chinese.

Finally, talked out and peopled out, I decided to get away on my own. I stood outside the guesthouse, taking in the beauty of the lush, green woodland and enjoying the unaccustomed, refreshing cool air. About two kilometers away, blocked from my view by the trees, were the massive, clear blue waters of Lake Victoria. I had been told the lake was even larger than the whole of Switzerland.

I looked around at the impressive array of buildings that made up the community. In addition to the missionary homes and guesthouse, there was a Bible school. The Bible school students were currently on vacation and the bungalow-style building, comprising a lecture hall and housing facilities, was where we would be holding the camp. It was also where the 300 young Africans would be housed when they arrived the next day. Beyond the Bible school was another large building. I was trying to work out what it might be used for when I heard a voice behind me.

"Welcome!" I turned to see a tanned, smiling white face. "I take it you are one of the YWAM team helping with the youth camp?" He stretched out his hand and introduced himself as one of the Canadian staff.

"It's quite an impressive set-up you have here," I enthused.

"Yes. We've been blessed all right. Have you seen around?"

"We had a quick look through the Bible school, but that's all." I pointed to the brick structure beyond the Bible school. "I was wondering what that building was used for?"

"Come. I'll show you." Without further explanation, the Canadian strode off in the direction of the building. I followed, curious to know what this large structure would contain. It looked almost like a small factory. But what would a factory be doing in a missionary compound? I guessed it was more likely to be a warehouse for vehicles or maybe an extensive work-shop for repairs. The Canadian unlocked a side door and opened it to let me in. "Everyone's gone for the day, so nothing is going on. But you can get a good idea of the operation." I stepped inside and let out an involuntary whistle.

Before me stood one large commercial Heidelberg printing press and several other smaller ones. There were folding machines: all the equipment needed for commercial printing. Reams of paper of various sizes were neatly stacked on shelves along one wall. Pallets lining the other wall were topped with newly printed books. I was stunned by the revelation. "So you are into book publishing?"

"It's fully commercial," the Canadian said with more than a tinge of pride.

"Do you do printing for outsiders?" I asked. In my mind's eye, I could see pallets of red-bound Gospels lining the wall.

"For sure," the missionary replied. "We supply books and Gospels for people all over the country, not just for our organization, but anyone who needs them."

"Mmmm. That's very interesting." We walked back outside and he locked the door. It had only been a week since Simon Malya and I had established our strategy for reaching the Chinese, and now, without even trying, God had answered our first major need of locating an African-based publisher and printer.

In the next week, we saw scores of young Africans touched by God and motivated for missions. But the aspect that thrilled me most about my stay in Kisumu was my discovery of the mission's publishing business. During my week there, I talked with the person in charge of publishing and negotiated some very reasonable prices for printing 10,000 red-bound Chinese Gospels. I now had just two other barriers to surmount in order to fulfill my commitment to Simon Malya. I needed permission from Brother Andrew to reproduce the booklets and thousands of Kenyan shillings to pay for them.

At the end of our week in Kisumu, I left the Round-the-World team, who were moving on to Ghana, and returned to Switzerland. It was strange to be back on European soil away from the flies, heat, smells and dust of Africa. Instead of standing out as the odd white face in a sea of black ones, I merged as a nonentity into the ordered crowds at Geneva airport. Back in Lausanne, it was wonderful to reunite with my SOE classmates. We chatted excitedly, sharing our stories. I heard details of Joe's spiritual conquests on the streets of Paris and Don's successful mission in Germany. Al told of the challenges he had encountered as he attempted to evangelize in Franco-dominated Spain, and Reona told of her attempts to reach the more conservative English. In turn, I kept them enthralled with my own adventures in Africa.

There were lots of mail to read. Of greatest interest, however, was a postcard from Bulgaria. Sent from the pastor in Sofia, it merely read: *The weather is nice in Bulgaria.* Those few words made all the tension, financial cost, emotional trauma, physical exertion and spiritual battles that we had gone through to complete our Bible-smuggling venture worthwhile. It bolstered my faith for the assignment that lay ahead.

Each student had his or her own plan for the future. Joe was heading back to France. Al had a call to Slavic ministry. Don and Deyon had a vision for a major outreach to coincide with the Olympic Games in Munich, in just under two years' time. With thousands of young people coming together for this single event, it would be the largest outreach YWAM had yet undertaken. Consequently, it would take considerable planning. Reona was staying on in Switzerland, but had plans to return to England later.

Exhilarating as it was to reunite, share vision and learn of each one's future direction, the most meaningful encounter for me during those final few days of the SOE was my reunion with Brother Andrew. I was thrilled to learn that he was to be our graduation speaker. When I heard late Friday afternoon that he had arrived, I went looking for him and found him in the downstairs dining room.

"Rudi! Good to see you." He put his cup aside and gave me a warm embrace. "And where did you go for your outreach?"

"Mainly in Uganda," I said, sitting at the table beside him. Andrew's eyes lit up.

"Africa? Tell me about it." I launched into a detailed description. I shared how God had used his remark to Floyd in India to ignite my own call to the Chinese working on the Tan–Zam railway project. I told him about my trip to Dar-es-Salaam, my amazing encounter with Simon Malya and of his willingness to join hands with me in this project.

"That's wonderful," Andrew encouraged. "It may seem an enormous undertaking, Rudi. But I tell you it's a great deal easier to reach the Chinese in Africa than to get the Gospel to them in Mainland China. If there is anyway I can help, please let me know."

I took a deep breath. Now came a sensitive issue. In my enthusiasm, I had already committed myself to the publishing house in Kisumu to print 10,000 copies of a red-covered, Chinese-scripted Gospel of John. In hindsight I should have gotten Brother Andrew's permission first. "Well, there is a way you could help." Brother Andrew's eyes locked with mine.

"How is that, Rudi?"

"As Simon Malya and I were discussing strategy on how best to reach the Chinese in Africa, I thought of your Chairman Mao style booklets. How would you feel about us reprinting them in Africa?" Andrew looked thoughtful. I held my breath. Was he going to refuse? He had every right to do so.

"Where would you print them?" Andrew inquired.

"There's a mission compound in Kisumu on Lake Victoria that has a commercial printing press. I have already checked it out. They'd be willing to print 10,000." Andrew's eyes opened.

"Oh. Really?" I wanted to bite my tongue. Had I overstepped the mark? "How much would they charge to print that many?" he asked. I gave him the quote the Kisumu publishers had given me. Andrew nodded his head slowly and then, looking passed me through the window, tapped his finger absently on his empty cup. "Mmmm."

I did not say anything. Inside, however, my heart was beating in time with his tapping finger. Did he think I had been presumptuous in making arrangements before I received Open Doors' official permission? After a few moments, but what seemed an eternity, Andrew looked straight at me. "I think we could do it. You arrange to get the red booklets printed in Kenya and Open Doors will pick up the tab." I stared at him, my mouth open like a goldfish.

"You'll what?" I sputtered.

"We'll pay the bill," he repeated calmly.

"Are you sure about that?" I asked, reluctant to accept. "It's a lot of money."

"I know. But the thrust of Open Door's ministry is to get the Gospel across uncrossable borders. What you are attempting to do in Africa is invaluable. We want to back you as much as we can." I stared at him stunned, overwhelmed by his generosity.

"Just get the books printed and have the publishers send us the account," Andrew said as casually as if he had just offered to buy me an ice-cream cone instead of paying for the printing of 10,000 booklets.

"For our part, we'll do everything we can to get them into the hands of the communist Chinese," I assured him. "Thank you. Thank you so very much."

I marveled at the ease with which God was dismantling seemingly insurmountable barriers. First, the discovery in Simon Malya of a bold Tanzanian Christian, one who was willing to put God's law of love above the restrictive law of his nation, a law that forbade any contact with the Chinese workers. Second, the provision of a publisher in Kenya who was prepared to print the literature at a very reasonable cost. And now third, Open Doors' permission not only to reprint their version of the red booklet, but their willingness to meet all the printing costs. When Jesus gives an instruction, then if we, like Peter, are willing to step out of the boat in obedience, God will perform the impossible. He will enable us to do what we cannot: walk on the water. No matter how impossible it is humanly speaking, nothing is too difficult for God.

Brother Andrew's offer gave new impetus not only for my assignment to reach the Chinese, but also for my whole missionary call to Africa. Over the next four months, I traveled throughout Europe, including Great Britain, speaking at churches, youth meetings, camps and Bible schools, sharing on the evangelistic opportunities in that continent and the need for people to be involved in short-term service.

These did not have to be people with special qualifications. All they needed was a passion to reach the lost with the Good News of salvation. The more people I could recruit the better. While in the United States speaking at Oral Roberts University at Tulsa, Oklahoma, I was encouraged to find students already prepared with a vision for Mainland China. Although the Bamboo Curtain remained tightly closed, some had been studying Mandarin in preparation for the day when it would open. I challenged them regarding the already open door in Tanzania. A couple eagerly signed up.

Typical of the caliber of the short-term missionaries I recruited during those four months was the wiry Scotsman and fully qualified accountant, Iain Muir. In his mid-twenties, Iain had a heart for missions, but could not see how he could be freed from his work to join us in Africa. I was staying with Iain and his mother in Edinburgh.

"It doesn't have to be long term, Iain," I challenged, attempting to warm my semi-frozen hands in front of the dying embers in the open fireplace. We had just returned from a meeting at Iain's home church. He picked up the poker and stirred the coals into life.

"When I hear your stories, Rudi, everything stirs within me." The orange, red flames danced merrily in the hearth, releasing their much-welcomed warmth. "I'd love to be on your team next year, but...."

"But what, Iain?" I asked, accepting a steaming cup of broth from Iain's mother. "Wouldn't your boss give three months' leave?"

"Yes, he would, but...."

"But what? What holds you back? Money?"

"No. I've got enough saved." He looked at his mother who had joined us. Since she had been widowed several years earlier, Iain had been her main support.

"Don't worry about me, son," she interjected. "I'll be fine."

"But what happens when...." She did not let Iain finish. "If I have any needs, there are plenty of friends and neighbors I can call on."

Iain gazed back into the fire. I sat holding my cup, letting its penetrating heat bring life into my stiffened fingers. I could imagine the struggle going on in Iain's heart. Africa was an unknown continent. While his mother said she would be okay, he knew how much she depended on him. And I guess there was also the financial commitment. Air tickets were not cheap and, although he had money saved, there would be no financial benefit to show for his three months' absence. As an accountant, he was well aware of that.

But like those dying embers in the fire, his vision had been stirred. In the service that night, I had told of Roli and my adventures into Bulgaria, the spiritual victories and revival we had experienced in Soroti, and my recent week-long Bible-smuggling excursion into East Germany and Moscow. I had particularly noticed Iain's reaction as I spoke. His eyes had been riveted on me, and I could see he was drinking in every word. But it was when I had started to talk about Africa, my call to the Chinese and my meeting with Simon Malya, that his eyes really opened. He was sitting on the edge of his seat as I challenged the congregation that mission was something *they* should be involved in. Had I given an altar call, I am sure Iain would have been the first to come forward.

Now as the immediate fervor of that moment had passed and he had begun to weigh up what it would really cost to join a three-month outreach to Africa, he was having second thoughts.

"It's taking the step, isn't it?" I said, seeking to rekindle his wavering zeal. "Stepping out from your regular routine?" Staring into the fire's dancing flames, he quietly admitted his real problem.

"I just need the courage to break out and follow my heart's desire."

"You can do it, Iain," I said. "Just make the decision to go for it."

"It's a great opportunity, son," his mother encouraged."I would seriously consider Rudi's offer." Iain nodded slowly.

"I can't get those Chinese out of my mind, but...." He sighed. Picking up his nearly cold broth and gulping it down, he looked back into the hearth. Then, placing his mug decisively on the table, he turned to me. There was a sparkle in his eyes. I knew he had made his decision. "I'll come with you to Africa, Rudi."

Having made that commitment, there was no stopping him. In fact, by the time I was ready to leave the next morning, he was so eager to go that he had decided to take four months off instead of three and join me in Nairobi in February, a full month before the rest of the team were due to arrive.

Iain's decision, as with every recruit, was a big commitment. Not only would it cost them time and money, but for some it meant putting their studies temporarily aside. For others, it required leaving their job with no assurance that their position would still be open when they returned. And for a few, Iain included, what would start as a short-term outreach would evolve into a life-long commitment. But what finally motivated their choice was the yearning to have a part in harvesting the vast fields of untouched souls in Africa, the excitement of stepping out in faith and the unique opportunity to take the Gospel to the communist Chinese.

By the time Iain and I were ready to leave in February, we had 20 who had committed themselves to join us in March. It was an international team of Americans, British, Swedish, Finnish and Germans ranging in age from 20 to 30 years and coming from a variety of backgrounds. Some were college students who were taking time out from their studies; others were professionals including a nurse, a couple of teachers and of course Iain Muir as our only qualified accountant.

In contrast to my first trip to Africa, flying into Nairobi was like coming home. With Iain tagging uncertainly behind me, I confidently pushed my way through the surge of African travelers. Making my way out of the turmoil of the departure lounge, I stepped into the heat and chaos of Nairobi's airport traffic and authoritatively hailed down a taxi. We loaded our luggage into the rusting vehicle. Along with my well-traveled gray case and Iain's gear was the box of literature samples I had collected during my travels. The most precious item was Brother Andrew's red-bound Chinese version of the Gospel of John, which I planned to take immediately to Kisumu to be printed. I also had other material, including a book for children that I had picked up in the States, which I intended to have translated into Swahili and also published on the mission's printing presses.

As our Kenyan taxi driver wove his way expertly between overcrowded buses, honking battered vehicles and open, melon-laden trucks, I carefully observed Iain's face as he took in his first sights, sounds and smells of an African city. "Bit different from Edinburgh, eh?" I smiled.

"Yes, and definitely hotter," he commented, wiping his forehead with his already damp handkerchief.

"Wait until you get to Dar-es-Salaam in Tanzania, then you'll really know what heat is," I smiled knowingly.

Our few days in Nairobi, before we headed inland to Kisumu, were hectic. My main task was to purchase a car. While in Europe, I had made the decision to sell my faithful red Saab and buy a new one in Africa. No more spring-prodding bus rides for me. With our planned literature distribution to the Chinese, I needed a car in good condition; one that could be relied upon to cope with the thousands of kilometers of often uneven, potholed, dirt-packed roads that lay ahead. After thoroughly investigating the market and traipsing from dealer to dealer, Iain and I finally chose a tidy, five-year-old, light blue Toyota, which seemed to meet all my requirements.

Stowing our gear in the back of my newly purchased vehicle, we left behind the now familiar bustling city roads of Nairobi and headed northwest towards Lake Victoria. Iain's eyes were wide as saucers as we entered the vast savanna plains with its endless sea of meter-high, golden, waving grass. Every new scene, each fresh clump of straw-thatched African huts and every distant, lone gazelle was an object to be photographed. But as one weary hundred kilometers merged into the next, the monotony of the journey took its toll. Iain's initial awe wore off and the camera was put aside unclicked until eventually, 12 hours after leaving Nairobi, we left behind the plains and began to climb up into the more lush vegetation of northern Kenya.

Finally we had our first glimpse of the waters of Lake Victoria. A few kilometers on, we turned in through the mission compound gates at Kisumu. My new Toyota had passed its inaugural test with flying colors.

In the next three weeks, before the rest of the team joined us, I concentrated my efforts on overseeing the production of the Chinese Gospels as well as other Christian books I had brought with me, including the yellow-covered children's book. By the time the entire team of 21—including myself—assembled early March at our base at the Kisumu mission guesthouse, the bulk of the printing was accomplished. My vision of pallets with 10,000 red-bound booklets lining the wall of the print house had become a reality.

I brought an unopened box into the guesthouse lounge where the team was having its first official meeting. "This is it," I said, dumping the newly sealed carton on the floor and dramatically ripping it open. Pulling out generous handfuls, I gave these out. There was a combined chorus of response. The stronger American accents rose above the softer Scandinavian tones and more clipped English voices.

"Great!"

"Fabulous!"

"Wow." Then all that could be heard were pages turning as each one flicked through the new, crisp paper. Only the two from Oral Roberts University could actually decipher the script, but for everyone the message was clear. In their hands was concrete evidence of a project of faith, one in which all of them were going to play an active role.

Although the 21-strong team was made up of strangers—the majority of which I had only met in the last 24 hours—there was an immediate bonding. We had been drawn together by a common concern: a desire to share God's love with the African, but specifically those communist Chinese workers assigned to the Tan–Zam railway project. Now the books had been printed, we faced the next vital step in that assignment: smuggling these books from the safe terrain of Kenya across the border into the nation of Tanzania, where such literature was strictly forbidden.

The next week had been assigned as a time of initiation, a chance for the team to get to know one another and be introduced to YWAM's fundamental, operating principles: in particular, the role of intercession. Our upcoming "smuggling" excursion into Tanzania became our major prayer project. Many hours were dedicated to praying not only for its success but also for God's overruling hand in the entire distribution of the red booklet in Africa.

At the end of the week, we planned to split up and go in

separate directions. Some would head north, returning to our old stomping ground of Soroti. They would also penetrate into other areas of Uganda. Another team would travel south to the unexplored territory—as far as YWAM was concerned—of Zambia. Only the remaining eight of us would be responsible for actually ferrying the forbidden literature into Tanzania. Although we would be many thousands of kilometers apart over the next three months, our hearts were united in our desire to see this project completed. All 21 of us committed ourselves to remain focused in prayer for the success of the outreach to the Chinese.

Our plan was to smuggle in 1,000 red Gospels and other newly printed literature at two different points. Iain, together with two Swedish girls and I, would drive my blue Toyota through the Serengeti Game Reserve and enter by a seldom-used border that cut through the middle of the park. The border was not used very often because, after crossing it, the road eventually petered out and turned into mere tracks through the bush. It seemed a precarious route, but the missionaries at Kisumu assured us that, if we used the mountain range as our guide, we would eventually hit the main road. The other four would go take an overnight ferry across Lake Victoria. We would meet together at the southern lake port of Mwanza.

Iain and I would then travel on alone to Dar-es-Salaam, where we would deliver our precious load to Simon Malya. The other six would remain evangelizing around Mwanza, working ironically with Fritz, the German missionary who had cast such negative predictions on my fact-finding tour into Dar-es-Salaam. That was the plan. The tricky part lay immediately ahead—getting the books safely across the border into Tanzania.

"Well, that's them off," I said, turning to Iain as we saw the last of the Uganda team onto their public bus and safely on their way. The team to Zambia had left an hour earlier. As I watched the overloaded bus disappear behind the trees with its baskets, cloth bundles and our own team's luggage precariously roped on top, I recalled my own spring-poking ride from Nairobi to Uganda. While our trip into Tanzania held potentially more risk, I breathed a silent prayer of thanks that at least I could travel in the comfort of my own car.

"Let's hope the girls have got our Toyota packed. I'd like to make it to Mwanza before dark." We headed back to the Kisumu compound in the van the missionaries had graciously allowed us to use in order to transport the teams down to the bus station.

"Do you think we'll have any problems at the border?" Iain asked.

"I hope not," I answered, looking out to admire our last view of Lake Victoria before it became hidden from view in the trees. "According to our information, the guards are pretty laid back at the Serengeti Park crossing. But one can never be sure. We need to be prepared for the unexpected." I glanced over at Iain and noted the glint in his eyes. It was almost as if he wanted something dramatic to occur.

We steered the van through the mission gates; and driving past the single-story bungalows, semi-hidden in their tree-studded setting, we pulled up in front of the brick guesthouse, just in time to see the Swedes loading the last box into my blue car. Each carton was identically sized and stamped with the same mission publishing logo. Their contents, however, were quite different. One of the five boxes held the yellow-covered Swahili translation of the children's book. The other four contained the red-bound, Chinese Gospels of John. "Where have you put the children's books?" I asked the fair-haired Swede as she staggered towards the car with the final box.

"In the rear of the trunk."

"Let's put the children's books towards the front of the trunk," I suggested. "If the border guards want to investigate, we can show them these. Hopefully they won't want to look further."

"Good thinking, Rudi," she said, helping me rearrange the cardboard containers.

"Just helping make seeing eyes blind, eh?" Iain grinned.

By the time we squashed our own luggage in the trunk and put the overflow in the back seat, there was barely enough room for the four of us to squeeze in. The Toyota was running precariously low to the ground. We would be riding on some pretty rough, gravel roads through the Serengeti Game Reserve. *Lord, just let the suspension hold up okay,* I prayed silently.

I backed the Toyota and waved to the remaining team of four. "See you off the ship tomorrow morning at Mwanza," I shouted through the open window. I sounded more confident than I felt. Groaning under its unaccustomed weight, the Toyota slowly grunted into action, then, kicking up some gravel, we were on our way. Driving out through the gates and onto the open road, I adjusted my glasses and relaxed in the driver's seat, thankful that after so many weeks of preparation, this crucial part of the operation was finally underway.

The Toyota purred steadily along the open road. After several hours of driving, we came down from the elevated, wooded green of Kisumu into the lowland bush and savanna grass of the Serengeti Game Reserve. This was my second and the others' first time to experience a game park. It was migrating season, the very best time to visit. For the next few hours, our attention shifted from concern about whether or not we would make it safely across the border, to focusing on the wild game. We were particularly enraptured by the sight of tens of thousands of wildebeest (an animal roughly the size of a zebra, but brown in color and of the cow family) moving in massive waves across the plains. We sighted at least 50 giraffe at one time as well as herds of buffalo. Gazelles were so common that at times they blocked the road. I had to virtually sit on the horn before they gracefully bounded off, loping over the low bushes. Everyone's eyes were straining the horizon to sight some more wild rhinoceros or maybe even a lion.

While the others were focused in camera-clicking excitement at the wild game, the lions looming in my vision were human ones: the guards at the upcoming border. By now I had entered a few communist countries. But even with that Bible-smuggling experience under my belt, I knew I could not afford to approach this frontier casually. There was always the chance that something could go wrong. We had been assured that the guards were pretty laid back. But they were like lions sprawled half-asleep by a watering hole. While they might appear harmless enough, these officials only needed to get a whiff that things were not in order and they would pounce, striking a deathly blow to our mission.

A couple of kilometers before we were due to cross from

Kenya into Tanzania, I stopped the car and we had a time of prayer, again committing our cargo into the Lord's protection.

"Lord, please make the seeing eyes blind," Iain prayed fervently.

"Amen. Amen." We all agreed. We had done our part. Now it was up to God.

As it turned out, our entrance into Tanzania was a low-key affair. There was none of the barbed wire or posted sentries I had become accustomed to when traveling behind the Iron Curtain, just a couple of sleepy attendants. One of them, a gun casually slung over his shoulder, ambled out of the small hut and over to where we had pulled up. Probably ours was the first vehicle that had gone through all day, possibly all week. The guard looked harmless enough, even bored. But like the lion at the water-hole, I knew I could not afford to relax, even for a moment.

He gave a half-yawn as he collected our passports, casually glanced through them and then gave them the official stamp. "You look well laden. What are you carrying?"

"Books," I said, opening the trunk for him to see. His eyes widened as he viewed the five boxes crammed in the back.

"What sort of books?" My heart missed a beat. Inside the car, the other three had their heads bowed. Was the lion about to pounce?

"We're Christian missionaries," I said. "This is literature for distribution." I opened the nearest box, and pulling out a yellow, Swahili children's book, handed it to him. How thankful I was I had taken the precaution of rearranging the containers. He flicked through the pages and after a few seconds handed it back. He then glanced at the other boxes. *Lord, don't let him ask to see their contents*, I prayed. Every muscle in my body tensed.

"Okay. Have a good day," the guard said, waving us through. As I got back behind the wheel and drove on, I started humming. We had passed the water-hole, and the lion, not aware of the prey under his nose, had failed to pounce.

"Lord, thank you for making seeing eyes blind," the girls shouted jubilantly in the back seat.

Just as we had been warned, the road petered out several hours beyond the border. By now it was late afternoon. We had only a few precious hours of daylight left. All we had to follow was a poorly defined grass track between the bushes and a mountain range that ran alongside us. The missionaries had warned that it was essential we reach the sealed road before Africa's night blanket covered us. If we did not, we would be hopelessly lost. No longer worrying about the potholes or trying to avoid the gazelles in our way, I put my foot on the accelerator and went for it.

With frightened gazelles leaping to either side of us, we bumped precariously over the uncharted terrain following the barely visible grass tracks. All chatter stopped and knuckles whitened as the other three grabbed the handles to steady themselves from my crazy driving. I was taking reckless risks. But no one complained. We all knew how important it was to reach the asphalt road before darkness enveloped us. Dusk was fast approaching and there was still no sign of the road.

Gazelles still leaping in every direction, I kept my foot on the accelerator. I thanked the Lord that the Toyota seemed to be handling the conditions okay. *Just keep it going,* I prayed. Then suddenly what I had feared most happened. There was a huge bang as the front fender collided with a young gazelle that had not been able to get out of our way in time. The car swerved precariously. I clung to the wheel and managed to keep us upright. "Oh no!" one of the Swedish girls gasped. "It's hurt." I glanced through the rear mirror and saw the stunned gazelle lying on the ground behind us. It would probably not survive.

Everything within me wanted to stop. But there was little we could have done anyway. This was the African wild, where the law is survival of the fittest. I hated to think I had caused the death of one of these gracious creatures, but our own survival was also at stake. We were a mixed team; and besides, we had no equipment to last a night in this game reserve. So leaving the wounded gazelle to its own fate, we pressed on. Darkness was fast rolling in. By now the mountain range was only a purple silhouette along the horizon to our right. We only had minutes before all visibility would be wiped out. *Lord, get us to that road,* I prayed in desperation. I could sense the same silent cries of the others as they too sent up emergency petitions to the Almighty. We were all acutely aware of the danger.

My faith was beginning to waver. Was God going to answer our prayers? Then, just as visibility was running out, I spotted the sealed road in the headlights. Relief flooded my heart as we bumped and bounced over the remaining meters of grass track. Reaching the road, I stopped the car. My heart still beating wildly from the pent-up tension of my crazy two-hour drive, we let rip in a time of exuberant, loud and very grateful praise to God.

Heading south, we drove in a much more subdued manner, until about an hour later we finally arrived in Mwanza. We pulled up outside the house where the German missionary Fritz had his headquarters. Although we had communicated by letter to arrange the team's visit here, I had not made personal contact with Fritz since our initial meeting in Soroti. He had heard no details about the outcome of my fact-finding trip into Dar-es-Salaam.

After hugs and introductions all round, I showed Fritz our treasure. His eyes were like saucers when I opened a box in the trunk of the car and showed him its carefully stacked contents of the red booklets. When I told him the story leading up to their production—my encounter with Simon Malya, my contact with the publishing house in Kisumu, Brother Andrew's generous offer to pay for publishing and even the ease with which we had made it through the border—he shook his head.

"I guess you have more faith than I have, Rudi," he admitted ruefully, taking the red-covered book from my hand and scanning its pages of neat Chinese script. "I must admit when you first shared your vision with me, I dismissed it as a scatter-brained scheme of an idealistic young man. I honestly didn't believe anyone would be willing to take the risk and help you. But I can see I was wrong. God really was in it." He gave me back the Gospel. "I have got to hand it to you, Rudi. It's a real lesson for me." I laid my hand reassuringly on his broad, stocky shoulder.

"What you shared was extremely important, Fritz. Without your words of caution, I could have blundered in and blown the whole project."

"Thanks, Rudi," he said.

"And we're not there yet," I added. "There's still the cartons that the others are bringing over by ferry tonight."

A broad smile creased Fritz's face. "I should be able to help there. I have had a lot of dealings with the customs. There is one officer with whom I've established quite a relationship. If he's on duty, we shouldn't have any problems."

Next morning, I watched nervously as the team staggered down the gangway of the overnight ferry, loaded not only with their own luggage, but each also carrying a heavy box of books. They entered the large, open-ended customs shed and dumped the cardboard containers on the table, ready for the dreaded inspection. We stood watching only a few meters away. The team looked at us all smiles. Outwardly they appeared relaxed. On the inside, however, I knew their hearts were pounding as wildly as mine had been at the Serengeti border the day before.

As a Tanzanian customs officer approached a team member, Fritz gave him a reassuring wave. "They're with us," he said.

"Fine," the customs officer smiled back. Then, without even a question as to what the boxes contained, he stamped the team's forms and allowed them all through. One thousand red-bound Chinese Gospels had been safely delivered into Tanzania. Now lay the next crucial stage: getting the booklets into the hands of the Chinese railroad workers themselves. Like the rough, grassy tracks we had followed out of Serengeti Game Reserve, it was uncharted territory. Thankfully though, we had another mountain range to follow: God's instructions to us through his Holy Spirit.

11

Contacting the Chinese

LEAVING the other six to work with Fritz at Mwanza, Iain and I set off early the next morning, heading southeast on yet another long, tedious trip through the savanna plains. By now not only the trunk, but also the Toyota's back seat was piled high with boxes.

"Phew, Rudi, I can see what you mean by humid conditions," Iain said as we neared Dar-es-Salaam. In the distance, we could see the lights of the coastal capital glowing in the tropical night air. His pale Scottish skin glistening with perspiration, Iain glanced at his watch. "Ten past ten. You'd think the temperatures would have cooled by now."

"They have," I replied. "You'll get used to it," I added not very reassuringly. I too felt hot and sticky, but my heat was generated as much by the anticipation of seeing Simon again as by the weather conditions. I could not wait to view his face when I showed him our Chinese Gospels. "Not far now. Temeke is right on the outskirts." Churning up dust, I turned off the main road and drove up the same narrow, sandy path the news reporter and I had first traipsed six months previously.

The difference this time: Simon was expecting us. His reaction on sighting the red booklets was everything I had anticipated. I dumped a carton down on the mat-covered floor of his living room, and he eagerly tore it open. "Rudi, this is marvelous," he exclaimed, gleefully plucking out a booklet and examining it carefully. "It's exactly what I had imagined." He lifted up the red

Gospel and shut his eyes. "Thank you, Lord, for the safe arrival of these books. We marvel at all you've done to get them here."

"Now Jesus, show us how to safely deliver them into the hands of the Chinese," I added.

"Amen! Amen!" Iain loudly exclaimed, bringing our impromptu prayer time to a close.

"I can't wait for the congregation to see these," Simon said as he sat in his thin, foam-cushioned lounge chair and took another careful look at the indecipherable script. "Our people have been praying for this project for so long."

The next Sunday, he brought a box of books into the church service and liberally handed them around. A strange quiet settled on the 200-strong congregation as each one touched and felt a copy for the first time. I watched with amused satisfaction as almost in awe they carefully examined its indecipherable contents. After all their prayers, it seemed almost unreal that they were actually holding the results in their hands. That morning, Simon preached a powerful word on evangelism. Although neither Iain nor I understood his Swahili, we could tell from his authoritative tone and the way he repeatedly waved around a copy of the red booklet that he was challenging his congregation to get it out. He was urging them to be the answer to their own prayers and to ask God to show them innovative ways to get these Gospels into Chinese hands. As I saw their faces light up and sensed their faith rising, I appreciated anew the caliber of this man and wondered afresh at the remarkable way God had brought us together.

Over the next week, Iain and I remained as house guests of Simon and his wife, sleeping in a church room especially built to accommodate visitors. In the following days, news began to filter back regarding various means the Temeke congregation had devised as they took up the challenge to distribute the Gospels to the Chinese.

Some members who worked as vendors at the marketplace where the Chinese shopped had surreptitiously slipped the red booklet in among the fruit and vegetables. A doctor in the congregation had plucked up courage to give a copy to one of his Chinese colleagues. What excited me most was the first direct contact that had been made with the Chinese working on the Tan–Zam railway project.

Simon shared the story with Iain and me over dinner one night. "Remember I told you how we have a church member working as an accountant with the workers on the railway project?"

"Yes," I said, helping myself from a communal bowl of well-cooked green vegetables, a variety I did not recognize.

"I had a visit from him today and I think you'll be interested to hear what he had to tell me," Simon said, also serving himself a generous portion of rice. My interest in food suddenly gone, I waited impatiently for him to continue.

"So what did he say?"

"Well," Simon said between mouthfuls, "I encouraged him to take some of the Gospels and see if he could give them to the Chinese he works with."

"If he got caught, wouldn't he lose his job?" Iain asked anxiously.

"Yes, he would, and that's why when I first suggested it to him, he was hesitant."

"But you still felt to ask him?" I questioned.

"I felt it was important to find out what the reaction of these communists really is," Simon replied.

"What, to sort of test the water?" Iain queried.

"Exactly. The Chinese are all supposed to be hardened communists, but we need to find out just how rigid they really are in their beliefs."

"And did he hand them out?" I asked, my uneaten food getting cold as I hung on Simon's every word.

"He got them into the camp okay without anyone detecting it; but he said he was too nervous to give them away, so he hid them for several days in his office drawer."

"But he did give them away?" Iain and I asked together. I noticed Iain's food was also sitting uneaten.

"Yes. A couple of Chinese dropped by his office yesterday to talk about a work-related matter. He took the opportunity while he was with them alone to give them each a booklet." I caught my breath.

"Wow. He really was taking a risk, wasn't he?"

"He certainly was," Simon answered. "Although I understand that in the course of his work, he has had quite a lot of contact with these two, so he felt relatively safe. Also, he had had a chance to talk with them on another occasion about spiritual matters and discovered they were sympathetic towards Christianity."

"So how did he broach the subject of our Mao-style Gospel?" I asked, anxious to hear all the details.

"It was after hours, so he was unlikely to be interrupted. He just took the books from where he'd hidden them in the drawer and said, 'Here's something you might like to read in your own language.'"

"What was their reaction?" Iain asked. The food on both our plates was now well and truly forgotten.

"Their eyes lit up when they realized what it contained, and they spent the next few minutes engrossed in its contents. One of them said that it was the first time he had seen the Bible in 20 years."

"Hard to believe, isn't it?" I remarked. "Did they keep them?"

"No, they felt it was too much of a risk to take them back to their living quarters."

"But at least we know there's a hunger there," Iain remarked.

"That's what really encouraged me," Simon agreed. "We just have to keep pressing in to find new ways to get the books through. I'm sure if we can get them into Chinese hands, they will read them."

The contact had begun, but we had a long way to go. The Temeke church members were faithfully doing their best, but we needed to get the literature out in bulk. For that, we required others to help and to use as many different methods as possible. During the next three months, I established a routine. Between visiting and encouraging the teams in their various locations of Zambia, Uganda, Kenya and Tanzania, I would reroute through Dar-es-Salaam. Whenever I could, I would bring extra supplies from the mission publishing house at Kisumu to stockpile them with Simon at Temeke. Each time we got together, Simon and I sought to find new and more effective ways to distribute our literature. Sometimes these opportunities came in ways we did not expect.

During one of my visits to Dar-es-Salaam, I learned that the Chinese national football team was coming in a few weeks to play against Tanzania. I recalled Brother Andrew's words, "If we can't get to the communist Chinese, God will bring them to us." Here was a golden opportunity to make contact with Chinese en masse. I immediately went out and purchased a ticket to the game. With so many Chinese working in Dar-es-Salaam, I knew the seats would sell like hot cakes and I did not want to miss out. I was not interested in the match itself, just the chance it gave me to get our version of Chairman Mao's red book into the hands of hundreds of Chinese workers. I did not have a strategy planned, but trusted that when the time came God would show me what to do. I then organized my schedule so I would be back in Dar-es-Salaam for the game.

I had hoped others would join me, but Simon had another commitment and Iain had rejoined the team in Mwanza and was some 500 kilometers away. As there was no one else available, I headed off alone. I reached the stadium a good half-hour before the match was scheduled to start. As I handed in my ticket at the gate, I looked like any other football enthusiast, the only difference was a pack on my back stuffed with as many red Gospel portions as I could carry. Although I had spent time seeking the Lord, I still had no idea how I would distribute these. It would be great if I could have stood inside the gate handing out my books to the Chinese as they came through. But such blatant disregard for Tanzanian law was far too dangerous.

I walked through the entrance and looked around. A few of the keenest fans were already seated and waiting. Before long, the trickle coming through the gate would swell into a torrent of eager spectators. The stadium would be filled with probably the largest, single gathering of Chinese Tanzania had witnessed, all cheering for their fellow countrymen. It was indeed a unique chance to reach them. But my window of opportunity was brief. The books were burning a hole in my pack. How could I effectively get them to these people?

Then an idea suddenly came to me. *Put the books out on the empty seats.* Instinctively I knew this was the directing of the Holy Spirit. I had no time to waste. The crowds were increasing by the minute. Working quickly and stealthily, I moved along the rows, placing my books on unoccupied seats. With over 300 Gospels in my shoulder bag, I had to work as inconspicuously as possible. Row after row I walked nonchalantly along, my bag in my hand. To the casual observer, it appeared as if I was looking for a seat. Keeping a careful eye out to make sure no one observed me, I cautiously slipped my hand into the pack, pulled out another few more copies and every half-dozen seats or so dropped one down.

I deliberately spread them out so as to cast the net as wide as possible. Also that made it less obvious. But the placement of more than 300 Gospel portions took time. As more and more people began to fill the seats, I was becoming concerned that someone would see what I was doing and report me. I still had a few more to get rid of when, towards the upper end of the stadium where I had already distributed, I heard some raised voices. I looked up to see a Chinese man holding a booklet and talking in high-pitched tones to the people around him. Someone else spotted another book and dived for it. This set off an immediate chain reaction, and within seconds the Chinese were fighting to claim a copy for themselves. They likely thought they were free copies of Mao's little red book which had been distributed as part of the match proceedings.

Fearful of their reaction when they found out the booklet's true content, and not wanting to be caught red-handed, I quickly placed the last few copies and hastily moved towards the exit. As I left, people were still grabbing for the books. It would have been wonderful to have stayed and struck up conversations with them, but I knew any attempt to make personal contact would be courting trouble. All I could do was trust the Lord to do his own follow-up. *Let them get into the hands of prepared, sympathetic hearts,* I prayed as I slipped out the stadium gates. Like a farmer, I had scattered seed far and wide; I just had to leave it up to Jesus to make sure that it found good, fertile soil. Such opportunities were wonderful, but unfortunately all too rare. We needed to find new ways of penetrating the Chinese camps.

"Why don't we load the car and take a trip along the proposed railway," I suggested to Simon during one of my return trips to Temeke. "I understand there are hundreds of camps spread out along the line. If we go and see, God may open up a way for us to penetrate them with our St John's Gospels."

The railway would eventually stretch 1,500 kilometers from the copper belt of Zambia right through to the coastal Tanzanian capital of Dar-es-Salaam. To date, the copper had to be transported overland, which meant it was not readily accessible to world markets. Land transport was both inefficient and expensive. Once in place, the railway would not only provide a quick and much cheaper means of transporting the copper to the coast, it would also bring a lucrative return to both Tanzania and Zambia, significantly boosting their entire economies. Without China's generous loan, however, this whole scheme would have never gotten off the ground. This is why both governments—particularly Tanzania, where the majority of the railway track was being laid—were so paranoid about protecting the Chinese from all outsiders. Although the government itself was not pro-communist, it did not want anything to upset the Chinese, and so jeopardize the scheme.

Always ready for adventure, Simon jumped at the idea of taking such a scouting trip. "Good idea, Rudi. Let's go tomorrow." We set out with enthusiasm but, as the hours slipped by and we continued to pass one lonely settlement after another, my faith started to sink. The camps, which were really depots for the tracks, sleepers and other material needed for the railway, were also being used as accommodation for the Chinese workers. Surrounded by barbed wire and rigorously controlled, these ghettos were set well back from the road. They were deliberately isolated from any Tanzanian village to distance the Chinese workers from the outsider, whether African or foreign. Unless one was actually working in the camp or had a legitimate reason for visiting, it was impossible to even get near them.

Then we came across a settlement that, instead of being set back out of sight, bordered right onto the road. Behind the barbed wire, which stretched for several hundred meters to our left, we could clearly see the wooden buildings. Their close proximity only heightened my frustration. "Isn't there some way we can get inside?" I said to Simon, gazing at the inaccessible buildings. They were so near yet so far. He shook his head.

"No way. You have to have a contact and I don't know anyone here." *God, open some way for us,* I prayed silently, staring longingly at the buildings. It all seemed so hopeless. I was feeling despondent enough by the apparent stalemate of our mission when, to add to my frustration, we had a puncture.

About five minutes past the Chinese camp, I saw a scrap of metal glinting in the sun on the road ahead. It was a long, straight stretch of highway and I assumed Simon, who was driving at the time, had also spotted it, so I did not say anything. But as the metal piece loomed closer, and Simon did not make an attempt to avoid it, I suddenly realized he had not seen it. "Look out, Simon!" I yelled. But my warning came too late. Simon looked up, saw the object directly in front, but had no time to swerve. There was an ominous bang as the car ran straight into it. I felt the metal tearing at our front tire. The Toyota zigzagged precariously back and forth across the road for a few moments as Simon struggled to bring it under control. Eventually it righted itself, and we came to a standstill on the side of the road.

We rushed around the front to inspect the damage, only to be greeted by a sadly deflated tire. "Oh no!" I said, wanting to kick the rubber and at the same time yell at Simon for his incompetent driving. Fortunately I kept my temper under control. Simon knelt down to inspect the damage more closely.

"There's no way we can drive on that," he said, straightening up. "We'll just have to replace it with the spare."

"And then what?" I asked, with more than a trace of irritation in my voice. "We're so far from anywhere, we can't risk travelling on without a spare." Simon shrugged.

"There was a sign pointing to a village just after the Chinese camp. Maybe someone there can patch it for us, at least temporarily."

To get to the village, we needed to take a slight detour down a dirt-packed road that ran alongside the Chinese settlement. The village was only a handful of round, wooden, straw-roof huts and no shops. An open, dirt-floor shack with some rusting machinery served as the local garage. Fortunately the garage owner was willing to repair the tire for us on the dirt floor. But he completed the task at his own leisurely pace. By the time he had finished, we had lost an hour and a half of valuable time.

Agitated by the unnecessary delay, exhausted by the intense humidity and angry at the added expense for the tire repair, I felt as if I had gone through a boxing match in which my opponent had won hands down. I took over the driving from Simon and, in stony silence, headed out the village back down the dirt-packed track. It was all I could do to stop verbalizing my frustrations.

Retracing our way back alongside the Chinese camp, we were nearing the main highway when I noticed an African man standing alone on the roadside. We had just passed him when Simon crashed through my sulky wall of silence. "Stop, Rudi. Stop!" In fright I jammed on the brakes, bringing the Toyota to a screeching standstill.

"What now?" I said, thinking there must be some obstruction that this time I had not seen. Simon pointed back excitedly to the African in front of the Chinese settlement. "I know that guy. He was a member of my church." He opened the door to let himself out. "Fancy seeing him out here."

"Oh no, Simon, we've wasted enough time as it is," I groaned, finally letting my annoyance surface. "We don't have time for socializing. Think of all the books we still need to get rid of." But he did not hear me. He was already out of the car and running back towards the African. I drummed my fingers impatiently on the steering wheel as, in relaxed African style, the two started up a conversation. Seemingly oblivious to our time pressure, Simon talked on and on. By now my fury was rising like a volcano nearing explosion. Finally they both walked back to the car. Poking his head through the car window, Simon introduced me to the man. Not bothering to get out, I just shook his hand through the open window. "Nice to meet you," I lied. Simon graciously ignored my obvious rudeness to his friend.

"Rudi, can you give me the car key, please? I want to open the trunk."

"Simon, we really need to get going," I said, ungraciously

jerking the key out of the ignition and handing it to him.

"I want to show my friend our little red book," he said calmly. "He is working in the camp here and said he would be willing to help distribute some."

Simon opened the trunk and the African man eagerly helped himself to handfuls of the Chinese Gospels. Within minutes he was striding off down the road with the bundle in his hands and a delighted grin on his face. I remained in the car feeling deeply ashamed at my rotten attitude and thoroughly rebuked by the Lord. What I had interpreted as an inconvenient delay and a victory for the enemy had in fact been God's means of bringing us in touch with this valuable African contact. Had we not had the puncture and taken the side detour into the village past the camp, we would never have met up with him.

I was coming to realize there were parts of the work we were responsible for, but there were other aspects which we had to leave solely in Christ's hands. While he had made me personally responsible for producing the material, it was up to him to select who distributed it. Sometimes the people Jesus picked out were not ones I would naturally have chosen.

Simon needed to get back to Dar-es-Salaam. So while he returned by public transport, I continued on by myself, seeking any opportunity, no matter how remote, to distribute the Chinese Gospels. As I drove south towards the Zambian copper belt, I began to notice cars and land rovers coming towards me with gasoline cans tied on top. At first I did not think anything of it. Then, as I realized how many vehicles seemed to be carrying these cans, it dawned on me that maybe there was a gasoline shortage around here. I had pumped gas before crossing the border from Tanzania into Zambia, but it had not dawned on me to bring any in reserve. But now the needle on the gas gauge was sinking dangerously low, and I was becoming increasingly concerned. I had to find someone who could supply me with gas. But every station I stopped at gave me the same response. "Sorry, sir. No gas." What was I going to do? I could drive safely for another five kilometers on what I had left in the tank, but no further.

I pulled up at the next village. Much like the one we had

stopped at to get the tire patched, it consisted of a few forlorn huts, but no garage and definitely not a gas station. I stopped an African man walking down the street and, pointing to my meter, sought to communicate with him through sign language and stilted English. "Gas?" He shook his head. "Where?" I asked, lifting my hands and shoulders questioningly. The man named a town I did not recognize. "How far?" I asked. "Ten? Twenty?"

He shook his head. "Two hundred."

"Two hundred?" I repeated, hoping desperately that I had misunderstood him. He nodded his head vigorously.

"Two hundred," he said, and named the town again.

"Anywhere else?" I said, looking at him as despairingly as I could in order to communicate just how desperate my situation was. He pointed to a cluster of buildings that I could faintly make out some distance away on the top of a hill.

"Mission. They give you," he said. A mission station seemed an unlikely solution to my problem, but seeking their help was my only alternative. Judging from the distance of the buildings, I should be able to get there on the gas left in my tank.

I turned off the asphalt onto a dirt track that snaked its way up the slope of a steep hill. My tank was on empty as I turned into the gate of what was in fact a Catholic mission station. It comprised of several large buildings around an open square. In the middle stood an impressive stone church, the spire of which I had seen from the village. As I drove into the meticulously swept, hard-packed dirt square, a European priest, dressed completely in white, came out to greet me. I got out of the car and explained my dilemma. "I am totally out of petrol and I understand the nearest station selling fuel is 200 kilometers away?"

"That's right," he confirmed. "But don't worry, we always keep spare gas. You're welcome to have some." He went off and a few minutes later returned with a can of fuel. As he generously poured the precious liquid into my thirsty tank, we started to talk. He explained that he was part of an order called the White Fathers, hence his white attire. "And you? Are you a tourist?" he asked politely.

"Well no. I'm actually a servant of the Lord too." I explained how I was making this trip because I had a burden for the communist Chinese, specifically the thousands assigned to the Tan–Zam Railway project.

"Yes, there are certainly a few of them," he said. "Our mission has quite a concern for them as well." My heart leapt. I had not expected a Catholic order to share my same interest in the Chinese. "Some of our priests have even made contact with workers in a railway settlement not far from here."

"Really?" I now faced another dilemma. Was this a God-directed opening or was this a trap? I had only just met this priest. I knew nothing about the White Fathers nor their theological persuasions. But instinctively I felt I could trust this man. There was something genuine and open about him that appealed, so I decided to share openly about the true nature of my mission.

"We have actually produced a Gospel in Chinese in imitation of Chairman Mao's little red book," I confided.

"That's interesting," he said. "We could do with something like that."

"I've got plenty with me," I said, "Here, let me show you." I opened the trunk and pulled out a sample from the box. He turned the booklet in his hands, looking at its bright red cover.

"What a cleaver idea," he said, opening the pages.

"It's a translation of John in the modern Chinese script," I explained.

"Very well done," he said, handing it back to me. "Would it be possible to buy some from you?"

"You don't have to buy them. I'll give them to you," I said, taking out a couple of bundles from the boxes. He protested mildly, but when I assured him that the money had been donated for their publishing and there was no cost, he accepted the books gratefully.

"That's wonderful. I can't wait until the other brothers see these." I gave him Simon Malya's contact details.

"Let me know how you get on with these and if you need any more," I said, getting back into the driving seat. "We can supply you with as many as you need."

"We certainly will. Thank you so much," he replied.

As I drove out the mission gate, I looked back to see him

standing there, the bundles of vivid red books tucked under each of his arms contrasting markedly with his spotless white habit in much the same way as the white cross stands out on our Swiss flag. I drove back down the hill, singing and marveling afresh at the amazing ways of God. Once again, he had turned a potential disaster into a window of opportunity. Had I not been low on gas, I would not have visited the White Fathers' compound and established what would become in the days ahead a key outlet for our red-bound Chinese Gospels.

Gradually other missions heard about our project and began to request the booklets. By the time I returned with the team to Europe after their four months' summer outreach in Africa, we were already considering a second edition. The following January 1972, I made my third trip to Africa to prepare the way for 20 fresh recruits who were coming for another three-month outreach and who would join the six from the previous team who had opted to remain as career missionaries, including Iain.

As well as continuing the process of transporting literature across the Kenyan border into Tanzania, the teams spread out from our base in Kisumu into a total of seven countries: South Africa, Ethiopia, Malawi, Kenya, Uganda, Zambia and of course Tanzania. While back in Europe, I had been able to raise funds to print another 10,000 copies on the mission presses at Kisumu.

It was now six months since I had seen Simon Malya. With my busy schedule back in Europe, which also included a trip into Nepal, India, Pakistan and Laos sponsored by Open Doors, our correspondence had been limited to a few brief lines, enough to let him know the date of my return to Africa but little more. I was anxious to fill in the gap and find out what had been going on, especially with regards to the distribution of our Chinese literature.

Although Simon seemed pleased to see me and assured me that the red booklets were continuing to get out, I found him in an uncharacteristically sober mood. "Remember the church member who was working in the Chinese camp?" he asked soon after my arrival. We were relaxing in his living room, enjoying a cool drink.

"The man who was our very first contact inside the camps?" I responded, sipping my drink and enjoying the welcome relief of the fan's cooling breeze.

"Yes. He got fired from his job," Simon said flatly. I sat upright and put my plastic 'glass' down on the floor.

"Oh no! He had quite a responsible position as I recall."

"Yes, he was an accountant."

"What happened?"

"He was accused of embezzling company funds," Simon explained. "But the man's work was impeccable. There was nothing in the records to discredit him."

"So it was a trumped-up charge?"

"I believe so. He was totally honest. The authorities used the embezzlement accusation as an excuse to get rid of him."

"So what was the real reason?" I asked.

"He had been quite bold in his witness among the Chinese and when the authorities found some of our red booklets in the workers' possession...."

"They put two and two together?" I said, finishing his sentence.

"Exactly."

"What a shame." I sat back in a reflective mood. Indirectly I was responsible for this man's dismissal. It would be easy to feel guilty. But I realized this was the price we all needed to be prepared to pay in order to communicate the Gospel to these politically manipulated atheists.

"What really shook me though," Simon added, breaking into my reverie, "was the visit I personally received a few weeks ago from the secret police." An electric current shot through my spine.

"The secret police?" I said, swallowing hard. It was one thing to have a church member falsely accused and fired from his job. It was another to have the secret police visiting Simon. That was getting too close for comfort. The bulk of the literature was stored in his church.

"It was a miracle that I was here when they arrived," Simon continued. "I was supposed to be guest speaker at an evangelistic campaign several hours' drive from here."

"So why weren't you there?"

"I was, but I had such a strong urge to return home, I informed the organizers I was leaving."

"They wouldn't be very happy about having their evangelist walk out."

"They certainly weren't and I knew it didn't make sense. But the urge was so great, I knew I had to obey. I had only been back in my house a short time when two secret police agents arrived."

"Praise God you were obedient to that prompting, Simon. What reason did they give for coming?"

"They accused me of hiding Chinese literature." I caught my breath as I visualized the scene.

"What did you say to them?" I asked almost in a whisper.

"I could have lied and denied it; but I knew if they searched the church and found the literature, I would be in worse trouble, so I admitted it." My mouth dropped.

"You told them you had Chinese literature?"

"Yes, but I made light of it. I showed them the boxes of other literature I had as well; the yellow-covered children's books and the others in Swahili, English and Arabic." I was amazed at his boldness.

"And they accepted that?"

"Our government keeps claiming we have freedom of religion, so I used that as my excuse. I said to them, 'Ours is a free country. What's unusual about me having literature in different languages? After all, I am a pastor and communicating God's love to people is my business.'"

"And of course they couldn't say anything to that."

"Freedom is freedom, Rudi. You can't claim we have freedom of religion on one hand and then accuse people of violating that freedom on the other. They knew I had them and didn't pursue it anymore."

Leaning back in my chair, I let out a low whistle, chuckling at the way Simon had so skillfully defused a potentially volatile situation. "Wow ... I really admire your courage and your wisdom." Simon shrugged, refusing to take any credit.

"It was the Lord, Rudi. After all, he does promise that when we stand before judges and courts he will give us the words to say.[6] But we are going to have to be much more careful in the future. They know we have the literature and will be waiting for one of us to step out of line so they can pounce."

[6] Mark 13:9–13: *"You must be on your guard. You will be handed over to the local councils and flogged in the synagogues. On account of me you will stand before governors and kings as witnesses to them. And the Gospel must first be preached to all nations. Whenever you are arrested and brought to trial, do not worry beforehand about what to say. Just say whatever is given you at the time, for it is not you speaking, but the Holy Spirit."*

12

Multiplication

LIKE corks bobbing in the water, it is sometimes easy to think of one's life as being pulled by the currents of human desire and circumstance. We make decisions that initially appear to have no significance. In hindsight, however, these prove to be major turning points. Only then do we realize that in fact all along God has been prodding and directing those apparently inconsequential choices to steer us in the right direction. Such was the case in my choice to go to Rhodesia, today renamed Zimbabwe.

I had visited seven different African countries: Kenya, Uganda, Tanzania, Malawi, Zambia, Ethiopia and South Africa. These were all the nations where our short-term teams had been operating. When someone suggested I visit Rhodesia, my underlying motive for going was somewhat carnal. It would give me a chance to notch up yet another country on my African belt.

I was visiting the team in Zambia at the time. From where we were staying, we could view Rhodesia. I was standing at the window, looking out across the border, when someone remarked, "You should make a trip there, Rudi." That sparked the idea and I used a visit to the Scripture Gift Mission as my excuse for going. Based in the capital Salisbury, the mission had been supplying our teams with literature for some time. The elderly lady in charge kindly invited me to stay at her home. We were enjoying fellowship over an evening meal, discussing the philosophy of YWAM and how our vision was to motivate young people into missions, when she said to me, her eyes sparkling, "Rudi, you need to meet Gary Strong. He is a key leader in the country. I believe he is someone who could help you."

"I'd love to," I said. I was eager to make acquaintance with anyone who could help us get YWAM launched in Rhodesia.

"He's a busy man, but I'll ring him right away and check if he can see you tomorrow." So it was arranged. I would meet with this Gary Strong, a Methodist minister, the next afternoon.

Situated on the third story of an inner-city commercial block, Gary's premises had the appearance more of a successful business than a church office. As I entered the simple but tastefully decorated room, an auburn-haired man, whom I guessed to be in his early forties, stood up from behind the modest, polished-wood desk and came to greet me.

"Welcome to Rhodesia," he said, giving me a firm handshake and directing me to one of two stylish leather chairs that graced his office. We were soon chatting like old friends. I was immediately impressed by his positive manner. He leaned forward slightly, his eyes fixed on me as I told him of our desire to recruit young people into missions. "Does YWAM run schools?" he asked.

"Yes, we do," I replied, referring to the SOEs operating out of Switzerland. "We have a three-month training school followed by a practical two-month outreach." Gary leaned back in his chair, his hands behind his head and sighed deeply.

"Well, we certainly need such training schools here in Rhodesia and I know just the place where you can hold it." Without giving me time to explain that Switzerland was the only country where SOEs were held, he rose from his chair. Going over to his desk, he pressed the button on his flip-up phone book and scanned the list for a number.

I opened my mouth to explain these schools were held only in Switzerland and we had no plans to hold one in Africa; but he already had his phone off the hook and was dialing a number. "I'll make arrangements to take you to see the facility," he said, holding the phone to his ear as it rang the other end. "It's a holiday retreat center and would be ideal." Before I knew it, Gary had organized for me to visit the facility later that same afternoon.

Situated ten kilometers from Salisbury, the retreat center, or Rest Haven as it was called, was indeed a beautiful facility. Really it was a small village set in a sweeping valley. Run by an inter-denominational foundation, the buildings were surrounded by well-kept gardens, complete with a swimming pool. Walkways meandered through native bush, where an occasional monkey could be seen swinging from branch to branch. The center had individual bungalows for accommodation, a chapel and smaller rooms that were usually used for seminars, but which would be ideal for classrooms. As I walked around taking it all in, something stirred within me. In my mind's eye, I could see young people sitting at the desks studying God's word much as we had in Lausanne, and then going out into surrounding nations to share the message of Christ's love.

The idea of running schools was not an entirely new notion. After two years recruiting short-term outreach teams from abroad, I realized the need for a permanent YWAM base and had already toyed with the possibility of running an SOE here in Africa. But it had seemed unrealistic. I did not have the staff. I had no finance and I did not have a suitable facility, at least not until now.

We had completed a tour of the grounds and buildings, and I was standing in the reception area reading some of the Rest Haven brochures. Gary was in another room talking with the manager. I looked up from the glossy pictures through the open door at the well-manicured gardens with its array of buildings and surrounding woodlands and sighed. It certainly was a perfect place for a training school, even the extra bonus of the swimming pool. Suddenly Gary broke into my thoughts. "It's available for three months during their low season, January through March," he said, a slight breathlessness in his voice. "And at a very reasonable price too." I looked at him, a little stunned by his dynamic salesman style of operating. He definitely was not one to let grass grow under his feet.

"That's fabulous," I said, but careful not to commit myself. To run a school would be a major undertaking. I needed to know this was of God and not just a good idea of Rudi Lack or Gary Strong. I left the retreat center that afternoon with all the pamphlets and information I would need to operate a training school in Rhodesia, but I refrained from making any final decision. The implications of taking such a step were too great.

During the two years I had been organizing outreaches into Africa, we had based our operations from the mission station at Kisumu. This was my first visit to Rhodesia. While I felt an immediate rapport with Gary, I knew that if I came to run a school here, I would need to make a long-term commitment. In order to stay on in Rhodesia, it was necessary for me to become a resident. While the facilities at Rest Haven were virtually being handed to me on a plate and, as Gary had rightly assessed, would make an ideal base for an African SOE, I was not sure I was ready to make that kind of commitment.

I returned to Germany in June 1972 to participate in the Olympic Games Outreach in Munich, the one Don Stephens had conceived during our SOE and which had taken two years to prepare. God had miraculously provided a castle at Hurlach an hour's drive from Munich, and it was this stone fortification that housed the 1,000 young people who assembled for the occasion. It proved a trendsetter for outreaches YWAM would organize in the future to coincide with other major international events. The Games Outreach elevated YWAM's status. Rather than a fringe organization of radical young "Jesus freaks" as some churches had perceived us, through this outreach we proved ourselves to be a responsible and internationally respected mission.

Initially we had planned a Jesus March through Munich, but the German authorities were concerned about possible crowd disturbance so they withdrew permission at the last minute. Then God turned the tragedy of the terrorist Arab attack (in which 11 Israelis, 5 Arabs and 1 German were killed) into triumph. The authorities not only relented in their hard-line approach and allowed us to march along our original inner-city route, they even provided us with flowers so that we could hand them out to the mourners who lined the Munich streets.[7]

Following the outreach in August, YWAM staff, who now numbered around 100, met in the castle at Hurlach for a conference. The Games Outreach had been a watershed experience and each of us had been stirred with renewed passion by the exciting,

[7] The full details are recorded in the books, *To Munich With Love* and *Is That Really You, God?*, by Loren Cunningham.

action-filled days we had just experienced. As we sat together under the open-rafted roof of the newly restored castle attic, which only days earlier had been crammed with rows of air beds and sleeping bags, Loren reminded us of YWAM's vision for waves of young people to spread across the world. He challenged everybody about the need to multiply. "We've seen one mighty wave with these Games, but we can't afford to rest on our laurels. One wave is retreating, but we must be prepared for the next even greater thrust forward."

That thrust, as the conference revealed, was a multiplication of new SOEs. We were at the height of the hippie movement when young people were being swept into the kingdom through the Jesus Movement. Many were coming with screwed-up backgrounds and, unlike those who had attended our SOE, had very little knowledge of the fundamentals of Christianity. I sat amazed as the different staff members began to share their vision for the future.

Many had a desire to start a school in their areas of service. Joe Portale wanted to commence one in France, David and Carol Boyd were eager to use the castle here at Hurlach as a base for an SOE and Don and Deyon Stephens were planning to continue running schools in Lausanne. Although she did not have a vision to start a school, Reona had a burden to expand her teaching ministry and instruct the upcoming crop of young Christians in the ways of God. As I listened to each one share, I got more and more excited. It was a relief to know that in thinking of operating a school in Rhodesia, I was not heading up a side tributary. If I went ahead, I would be flowing with the main stream of where the rest of YWAM was heading.

"What about you, Rudi?" Loren asked, turning to me. "What are your thoughts for the future?" After weeks of procrastination, I had finally made up my mind.

"I'm going to start a school in Rhodesia."

My decision had been made and my course was set. Some seemingly insurmountable barriers, however, still needed to be dismantled before we could proceed. The most pressing was my need of finance. I had worked out that I would require a minimum of 2,000 Swiss francs to get a school off the ground. But large as that sum appeared, I was confident of God's provision. He had already amazingly provided for the printing of literature, while a German businessman had recently donated 10,000 Deutschmarks to buy a van. Surely with that record, I could believe for God to come up with a mere 2,000 Swiss francs for the Rhodesian SOE.

As I preached and shared my vision for the school in various churches around Europe as well as back in my stomping ground of Switzerland, where the people had always been so supportive, I fully expected the money to come in. I was sure I would easily have the 2,000 Swiss francs in hand before I returned to Africa in October. But although everyone seemed interested and wished me all the best in my future plans and even promised to pray, only a tiny portion of my school budget had been supplied. Although I had the generous donation to purchase a van, I left Europe with virtually no other funds in hand. I still did not have any staff, and as yet not a single student had been recruited. All I had was a clear conviction that Jesus had called me to start the school.

At the Olympic Games, I had reunited with Brother Andrew. He was planning a 12-city evangelistic campaign in South Africa later that year, and invited me to assist him in praying for people after the meetings. So instead of heading directly to Rhodesia, after my time in Europe, I flew to South Africa via Nairobi. There, as well as meeting up with a small YWAM team who had set up a permanent base, I also purchased a second-hand, white Volkswagen van for our use in the new school. One of the Nairobi YWAMers offered to drive it to Rhodesia while I flew on to Johannesburg to meet with Brother Andrew.

The campaign with Brother Andrew was an awe-inspiring experience. Every night, he spoke to capacity crowds of up to 8,000 in stadiums and public halls in each one of the 12 cities. Over the two weeks, around 50,000 people attended the meetings. Night after night, Brother Andrew stirred the congregation with a challenge to be involved in missions, and at every meeting hundreds stood in response. In all about 4,000 committed themselves. The campaign gave me an ideal opportunity to share about the training school that I was starting in Salisbury the following January. Many expressed interest and wanted to know more details.

Typical of those inquiring was a young man named Logi. Dressed in jeans, wearing an up-market, open shirt and sporting a fashionable, slightly longer than usual hairstyle, Logi was what we would describe today as a yuppie. He was not the clean-cut, young church person one would normally expect to recruit for missions. He responded along with the scores of others to Brother Andrew's call for salvation, coming forward at the end of a meeting in Cape Town. There was something about this young man in his mid-twenties that made him stand out and drew me to him.

"How can I help?" I said, going over and laying a hand lightly on his shoulder.

"I don't know much about this Jesus stuff," he said, looking me straight in the eyes.

"In fact, I would not be here if my friend hadn't dragged me along." His direct bluntness instantly attracted me to him.

"So how did you enjoy the meeting?" I asked.

"Well, it's certainly different from church. But there's reality in what that man spoke tonight and I want it." I explained that what he needed was Jesus in his life, but before he could invite him in, he needed to turn from his sin."

"I have led a pretty rotten life," he said with frank honesty. He explained how he had been brought up in a middle-class family in South Africa, but had rebelled against his parents' values and way of life.

"My aim has been to get ahead and make money—heaps of it," he confessed. "I thought I was free and really going places. But lately I've begun to wonder."

"True freedom can only be found in Jesus Christ," I responded.

"Most of the people I mix with are phony and artificial. What I saw tonight was real," Logi replied. "That's what I want."

"If you are willing to turn your back on your old way of life and accept the gift of salvation that Jesus gained for you through his death on the cross, then you can have it," I assured him.

Tears streaming down his cheeks, Logi knelt down and in

childlike simplicity gave his life to Jesus. He rose smiling through his tear-stained face. I was convinced his conversion was genuine. But I also knew the pressures ahead and the temptations he would face to persuade him to return to his old life.

"What do I do now?" he asked.

"I'm starting a training school in Salisbury in January. If you came, it would help lay a solid foundation in your Christian faith." Logi seemed keen and took down the details. He was just one of many who had expressed interest in my Salisbury-based SOE. If everyone who inquired showed up, I would have well over 200 students. I still did not have the necessary finance or staff. But I was confident that the Lord would provide all I needed.

Following the campaign in South Africa with Brother Andrew, I headed north to Salisbury to prepare for the school. By the time it was launched in January, I had 30 committed students, including the newly converted South African Logi. I wondered what had diverted the attention of the other 170 who had also shown such keen interest. But I thanked God for those who signed up. I was especially grateful for the high caliber of students he had provided. They ranged in age from 18 to 30. A few were from America and Europe, but the majority came from white, middle-class South African and Rhodesian homes, but some like Logi had had their season of rebellion. The common factor that bound them all together was their zeal to serve Jesus Christ.

When I started the school, I still did not have any staff; so I recruited the more capable and mature students to help with administration and leading small groups. The 2,000 Swiss francs I had felt so essential to run the school never materialized. But in the end I found it was not needed. The students' fees more than covered all our expenses and with the Rest Haven's charges so minimal, we were even able to hire a cook and another helper for washing up. This released the students from any duties and enabled them to concentrate on their studies. We had a number of visiting speakers, including Brother Andrew and my dad, while I took a large chunk of the teaching myself.

The school had its difficulties. I quickly discovered that administration was not my strong point. Fortunately I was able to have students assist in the areas where I was weak. Along with running the school, I continued our literature distribution throughout Africa, including our specialized outreach to the Chinese. During the campaign with Brother Andrew, I had also started a tape-duplication ministry. Orders continued to come in from people who had either attended or heard about the campaign and wanted a cassette of Andrew's messages. But all this took time and commitment to do well, and I soon realized I had taken on more than I could personally handle.

What I lacked in administration skills, however, I was able to make up for in enthusiasm. Day after day, I was able to impart to the students my passion for missions. I shared about Roli and my adventure into Bulgaria as well as the other Bible-smuggling excursions I had taken into the Soviet Union. I told them about the unique doors of opportunity that had opened to the short-term teams in Africa: for example, our exposure on nationwide television in Uganda. Above all, I encouraged them not to limit God.

One of the stories that had them on the edge of their seats was the account of a daring day trip that I had taken into the capital of the small spice island of Zanzibar, two years earlier. A mere 80 kilometers long and 35 kilometers wide, Zanzibar lies 40 kilometers off the coast of Tanzania. Originally a British colony, Cuban-trained communists had taken over the island in a violent, bloody coup in 1964.

Iain Muir, the Scottish accountant, made the initial foray. It was during the time when he and I were in Dar-es-Salaam delivering our first batch of red Chinese Gospels to Simon Malya. I had gone to visit the team in Zambia, so he decided to make a day trip on his own. He flew in from Dar-es-Salaam and boldly handed the Swahili translation of our yellow-bound children's book to kids on street corners. He came back so ecstatic at the response he had received that Simon and I made arrangements a few weeks later to make a follow-up visit ourselves. By this time Iain had returned to Kenya to join the team there.

Our journey got off to a shaky start. Confused about which plane we were to take, we almost missed our flight and only managed to scramble aboard the tiny craft minutes before take-off.

After an extremely turbulent 20-minute flight, we safely landed on the lush, green island. The rich fragrance of vanilla and clove spices—the island's main export—hit our nostrils the moment we emerged from the plane. Then, carrying heavy shoulder bags full of literature including copies of the red Chinese Gospel, Simon and I hailed down a taxi. We were about to get in when two men stepped forward and stopped us. They were waving their hands and jabbering in Swahili. I looked questioningly at my Tanzanian companion.

"What's the trouble?"

"They won't let us go in the same taxi," Simon whispered.

"Why?"

"Because you are a foreigner. They are suspicious that you might be a spy."

I could not understand what difference it made if we traveled together, but I was not in a position to argue. We quickly arranged to meet in the center of town at the famous Anglican cathedral, Christ Church. It was here in one of the back pews that Iain had told us he had dumped his last few books before rushing back to the airport to catch his flight out.

A heavy depression settled on me as I traveled alone to the cathedral. I still felt shaken from our last-minute hitch in catching our plane, the turbulence of the flight, and then the confusion at the airport. The spiritual atmosphere seemed to be more oppressive than any country I had ever visited. This, I surmised, was due not only to its current communist regime, but also to its dark history of wealthy, dictatorial sultans who had ruled in opulence and lived in palaces that could accommodate more than 100 concubines. A little over a century ago, Zanzibar had also been the clearing-house for hapless slaves who had been captured from East African countries, shackled in irons, hoarded together like animals and auctioned off to the highest bidder in the world's flourishing slave market.

Dragging my heavy overnight bag from the back seat, I paid the taxi driver, glanced around to make sure I had not been tagged and followed Simon, who had arrived in his taxi just before me, into the impressive Christ Church Cathedral. I was still puzzled by the scene at the airport. That issue never was resolved. My eyes adjusted to the dimness of the darkened interior. Because of its great historical and architectural significance, the cathedral had been allowed to continue functioning after the communist takeover.

Simon and I had devised a plan. We would leave our bags here and then, following Iain's example, take small bundles and distribute them on the streets. We figured this would be our safest temporary distribution center on the island and the Anglican priests the most sympathetic to our cause. We were in the process of looking for an inconspicuous place to leave our bags when an African priest approached us.

"May I help you?" he asked in impeccable English. I extended my hand.

"I'm Rudi Lack and I'm with an organization called Youth With A Mission." Our time in Zanzibar was short, so I decided to take a risk and share openly with him the true purpose of our mission. His next words, however, stopped me short.

"Well, I hope you're not here to try and evangelize. Just days ago I had the secret police visit and accuse me of distributing Christian literature. Some foolhardy person had been handing it out to kids on street corners. They even had the gall to leave some here on a back pew." I gulped. Simon and I eyed one another. The priest turned and went over to a cupboard at the rear of the building, and returned with a small package of our yellow-bound children's books, the very ones that were in our bulging bags at his feet. "Fools," he said, throwing the books with disgust on a nearby pew. "If only these people knew how much trouble they caused."

We managed to mumble some words of commiseration, then quickly excused ourselves. Very thankful that we had not said anything to incriminate ourselves, we made a rapid retreat onto the street. That door closed, now what do we do?

Simon steadied himself against the cathedral's exterior stone wall. "Rudi, I don't feel very well." I looked at him in concern.

"What's the problem?" I knew it could not be the heat. He was well used to the humid conditions in Dar-es-Salaam.

"I feel really nauseous and I have got a splitting headache."

"Let's find a place to sit and get a drink, Simon. Maybe that will make you feel better."

Sitting in the shade of a small roadside stand, we sipped from a bottle of Coke and discussed our next move. "Our only choice is to book ourselves into some cheap hotel, and wait till dark to get rid of our books," Simon said. I agreed. The place was clearly crawling with secret police; and while Simon merged in with the populace, my white face stood out like a white sheep in the midst of a black flock. We found a cheap guesthouse called Zanzibar House, where we dumped our heavy bags safely in a wardrobe. We then spent the next few hours exploring the city, praying and checking out the best spots where we could make our night delivery.

Simon was unusually quiet. Although he did not complain, it was apparent that he was struggling with whatever was ailing him. Finally in the late afternoon, he turned to me. "I can't make it, Rudi. I'm going to have to go back." I looked at him in disbelief.

"What, to Dar-es-Salaam?"

"I'm feeling too sick to keep going."

"But what about the literature?" This was not the bold, dare-devil man I knew who was willing to face all odds to get the Gospel out. I was sure his sickness did not have a physical cause, but was triggered by the extreme spiritual oppression of this place.

"Let's pray. You'll be all right," I encouraged him. But Simon shook his head.

"It's no good, Rudi. You stay on if you want, but I'm catching a taxi and taking a plane back." My stomach was in a knot. What was I to do now? Should I return with him and forget about try-ing to saturate Zanzibar with Christian literature? We were going to be hard-pressed as it was with the two of us trying to get rid of it all. How could I possibly manage to distribute it on my own? But the thought of taking even one of our books back undelivered was more than I could bear.

"All right Simon, you go, but I'm staying," I said.

I bundled him into a taxi and as it wove its way out of sight between honking cars, bell-ringing cycles and even an occasional horse and cart, a wave of desperate loneliness overcame me. I spent the next couple of hours wandering forlornly through the dirt-packed city streets until, feeling tired and realizing the need to reserve my strength for my night delivery, I retired to the dilapidated Zanzibar House. Sitting on a half-broken cane chair on the verandah, the island's spice scent wafting in my nostrils, I looked out over the sea waiting for the sun to set and darkness to take over so that I could safely begin disposing of my literature.

Eventually the sinking sun slipped from view under the horizon. Then quickly packing as many books as I could into one of the smaller and less conspicuous shoulder bags, I went out into the dark, ill-lit alleys. I walked along placing small piles on the raised stone ledges at the entrances of the run-down, ancient stone houses that backed right onto the street. An occasional gas-lit street lamp was my only light. It cast an eerie shadow across the narrow, dirt-packed alleys, adding to the already spooky atmosphere. Soldiers with guns were positioned intermittently at street corners. As I crisscrossed the town carefully depositing my books, I had never felt so petrified in all my life. I was already exhausted from the accumulated tension of the day, and every strange noise or unexpected footstep made me freeze. At any moment, I expected to hear one of the gun-toting-soldiers shout, "Hey, you there! What are you doing?!" What would I say? What would they do with me? Would they cast me into prison?

Yet, the sense of urgency to get all the books out kept me going. After four hours of crisscrossing the town, exhaustion finally overwhelmed me. I was so weary, I could not take another step. But I still had a good number of books to deliver. I did not want to give up now. I decided therefore to take a few hours' rest. I worked out that if I woke at 4am, I would have enough time to deliver the last of my books before sunrise. There was just one problem with this plan. I did not have an alarm clock. I could not risk asking the hotel to give me a wake-up call. That would arouse too much suspicion. But my feet were blistered and my back ached. I had no more energy to keep going.

If I was supposed to deliver the rest of the books, then God himself would have to give me a wake-up call. As my head hit the pillow, I prayed, *Lord, you wake me at four.* I fell immediately into a deep sleep. I was so weary, I did not even dream. The next thing I remember was the penetrating crow of a rooster. I woke with a start and, fumbling for my watch, looked at the time. It was exactly four o'clock!

Grabbing my small bag, I stuffed it with the remainder of the literature and crept out the guesthouse door. For the next two hours, still under the cover of darkness, I continued to deliver my booklets, placing them in any crevice or on any suitable ledge I could find. I even daringly threw copies of our red-bound Gospel over the high barbed wire stone fence that surrounded the Chinese embassy. By six o'clock, I had crisscrossed the city several times and the sky's pale pink hue was signaling the start of a new day. Lacing the streets with the last of my books, I littered them liberally between trees and along the roadside. I placed the final lot on a doorstep just as the sun's bright red streaks painted the sky, evaporating the darkness and exposing my night's clandestine "delivery".

As I hastily retreated to Zanzibar House, the city was already stirring to life. Soon people would emerge from their houses and spy my booklets. It had been a tough night's work, probably the most difficult assignment I had yet undertaken and one I could easily have shirked. But as I noticed a few people spot the books, pick them up and immediately begin to read, I felt a deep sense of satisfaction. I had accomplished my part. Now it was up to God to complete the task.

I looked around the SOE classroom of students who, sitting in the safety of the Rest Haven Holiday Retreat, had been hanging on my every word. "What happened to Simon Malya?" one of them asked.

"By the time his plane got back to Dar-es-Salaam, the nausea had lifted and it never returned," I answered.

"Which proves that his sickness probably did have a spiritual cause?" one of the girls commented.

"I believe so. In fact that was a key lesson both Simon and I learned that day. When we are about the Lord's business and get sick, it's crucial to find out the real cause. It may be physical. More often than not, however, what we are suffering is a direct satanic attack and we need to push through. If we are willing to resist, there is no obstacle that we cannot overcome, just as there is no border that cannot be crossed," I said, bringing my lecture to a close and challenging them to a new level of commitment.

"All it takes is faith and a willingness to be used by God. Here in Rhodesia and South Africa, we have so many resources at our disposal. Yet, even in our neighboring northern nation of Zambia, there are communist Chinese working on the Tan–Zam railway project who are being denied the Gospel. It could be dangerous, but are you willing to take the risk and reach out to them with God's message of love?" There were some vigorous nods and a few *Amens.*

A thrilled smile creased Logi's face, "I'm ready, Rudi." I smiled at his willing enthusiasm. He was a different person from the ambitious, career-driven, young man who had stood before me in the Cape Town stadium tearfully giving his heart to Jesus Christ. In the last few months, he had eagerly absorbed all the teaching. His faith strengthened and matured, the driving motive of his heart now was to serve God, whatever the cost and wherever he might send him.

Earlier in the school, he had approached me after lectures one day, greatly excited with what he believed was a word from God. "The Lord's told me I'm to go to Ethiopia, Rudi." I looked into his exuberant, faith-filled eyes. I did not want to dampen his zeal, but neither was I convinced he had really heard from God. Ethiopia was completely closed to South Africans. There was no way, humanly speaking, that he could cross that border. I was sure he had not heard properly. But I did not want to discourage his faith, so I merely responded, "Maybe it's just a matter of time, Logi." Now, seeing his earnest response to my challenge, I realized it was time to release him, if not to Ethiopia, at least on an evangelistic outreach.

Logi was not the only one who needed to be released. The lecture phase of the school was fast drawing to a close, and the three-month practical outreach loomed ahead. All the students were like eager racehorses lined up at the starting gates, rearing to be let go. As I helped them load their gear into our assorted fleet of vehicles that ranged from students' private cars to our newly purchased second-hand VW van and even a pick-up, I felt the pangs of an apprehensive father watching his children leave home for the first time. Would they cope? Had I prepared them adequately? The three teams were headed for the surrounding countries of Malawi, Zambia and South Africa. I longed to split myself three ways and go with each team. But of course that was impossible, so I had decided, at least initially, to join the team that faced the greatest potential risk: the team going into Zambia.

I put a South African guy named Art over the team going to Zambia. A talented musician and guitarist, Art had led a number of street meetings during the lecture phase of the school. I felt confident he had the leadership qualities necessary. The seven students, including my South African convert Logi, and I set off in our white VW. Instead of heading directly north into Zambia, however, we took a westerly route into the neighboring nation of Botswana. The newly independent black dictatorship of Zambia led by Kenneth Kaunda had no political relationship with the white-dominated, democratic government of Rhodesia led by Ian Smith, so the only way we could enter Zambia was through Botswana.

On board were boxes of tracts, books, Bibles and our yellow-bound children's book, and some from the latest 10,000 edition of the red-bound Chinese Gospels, hot off the press in Salisbury. While the Kenyan mission station at Kisumu continued to print and supply the northern African countries, it had become more practical to find a printer in Rhodesia who could supply the south. We joined up with the same mission organization that previous short-term teams had worked with in the southern Zambian city of Lusaka. Our team was spread out among different missionary families. I was staying in a home with Art.

A pattern similar to those developed by earlier short-term groups emerged. There were street meetings led by Art on the guitar, preaching at church services and distribution of literature both door to door as well as in the markets. Art's singing and exceptional guitar skills opened doors into many school assemblies. As our group's reputation grew, more schools invited us to perform. During these three months, we sang, preached and shared testimony before a captive audience of close to 30,000 Zambian schoolchildren.

The greatest opportunity that presented itself, however, was the chance to attend the national trade fair in Ndola. In talking with the locals, I learned that this national event, held in the copper-belt town of Ndola, drew thousands from around the nation. As I realized its significance, I got excited at the potential it offered us. Here was a unique chance to share the Gospel and reach many lives for the Lord. We could distribute literature and engage in personal evangelism with people from all over Zambia.

There was only one problem. Ndola was in an area where we had no contacts. It was a five-hour journey north of Lusaka, and we would be gone for several days. I had no idea where to house the eight of us. Our budget would not stretch to guesthouse or hotel accommodation, even a cheap one. Since coming to Africa, I had personally stayed in all kinds of places. I had slept under a haystack, in a stable, bedded down in hall corridors, slept on buses and train stations and on one occasion even spent the night in a public bathroom. But while I did not mind roughing it myself, I did not feel I could I make the same demand of the seven young Rhodesians and South Africans on our Zambia team. All of them came from good, middle-class homes. Not one had likely experienced anything rougher than a tent-camping holiday. Yet, it was such a wonderful opportunity. I had pondered for several days about the possibility of going, but did not say anything to anyone. Now it had come to a point when if we were going, we had to make a decision. The fair was the day after tomorrow, and Ndola was a half-day's drive away. But this was not something I could decide alone. As student leader, Art needed to be involved in making the decision.

With the two of us being housed in the same missionary home, I took the opportunity that evening to raise the subject with him. "What do you think, Art?" We were standing outside enjoying the cooler, balmy tropical night air. "Evidently thousands from all over the nation attend this trade fair. It's an amazing opportunity for evangelism."

"Yes, it would certainly be a unique experience, Rudi, but…" Art's voice trailed off.

"But what, Art?" I guessed he was tussling with the same issue that had concerned me: a lack of suitable accommodation.

"Do you know anyone in the area?" he asked. I had to admit I did not.

"So how are we going to house the eight of us? Our budget won't stretch to paid accommodation."

"I've thought about that. The girls would probably have to sleep in the van and the guys out in the open." Art looked up at the night's brilliant array of stars.

"Mmmm." He slowly stroked his chin. "I'm not sure, Rudi. I just don't know what to say."

"Let's put the idea to the rest of the team and see how they feel," I suggested.

When we shared with the others the next day, they expressed the same reservation that Art had. "Where will we wash?" one of the girls quizzed.

"And how will we fix our meals?" another asked dubiously.

"Something will work out; you wait and see," I replied with a great deal more confidence than I actually felt. The students had been enthralled listening to my adventures of faith in the classroom. Now that it was time to take some steps of faith themselves, they were not so sure. "Here's a chance to step out in God and really prove him," I said, seeking to stir their lagging spirits. "If we aren't prepared to take risks, the Lord will never be able to prove himself to us."

I knew that by encouraging them to go, I was stepping out on the edge myself. But I was not prepared to pamper them. With some gentle prodding and more than a little gentle persuading, they all agreed—some reluctantly—that we should go as a team to the Ndola Trade Fair. "What if we do have to sleep in the VW and out in the open," I argued. "It's not going to kill anyone."

We left very early the next morning. By the time the eight of us arrived at Ndola five hours later, the trade fair was already well underway. Held in an open field outside the town, there were hundreds of stands as businesses, large and small, displayed their wares. Some were under crudely erected plastic covers. Others had more sophisticated displays, while for some their stall was just a table in the open or some rags thrown on the dirt. As we had been correctly informed, many tens of thousands had gathered for this national event.

We drove our white VW into the midst of the milling African crowd, the largest I had ever seen, jumped out and quickly, unloading our boxes of books, set up our own stall. Art grabbed his guitar and started strumming. The music and our white faces instantly drew a crowd. Books are scarce enough in Africa, but to get something for nothing was almost unheard of. As we sang, preached and gave out free literature, everyone scrambled for our giveaway tracts and happily paid a few pennies for the more expensive books. Within hours our total supply (except for some boxes of Chinese Gospels) was depleted. It had certainly been worth taking the effort to come.

I looked proudly at each student as they mingled with the crowd, their fair features standing out amongst the sea of black faces. Each had a small group around them and was involved in intense conversation. Using simple, comic-style tracts, they were expounding to these Zambians why they needed to put their faith in Jesus. Meanwhile, Art continued to strum his guitar. A couple of the team sang with him and an ever-increasing number of black bodies pressed around to hear.

The temperatures had soared. There was no shelter in this open area, barely even a tree. I had confidently told the team God would provide. Now as I faced the reality of a mixed group of middle-class South Africans and Rhodesians sleeping in a van and under the sky in the open Zambian countryside, I was beginning to have second thoughts. Had I been foolhardy in persuading these raw recruits to attend the fair?

I was standing by our van struggling with my doubts when a European, a total stranger, came over to me smiling. "Are you the leader of this group?" I looked at him startled. I had not expected to see another white face in this sea of dark-skinned Africans.

"Yes. I'm Rudi Lack, and these are students on an outreach from our Youth With A Mission school in Rhodesia."

"Pleased to meet you," he said, extending his hand. "I am a

missionary here in Ndola and I've been watching these young people. I want to let you know how impressed I am with what you are doing."

"Thanks," I said. We talked for a few minutes, exchanging general pleasantries, and then he asked, "And where are you all staying?"

"We don't actually have anywhere to stay at the moment. We thought we'd just sleep out in the open."

The man looked at me horrified as he eyed the young girls on our team. "You can't do that, Mr. Lack, not here in central Zambia. Come and stay with my wife and me. Our place isn't fancy, but we do have a big house. You are welcome to spend the night." I was staggered by his generous offer and from a complete stranger.

"Are you sure?"

"Honestly. It will be fine. My wife and I would love to have you," he assured me. A weight lifted from my shoulders.

"Thank you. Thank you very much." Once again, in spite of my wavering faith, God had proved himself.

From a few days' visit to a trade-fair, the group's outreach in Ndola extended into a couple of weeks. The missionary introduced us to other churches in the area. Ministry opened up and the team decided to stay on. I left after we had been in Ndola a couple of days and returned to Salisbury where a skeleton staff had been carrying on the tape-duplication and book-distribution ministry. By now we had acquired an office sharing third-story premises in the same downtown block as the Methodist minister Gary Strong had his office.

After three months of outreach, the teams reported back to the Rest Haven Holiday Retreat. As the vehicles drove in, they sported a few more dents; and their occupants' faith had also been stretched to the hilt. Yet, despite difficult and often testing times, the students' enthusiasm remained high and their zeal for God unabated. I listened, my father's chest swelling as one by one my kids told how the Lord had provided for them and led them every step of the way. In true pioneering spirit, the team to Zambia had made a side-excursion to the Congo where no other YWAMer had ventured. Art's remarkable talent on the guitar had paved a way for the Zambia group to perform on national television.

But what really made my mouth drop was Art's report on what happened after I had left them in the copper-belt town of Ndola. "Rudi so inspired us with his vision for the communist workers on the Tan–Zam railway project, that since we were in the area and had boxes of Chinese Gospels with us, we decided to take them to the camps ourselves," he explained. Now it was my turn to sit on the edge of my seat.

With the boldness and seeming foolhardiness of youth, they had taken no precautions but just rolled up to the camp's barbed wire and started giving out books to the African workers. They gave them some in English and said, "Here is something for you to read." Then they gave them the red Gospels and said, "Here are some for you to give to the Chinese." I was staggered by the simplicity of their strategy.

"And they just took them?" I asked.

"Yep," Art grinned. "They seemed more than happy and quite willing to hand them on to the communist workers." These young students had gone further and been even more daring than I had. It stirred me to greater boldness and rekindled my own burden for the Chinese communist workers in Zambia and Tanzania. *Lord, open the way for me to take another trip and deliver more Gospels to the Chinese*, I prayed. It would be another year, however, before God would answer my heart's cry.

13

Black and White Do Mix

"RUDI, you're training the white middle class but forgetting the black Africans." I was sitting in YWAM's third-story downtown Salisbury office taking a coffee break with Gary Strong. By now the two of us had become close friends. It had been a year since Gary had catapulted me into starting the Rhodesian SOE. Now God was using his direct and penetrating observations to once more redirect my life. His words stung deep and I shifted uneasily in my seat. "You mean run a multiracial school?" Gary nodded his crop of auburn hair.

I looked at him doubtfully. What Gary was suggesting was revolutionary. "It's never been done before," I objected. "There are no mixed racial schools in the country, even secular ones."

"I know. But we have got to start somewhere. If the church doesn't set the example, who will?" Gary commented. He was not talking from theory. His own church had led the way as a multiracial congregation. I turned in my swivel chair and stared through the window over the skyline of high-rise office buildings. I could have been in any Western city. But I was in Rhodesia. And like its neighbor South Africa, it was a dominating, white-minority conclave surviving in a black-majority population only by its strict laws of apartheid.

"You're right, Gary," I agreed. "But we are in a country where whites and blacks don't mix. It won't be easy."

"That's true," Gary admitted. "And because the Rest Haven is in an exclusive white area, you wouldn't be able to use that. But there are other places. The YWCA, for instance."

"It's not exactly the best area of town."

"No. But it would suit your purposes."

I reflected on the contrast between the beautiful facilities of the retreat center on the outskirts of Salisbury and the decidedly less affluent suburb where the YWCA was situated. In other ways, however, this 100-room hostel would make an excellent facility, and it had another added advantage. It was one of the few areas where whites and blacks were permitted to live side by side. Despite the difficulties it posed, I knew Gary was right; and even though blacks and whites did not mix in this country, I knew it was right to go ahead and run a multiracial SOE.

Shortly after making this decision, I was in the town of Bulawayo, a five-hour drive south of Salisbury. We had shown a film *Breaking the Bamboo Curtain*, which told of the persecution of Christians in Mainland China, and I had challenged the mixed audience of their need to be involved in missions. I also mentioned our forthcoming multiracial school to be held in January. After the meeting, an African teenager came up to speak to me. "My name is Salu Daka. I'd like to come to your school," he said forthrightly. I looked dubiously at this tough, young man. He had clearly had little education. I was doubtful as to how he would fit. But I also caught his sincerity. I questioned him about his background.

The eighth of ten children, Salu had been born in a cow-dung hut in the small mining village of Shabani, outside Bulawayo. His parents were so poor that when he was born, his mother could not even pay for the subsidized midwife care, so she had delivered him on her own.

"My dad works on building sites," Salu explained. "But he's not home much. I hardly saw him as a kid growing up. Me and my brothers used to look after our family vegetable lot." With more than a little pride, Salu told me how as a lad he used to ward off the elephants. "It wasn't until I was 16 and came to work here at Bulawayo that I wore my first pair of shoes."

"How old are you now?" I asked.

"Eighteen."

Salu went on to explain how he had been able to get a job as a mechanic but how the lure of city life had drawn him away from his mission-school upbringing. Like his brother, he had got caught up in the black-resistance movement. Then in May, just a few months earlier, Salu had attended a tent mission. "That's when I received Jesus into my life. I had been having really bad nosebleeds and even gone to a witchdoctor for help," he explained. "But at this meeting, Jesus healed me."

As a result of his conversion, Salu told me there had been a total turnaround in his life. In the last few months, he had spent every spare minute studying the Bible. He had been out distributing Christian pamphlets to his non-Christian friends, joined a team from his church and even went out preaching in surrounding villages.

I looked into the eyes of this young, zealous man. He had been deeply affected by the film we had just shown. But coming to a school in Salisbury far from home, and mixing with mainly middle-class students, would be a major adjustment. I was not sure he had the maturity to make it. Yet I was drawn by his sincerity. I could see that he was a rough diamond who, with some cutting and polishing, had the potential to be effective for God. "Put your application in for the school, and we'll pray about it," I told him.

Salu's letter arrived. I prayed, but still felt unsure. Would he fit? He had no financial backing and no means of support. Despite my misgivings, something drew me to this young man. Just days before the school was due to start, I decided to risk it. I sent back a letter of acceptance and Salu Daka became our first black, male Rhodesian student. The other four blacks—all female—came from South Africa.

Running a multiracial school, the very first in the country, was indeed a whole new ball game. Held in the YWCA, it got off the ground in January 1974. Not only did we have to relocate to a less exclusive area, we also had to lower our standard of living. There were no more paid workers to do the cooking and scullery duties. We could not afford them. In our first school at the Rest Haven Holiday Retreat, the fees had been set at a rate equivalent to other Bible schools. Now in concession to our black intake, we lowered the fees. Even so our five black students who, like Salu, came from poorer homes struggled to pay the minimal, reduced rate of 15 Rhodesians dollars a month. This was a mere portion of the total fee.

I decided to take the bold step of putting black and white students together in the same room. For many, particularly the white Rhodesians and South Africans, this was the first time they had had any close social contact with blacks. They were used to servants in their home but not to treating them as equals. It took humility and in the first few weeks caused a few upsets. But to their credit, none of the students pulled out. Even though it was a major adjustment, they all stuck with it. I had expected my greatest resistance to come from the white students. To my surprise, those who found it hardest to adjust were the blacks: in particular, the black Rhodesian teenager Salu.

My initial assessment of Salu proved to be true. He was a rough diamond. But it was not until he got into the school that I realized just how much polishing and cutting still needed to be done in his life. The first hint of his problems emerged in the classroom. Whenever any issue of a remotely racial nature arose, Salu was quick to inject his black viewpoint. In running a multiracial school, we were slashing into a jungle of prejudice and I had expected differences. But it took a few weeks before I realized just how deep Salu's racial hatred ran.

A few weeks into the school, I was packing away my notes after a lecture when Salu's white roommate approached me. "Rudi, can I talk with you in private?" I picked from the agitation in his voice that it was serious and agreed to see him straight away. Our YWCA facilities were limited and my bedroom one of the few places where we would not be disturbed.

"Come. We'll talk in my room." As I perched on my bed, Salu's white Rhodesian roommate sat on the lone wooden chair in my room.

"What's the problem?" I asked.

"It's Salu," he burst out, his jaw set in determination. "I cannot continue rooming with him. I've really tried. But it's impossible."

I sat stunned by his adamant declaration. A normally easygoing young man, I had deliberately chosen him as perhaps the most suitable person to share the intimacy of a bedroom with

Salu. I knew Salu was a tough nut and I felt this young man, of all the students, would get along with him. Obviously I was wrong. Dismissing it as nothing more than a personality clash, I moved Salu into another room. But when, after a few days, his new roommate came complaining that he also found Salu difficult to live with, I realized the problem ran much deeper than I had anticipated. I began to really pray.

I decided to take Salu aside. It was the weekend and we had been working with some of the other students, packaging tape-cassettes in our downtown Salisbury office. "Let's take a break and go for a walk together," I suggested. As we dodged the empty glass bottles and cigarette packs carelessly tossed on the pavement, and strode along plaster-peeling shopfronts, I turned to him. I had decided to take the direct approach. Of all the students, I surmised he was one who could take it on the chin.

"What's the problem, Salu?" I liked this young man. He had a zeal for God and so far he had always been respectful towards me. But I was about to witness a side of him I had not seen before. He continued walking, staring sullenly at the rubbish-strewn pavement but not speaking. I kept in step, saying nothing and waiting for him to answer. When there was no response, I decided to dig further. "Two of your roommates have come to me complaining that they can't get along with you. But I want to hear your side of the story."

"I'm okay." He kicked an empty bottle out of the way and stared at the ground. We continued walking on in silence. Approaching one of the few inner-city parks, we sat down on a rusting iron seat. I tried another approach.

"I know something's bugging you. Can't you tell me what it is?" I gave his thigh a friendly tap. Salu brushed my hand angrily aside and looked me direct in the eyes. There was a darkness emanating from them that startled me. But I knew I was getting through. "Is it the white/black issue?" I asked in an attempt to dig deeper into his rocky resistance. I struck oil. For the next hour, I sat listening as a torrent of bitterness gushed out of his mouth and I came to appreciate with new understanding the philosophy that motivated this young man's life.

For him white people symbolized oppression, something to be

despised. Whites were exploiters. He saw the minority white Rhodesian farmers tilling vast tracts of fertile land, while the poor blacks eked out a living on a few poorly cultivated acres. His hatred towards anyone with white skin had been so ingrained into him as a child that Salu had never conceived of socializing with a white person, let alone having one as a friend. To consider them as an equal was unthinkable. As with so many of his fellow blacks, he had retained a sullen attitude of servitude towards whites but had kept well away from them.

His three years as a Christian had brought only a veneer of change. He had always attended a black church and had minimal contact with whites. Before coming to the school, his abject hatred of whites had remained rooted deep within and largely unrecognized as a problem. It was only now in the multiracial soil of the school that his true feelings on racial issues began to surface.

As he poured out his bitterness, expressed his hurts, feelings of rejection and sense of inferiority as a black, there was little I could say. His emotions were real. What Salu was expounding was not just his own hurt. He was speaking for perhaps the majority of his fellow blacks. I placed my hand softly on his shoulder. It was rigid and tense. But I knew that even by letting his true feelings erupt, a breakthrough had been achieved. It would take time, a lot of love and a great deal of patience, but I was hopeful that eventually God would be able to break through and soften the stony resistance that was so much a part of Salu's life.

The change was gradual, but it happened. During the next few months, the school cemented together and genuine friendships between black and white students were established. This mostly occurred in very natural ways: sitting together at meals, discussing the latest teaching, enjoying a joke together, doing work duties, scrubbing floors and even cleaning toilets. It all helped to break down the barriers. Probably for the very first time, our black students saw whites not as the superior race, but as normal human beings; whites who, because of our limited budget, were willing to eat substandard food and carry out menial tasks which in this culture were usually assigned to blacks.

For their part, the white students gained a new perspective

and respect for the blacks, recognizing them to be equals in intelligence, whose ideas needed to be listened to and not ridden over or downgraded. Just mixing with one another, and fully participating in all the school activities together, helped to bring about that integration.

For the first few weeks of the school, Salu kept company mainly with the female black students. He would sit with them in lectures; and if the program of the school forced him to mix with white students, he associated with them out of necessity rather than choice. As we got into the school, however, a change started to take place in Salu's heart. Almost in spite of himself, his genuine love for Jesus—his eagerness to learn his ways and his longing to lay down his life in the Lord's service—began to take precedence over his long-held attitudes of racial hatred and reserve.

The changes surfaced in little ways. I noticed him one day, for instance, smiling as he was drying dishes with a white student. Obviously something had occurred that amused them both. On another occasion, I saw him deep in conversation at the dining table with a white South African. They lingered long after the rest had left. Initially the signs were intermittent, but it was clear his hardened attitudes had begun to soften.

Then there were those definite moments of change. For example, the day I shared a message on Giving Up Your Rights. I watched Salu closely as I explained that none of us have any rights, even the right to hold on to anger and bitterness at racial inequality and injustice. Although Salu gave no outward show of emotion, I knew the message had touched him deeply when over the next few weeks his behavior towards the other white students dramatically altered.

While he remained the tough, young man I had first encountered in Bulawayo, by the time the lecture phase came to a close, I was confident that a genuine change of heart had taken place. I was totally relaxed about letting him join the outreach team that was heading for Rhodesia's western neighbor, Mozambique. Salu himself had felt strongly that God had called him to Mozambique. Besides, this was one of the few foreign nations where he was permitted to travel. White Rhodesians were issued with British passports that gave them free access to the world. As a black, Salu only had an ID card, which allowed him to visit only Angola and Mozambique. Salu would be the solitary black on the team. But I was so confident of his transformed attitude that I was sure there would be none of the blow-ups we had experienced at the beginning of the school.

The blow-up I was more concerned about was a political one. In April 1974, the nation of Mozambique was in political turmoil. For ten years, a fledgling black, Moscow-trained, communist, resistant movement called FRELIMO[8] had been waging guerrilla warfare in an attempt to overthrow their hated colonial rulers, the Portuguese. The better-equipped Portuguese government forces had held out against the resistance fighters, but recently a revolution in Portugal had weakened their power and the Marxist communist FRELIMO was steadily gaining ground. But they had not yet tightened their atheistic grip on the country. Under Mozambique's old colonial power, evangelism was greatly restricted. Right now there was an open window of opportunity. In the atmosphere of change, with their old Portuguese bosses rapidly leaving, the general populace was in the mood to listen.

I had first visited Mozambique on my own in 1971 when it was still firmly under colonial rule. The previous September I had joined a team from South Africa, and we had gone in on a brief weekend campaign. By then the iron grip of the Portuguese colonial power had started to weaken. We had wonderful freedom to share the Gospel and had saturated the town with literature. We held open-air meetings and prayed with people on the streets for salvation, something that would previously have been impossible. The people were amazingly hungry and I recognized Mozambique was a ripe harvest field for the Gospel.

During the lecture phase of our multiracial school, Don Milam, an American who I had met during that outreach, came to visit us in Salisbury. He had set up a Teen Challenge Center and was working with drug addicts in the capital Lourenco Marques.[9] He told us how the FRELIMO were fast gaining control and that the door of opportunity could close any minute. They

[8] Front for the Liberation of Mozambique.
[9] Today renamed Maputo.

urged me to send one of our school outreach teams to help them. I knew I was taking a risk in sending my students into such a volatile area, but recognized this was Mozambique's time for harvest. I did not want to miss it.

I chose the team carefully. The leader was a former hippie named Tom Bauer from California. Long-haired and easygoing, Tom had been traveling the world when God caught up with him in Rhodesia and he committed his life to the Lord. He attended our first school and then joined our school staff. I felt confident of his leadership. Another advantage: he had a mini-van. He and two others would drive in the van via South Africa. Salu, because he was not permitted to enter South Africa on his black Rhodesian ID card, had to take a train direct to Mozambique by himself.

As I waved the gray mini off and put Salu on his train, my heart was full of expectancy for them. There was a great harvest ahead of them in Mozambique and thankfully the team would not be on their own. They would be working in Lourenco Marques with Don Milam and his team. Even so I still felt some concern. Mozambique was fast coming under the grip of FRELIMO's communist control. At any time, the door would close.

As in the previous school, we also sent teams into Zambia and South Africa. Instead of joining up with any of the outreaches, however, I had opted to stay in Salisbury where our tape and literature ministry needed my attention. Along with my YWAM work, I was now the official Open Doors representative in Rhodesia and, as a result, getting more and more invitations to minister in churches and speak on missions. My particular focus continued to be our literature outreach to the Chinese working on the Tan–Zam railway project. The red-bound Gospels were still getting out to them through the Catholic White Fathers and other missionary organizations that had captured the vision. While Simon Malya's church in Dar-es-Salaam remained the hub and main outlet for the books into Tanzania, our YWAM teams, such as the one currently in Zambia, were also servicing the Chinese in the copper-belt area.

My position as Open Doors representative gave me contact with overseas Chinese Christians in South Africa. I visited their churches and exhorted them regarding their responsibility to pray for the Chinese who were captive behind the Bamboo Curtain and barred access to the Gospel. I also informed them about the opportunities they had right on their own doorstep and how they could get involved in our literature outreach to the Chinese Tan–Zam railway workers. "We may not be able to be missionaries to Mainland China, but God has brought them right to us," I challenged.

At the same time as exhorting them, God was rekindling my own vision for the Chinese. It had now been two and a half years since I had had any hands-on experience in distributing the red-bound Gospels. How I longed to make another trip. But that would have to wait. In the meantime, I was preparing for the students' return from their two-month outreach.

Impressed by the example I had set through our multiracial school, the owners of the Rest Haven Retreat Center had taken the bold step of allowing us back into their beautiful facilities. Admittedly, we were assigned to a camping area on the edge of the extensive valley that housed the rest of the center's facilities, set apart from the main buildings. The students would need to sit on hard, wooden benches for their final week of reporting back instead of the comfortably molded chairs used in our first school. Paint was peeling off some of the walls and, instead of the fully equipped kitchen, we would be cooking camp-style on gas rings and were without ovens. But even to be allowed back into Rest Haven as a multiracial group was a major breakthrough.

It was with excited anticipation that I waited for the vehicles to come rumbling through the gate. I could not decide what I liked best: seeing the exuberant students excitedly wave goodbye when leaving for outreach; or when their vehicles came limping back, more bumps and bangs than when they had left, but filled with students who were brimming with wonderful stories of God's faithfulness to them. They tumbled out and, unable to wait for the official report time, began immediately relating experiences of God's provision, the people they had led to the Lord and all the literature they had distributed.

It was great to have them back, but there was one car that I still waited anxiously to see: Tom's gray mini-van. During their two months in Mozambique, I had no communication with them. I carefully followed newspaper and radio updates. News on Mozambique was not good. FRELIMO's leader Samora Michel had tightened his communist grasp on the country. Freedoms had already been taken away. I prayed daily for God's protection and for the team's safe return. No news is good news. I was confident my prayers had been answered, but I would be comforted to see them and know they were safe. I breathed a great sigh of relief when finally I saw the gray mini turn through the Rest Haven gate and head towards the campsite where we were housed. A shout went up from one of the students, "Tom and the Mozambique team are back!"

Along with the other students, I crowded round to welcome them, offering a silent prayer of gratitude. *Thank you, Lord, for bringing them back.* They emerged from the van, and there were hugs and shouts of reunion. Then I noticed to my horror that the one black face was missing. Salu was not with them. The team had driven direct from Mozambique to Rhodesia. I could see no reason why Salu could not have traveled with them. Had my confidence in him been misplaced? Had he had a disagreement with his three white teammates and gone his own way?

I stood back as chatting and squealing students greeted the team. Then as they faded away, I went over to Tom. I gave my scrawny long-haired co-worker a friendly hug. "Great to see you back, man. We were getting worried you wouldn't make it." He beamed at me.

"We had a wonderful time, Rudi. You wouldn't believe it. The people in Mozambique are so open. We literally plastered Lourenco Marques with Jesus posters and lost count of how many books and Bibles we sold on the streets and literature we gave away."

"We led so many people to the Lord," one of the girls added, coming over to join us.

"Yes. It's certainly a ripe harvest field," Tom agreed. I grinned at their enthusiasm.

"Had a good time, eh?"

"Honestly, none of us wanted to come back," another of the girls piped up.

"Well, it looks as if you didn't all make it. What happened to Salu? He didn't cause any trouble, did he?

"Oh no," Tom quickly replied. "He had a wonderful time. He felt such a strong call to Mozambique, in fact, he decided to stay."

"He's already learning Portuguese at the university," one of the girls enthused. Tom looked at me anxiously. "Don Milam said it was okay for him to remain with them. I hope I did the right thing leaving him, Rudi?"

"That's fine, Tom." I was just worried when I saw he wasn't with you."

"He was so determined, even if I had tried to make him return, he would have refused," Tom added.

I nodded. "I can understand that. When Salu sets his mind on something, he can be pretty tenacious." Salu may have softened in some areas, but he was still the same tough, young man I had first met at the mission meeting in Bulawayo. I was just glad that the Lord had gotten hold of him and that his zeal had been redirected.

The report week over, the school broke up and the students scattered. A little later, Tom also decided to return to Mozambique and work with Salu and Don Milam in the Teen Challenge Center for drug rehabilitation. News of them was sparse but from the little that did seep through, it appeared God was continuing to move in Mozambique; and in the chaos of the political turmoil, people remained open to the Gospel. In the meantime, I was preparing to make some changes myself.

14

Arrested

It was with mixed feelings of nostalgia and anticipation that I prepared for a new phase in my ministry. I had pioneered two schools in Rhodesia and established the YWAM office in Salisbury. But I was a tracker, not a settler. The time had come for me to hand the leadership over to those who would take YWAM in Rhodesia on to its next stage. I had taken up residency and in many respects put my roots down in this nation. Both schools I had overseen had been pioneering ventures and most of the students were doing well. It had been a satisfying two years. But it was now time to move on.

In March 1975 I said my final farewells. I was especially sad to say goodbye to my auburn-haired office neighbor, Gary Strong. Over the last two years, we had grown to be close friends. God had used this man to bring major redirection in my life and I was going to miss our energy-packed chats.

Before I returned to Europe though, I still had one piece of unfinished business to attend to: my long-awaited return trip to the Tan–Zam railway project. Because the white Volkswagen had been purchased in Nairobi, it needed to be taken back for re-registration. I had therefore decided to take this opportunity to load the van with Chinese Gospels and drive to Kenya via Zambia and Tanzania. By now the railway project was nearing completion. This would probably be my last chance to distribute the red-bound Gospels to the communist Chinese in Africa. With the seats as well as the back of the VW van piled high with boxes of books, I headed north for Kenya via Botswana, Zambia and Tanzania.

The political relationship between black, independent Zambia and white Rhodesia had continued to worsen. Black Rhodesian terrorists had their headquarters in Zambia and would make raids into Rhodesia attacking white settlers. As a result, the border between the two countries was now tightly closed and carefully guarded. They were virtually at war. Zambia's President Kenneth Kaunda considered Prime Minister Ian Smith his arch-enemy. Rather than a thaw in political relationship, the resistance between the two nations had hardened. There was therefore only one route I could take into Zambia from Rhodesia, and that was through Botswana. The only reason I could even contemplate traveling as a Rhodesian resident by motor vehicle was due to the fact I had a Swiss passport and the van had Kenyan registration plates.

I broke my journey from Salisbury at Bulawayo. As I drove into the city, with its wide streets so designed to allow an ox wagon to make a U-turn, my thoughts turned to my tough, black Rhodesian student, Salu. Bulawayo was where we first met. Salu had been in Mozambique not quite a year now. Although news of him was intermittent, any reports I had heard had been encouraging. He along with Tom Bauer and Don Milam had been taking full advantage of the political chaos in Mozambique. They had been out on the streets distributing literature and boldly sharing the Gospel. But things had been heating up in Mozambique. There had been some horrifying reports coming through of club-wielding freedom fighters massacring fleeing white Portuguese. Women had been raped; men, women and children shot and bayoneted to death in cold blood. It was not a safe time to be in Mozambique. As I drove into Bulawayo, I offered up a prayer for Salu, Tom, Don and the other workers, *Protect them, Lord.* Let your angels take care of them.

The next morning after an evening spent with friends, I headed northwest and mid-afternoon crossed from Rhodesia to Botswana. I was now about two hours from the Zambian border that stretches for about 400 kilometers along the Zambezi River. A diesel, iron barge was my only means of transport across the broad-flowing river. I eased the VW down the gravel ramp onto the barge. It clanged as the wheels hit the open deck. The hand-brake secured, rusting iron gates were pulled up either end to prevent my van and the only other vehicle on board from rolling off. The diesel motor burst into life, emitting a cloud of black smoke, and we commenced our ten-minute journey across the steady-flowing river towards the flat horizon of Zambia.

I got out of the van and stood clasping the single, steel railing, which provided my only protection from the hippopotamus that, I had been informed, lurked below. I looked down into the blue green waters and shuddered slightly as I recalled the story, recently recounted to me, of a hippo that had overturned a boat and used its powerful jaws to crush an unfortunate tourist to death. Our rusting barge was pretty sturdy; and although this was not the normal tourist entrance into Zambia, I had no doubt it had safely crossed this river hundreds of times. I gripped the railing, my hands sweating. My concern was not so much of falling into the hippo-infested waters, but of the potential danger awaiting me on the other side.

In these times of political unrest, entry into any African country was strictly regulated. I was not just crossing a border, but was seeking to enter as an unacceptable Rhodesian resident carrying illegal Chinese literature. I had smuggled books across borders many times, but the tension never got any less. So far I had never been stopped. Today could be the exception. *Lord, make those seeing eyes blind*, I silently prayed once again.

The ten-minute trip across the river completed, I got back in the van, drove it up another gravel incline and parked outside the moss-streaked, plaster-walled customs shed. Walking inside, I was greeted by a uniformed Zambian customs official. He was seated behind a crude, wooden table. Handing me a form, he pointed to a chest-high wall-shelf. "Fill this in over there. We need a detailed list of everything you are bringing in."

I stood scanning the form and, using my own pen as none were supplied, copied the relevant information from my Swiss passport. I laboriously listed all my personal belongings. I also declared the different English books and tracts I had brought with me. But I did not mention the Chinese literature.

That would only be asking for trouble. Returning to the table where the official sat, I handed him my completed form. He took it and carefully checked my answers. "So you are from Switzerland, Mr. Lack?" Every muscle in my body tensed. Was he going to ask me where I had originated my journey or how long I had been in Botswana? I would have to tell him I had only been there two hours. That would immediately arouse suspicion. But he did not ask such awkward questions and I did not offer any unasked-for information.

"I see you're carrying Bibles and Christian tracts," he commented. I caught my breath.

"Yes," I said slowly. "It's not illegal to bring them in, is it?"

"Oh no, that's fine," he answered. "I was just interested because I'm a believer in Jesus myself." My tensed muscles relaxed and I breathed easier.

"You are? That's wonderful." It was the first time in all my border crossings anywhere in the world that I had encountered a Christian customs officer. Once more God had gone ahead and paved the way. *Thank you, Lord.* We started chatting about our mutual faith. I told him about YWAM and what we had been doing in Africa although I carefully avoided mentioning our work in Rhodesia. All the time the customs official kept hold of my completed but as yet unstamped declaration form.

After a few minutes he scanned the list again. "Do you have any other literature?" he asked. I looked at him hesitantly. What should I say? If I said, "No," I would be telling a deliberate lie. But he was a believer. Maybe he would let me away with it. So I reluctantly confessed.

"Well, I do have some Chinese Gospels."

"Then you need to add that to your list," he said politely but firmly and handed the form back to me. Reluctantly, but with no other choice, I pulled out my pen again and wrote on the form, "Chinese Gospels".

"Fine," he said, finally giving my form the official blue stamp. "Enjoy your trip. May God go with you." I looked at him incredulously. He knew I had illegal literature. He had even made me list it. Yet he was letting me through without any further questions.

For the first time ever, it seemed God had orchestrated events in reverse. Instead of making the seeing eyes blind, I had been made to officially expose my clandestine load. And it had been a Christian who had made me declare it. Yet he had still let me bring them in. *Why, Lord? Why was it necessary to declare those books?* It did not make sense. Only later would I understand why God had arranged for that Christian customs officer to be at the border that day, and why it was so crucial for me to have included those Chinese Gospels on my declaration form. Had I not done so, things might have turned out very differently.

It had been a long day, and it was late afternoon by the time I had cleared customs. That night I stayed with an African pastor I knew not far from the border. The next morning I set off early, my heart singing. I felt a freedom and special awareness of God's presence. The weight and responsibility of running schools and operating the YWAM base in Rhodesia was behind me. I was doing what I loved most, distributing God's Word. I drove along the flat, low bush land, heading north. Beside me on the passenger seat was a box of English tracts and booklets. When I came to a village, I slowed down to a crawl and tossed books out the window to the crowds in the markets and to people walking along the roadside. The Africans scrambled to pick them up. Books were such a rarity for them, they were eager to accept anything. I looked back through the rear-view mirror, smiling as I saw them open the books and tracts and curiously start reading their content.

The second night in Zambia I spent with missionary friends in Lusaka, and then proceeded on for yet another day of literature delivery. In every village I passed through, I distributed literature out the van window to the passersby. It was slow work, but I loved it. I was getting God's Word out. My main target for this trip, however, was the Chinese. Towards the end of my third day in Zambia, I neared the central Mikushi River district and had my first view of the Tan–Zam railway project. I kept my eyes alert for any Chinese and African gangs. But it was late afternoon. The workers had finished for the day. It was nearing dark when I spotted my first barbed wire Chinese compound. A couple of uniformed Africans were guarding the camp. Night was closing in and, exhausted from my long day's drive, I decided here was as good as anywhere to spend the night.

There was nowhere to wash and I had nothing with me to eat, so I just cleared some of the boxes from the back, pulled out my sleeping bag, crawled into it fully clothed and fell asleep. I woke with the first rays of sun beaming through the window. I sensed a wonderful glow, not just from its warming rays, but also from a deep awareness of God's presence and the knowledge that I was in the very center of his will.

I pulled myself up in my sleeping bag and looked bleary eyed out the window. I could see the Africans still guarding the barbed wire Chinese camp. Through the bushes, I could just make out the outline of the wooden barracks where the workers were accommodated. A wave of compassion and love for them flooded my spirit. I sensed something different about this day. I felt tense, probably because of all the camps and railway work gangs that I planned to visit and distribute literature to that day. Yet there was something more—an inner orange light warning that everything ahead might not be smooth sailing. Putting on my glasses, I reached for my Daily Light devotional and read the assigned Scriptures for the day, March 28.

Be strong and courageous.

The Lord is my light and my salvation—whom shall I fear? The Lord is the stronghold of my life—of whom shall I be afraid? He gives strength to the weary and increases the power of the weak. Even youths grow tired and weary, and young men stumble and fall; but those who hope in the Lord will renew their strength. They will soar on wings like eagles: they will run and not grow weary, they will walk and not faint.

My flesh and my heart may fail, but God is the strength of my heart and my portion forever. If God is for us, who can be against us? The Lord is with me, I will not be afraid—what can man do to me?

I shut the Daily Light and turned what I had just read into prayer. *Lord, you go before me today. I don't know what lies ahead, but your Word tells me if you are for me, no man can be against me. Thank you that you are my salvation. I will be strong and courageous. I will not fear.*

I wriggled out of my sleeping bag, took my place at the

steering wheel and drove 100 meters to where the two Africans stood guarding the entrance to the compound. Emboldened by my students' example, I decided to try the direct approach. I grabbed a half-dozen English books and sandwiched some red Chinese Gospels between them. Then, getting down from the van, I went up to one of the African guards. He frowned as I approached and appeared even more uncertain when I handed him the bundle of books. "Here, these are for you."

"Well, thank you. Thank you very much," he said, coughing slightly and clearly taken aback by my unexpected gift.

"Give the red booklets to the Chinese."

"I'll do that," he promised.

Having made my delivery, I did not hang around, but jumped back into the VW, turned the key, pumped the accelerator and shot off down the road. I was anxious to put as much distance between the camp and me before anyone discovered what I had done. The camp well out of sight, I slowed down and started looking for Chinese and African workers. But the crews were generally some distance from the main road and not easy to spot. After driving for about half an hour, I sighted my first railway laborers. They had been up well before dawn. Wielding picks and shoveling dirt, the Africans were laying down the sleepers, while the Chinese, dressed in their drab ill-fitting gray Mao uniforms, were supervising the work. Playing on the laboring African's ignorance—only the politically educated African understood it was forbidden to give literature to the Chinese—I drove up to a small group of Africans who were working slightly apart on their own. "Would you like some books to read?" I asked out the window. As with the African guard, I had sandwiched red Chinese Gospels between English books.

"Yes," they replied, putting down their shovels and coming over to the van.

"These English ones are for you and the red books for the Chinese," I explained, handing the books out through the window. Like children receiving free sweets, the Africans took them eagerly. The wheels churning up a cloud of dust, I beat a hasty retreat before their Chinese supervisors could see me and question what I was doing or read my number plate. For the next few kilometers, I kept one eye trained on the rear-view mirror to make sure there was no vehicle following.

I tried the same tactic and received a similar positive response when, half an hour down the road, I came across another work gang. Then I began to get concerned. My actions could draw suspicion. Perhaps I should be less direct. So when I came across the next group of workers, I tried a different approach. Driving up beside them, I wound down the window and stuck my head out. "Do you have any petrol I could buy?" I asked. The African worker shook his head.

"Sorry. We don't sell petrol." I pretended to look disappointed.

"Oh, that's too bad." Then, as if an afterthought, I casually added, "By the way I have some books you might like to read." Glancing round to make sure no Chinese supervisor was watching, I handed him a bundle through the open window. The African's eyes lit up.

"Thank you very much," he said, taking them from me. Another African came over to see what was going on. I gave him some books as well and I repeated the now familiar instructions. "The English are for you. Give the red ones to the Chinese." They nodded and went off delighted with their unexpected treasure.

I would love to have stopped and talked more. But it was too dangerous to hang around. Having made my illegal delivery, I needed to be away as quickly as possible. Speed was my greatest protection. Within seconds I was down the road with the railway workers well out of sight. If either of the Africans were asked what I was doing, they would hopefully say I had stopped to ask for petrol. *Lord, just let those books get into the hands of prepared hearts*, I prayed.

My new approach worked well. The book-starved workers took them eagerly and appeared to be more than willing to pass the red-bound Gospels on to the Chinese. Unfortunately though, the railway gangs were not easy to spot. I did not know which side roads to take to find them, and it was frustrating to think how many I had unknowingly bypassed.

The excitement and tension of my morning's activities were beginning to take its toll. Every time I approached another Chinese–African railway gang, it was like coming to a new border crossing. I had no idea what the African workers' response would be or if the Chinese supervisors would figure out what I was up to and come after me. I had not had any breakfast or dinner, only grabbing a quick snack of fruit in one of the villages along the way. By late morning, I reached the town of Serenje. Feeling hungry and tired, I decided to stop and seek out a local Christian minister. There were many Chinese living in the area. Maybe his church would be willing to help distribute the Gospels to them.

Serenje is quite a small town. I stopped an African walking along the road, and he directed me to the home of a Presbyterian minister, Reverend Bulangano, who evidently had the largest church in town. Parking the VW in front of a corrugated, iron-roof, white, brick house, I went up and knocked at the front door. A well-dressed African, who I guessed was Reverend Bulangano, answered. I introduced myself. "I'm Rudi Lack, and I'm a missionary with an organization called Youth With A Mission. I am involved in a project you might be interested in."

"Come in," he said, graciously ushering me through the door into a pleasant, light blue living room. He directed me to an easy chair. "Please take a seat, Mr. Lack."

"Now how can I help you?" In the past, I would have been more hesitant about sharing openly with a complete stranger. But emboldened by my morning's activities, my faith was high. I decided to trust myself completely to this man. I explained to him about our outreach to the Chinese and our production of St John's Gospel in the style of Chairman Mao's little red book. His eyes lit up with interest.

"That sounds like a wonderful idea, Mr. Lack. We have a lot of Chinese here in Serenje. I am sure my people would be willing to give your booklets out." I was thrilled by his enthusiastic response, especially when I compared it with the fear-ridden rejection I had received from the Swedish shop assistant in Dar-es-Salaam or the indifference of the Baptist minister. A fleeting thought passed my mind. Did this Presbyterian minister know how inflammable this material was or that it was illegal to give out Chinese literature?

"I'll go and get some to show you," I said. I returned with two boxes. I opened one and handed him a sample. He smiled as he turned the book in his hand and examined it carefully.

"A very clever imitation, Mr. Lack. Yes, I'm sure my people can use these." He returned the book to the box and closing the lid put it against the wall. "Now, how about joining us for lunch?" The familiar smells of cooked banana had been wafting in from the kitchen and I gratefully accepted his invitation.

"That's very kind of you. I'd love to." His next words, however, made me wish I had not been so eager to accept.

"We've got another guest coming as well. The district commissioner. I'm sure you'll enjoy meeting him."

The last thing I wanted was to meet some government official. My aim was to keep as low a profile as possible. But it was too late to pull out now. I could only hope the district commissioner would not ask too many searching questions. I certainly did not want him to find out the true purpose of my visit to Zambia.

Minutes later there was a knock at the door. Going to answer it, Reverend Bulangano ushered into the room a dignified and smartly dressed uniformed African. "Mr. Lack, I'd like you to mee-tour district commissioner." We shook hands and then both took a lounge seat as the reverend's wife served us drinks.

"We haven't seen you in church for a while," the reverend said breezily. The district commissioner shifted uncomfortably in his chair, making some weak excuse for his non-attendance. "I just want to let you know you are always welcome," the reverend smiled. Then changing the subject, he walked over to the open box of Chinese Gospels. Lifting up the lid, he pulled one out. I looked at him as I froze in horror. What was he doing? He came back and handed the red booklet to the district commissioner. "Look, Mr. Governor, what my friend from Switzerland has brought me! Bible portions in Chinese to give to the Maoists." I stared at him in horror, hardly able to believe what I had heard. How could he be so naive? He had blown my entire cover. I did not know where to put myself.

The governor took the booklet from the reverend and looked at it closely. I braced myself for his interrogation of my illegal activities that would inevitably follow. Instead he handed it back to the reverend. "That's nice. Those people certainly need the Scriptures. They are atheists." He did not have any words of recrimination. He said nothing about literature distribution to the Chinese being illegal. To the contrary, the governor openly expressed his concern about the political activities of the Chinese.

Over the meal, he freely shared his opinions. He recognized the Chinese were using this Tan–Zam railway project as a means of propagating their communist propaganda, and he readily declared his disapproval. "Many Africans are coming under their sway and believing their propaganda," he admitted. "The African division of the secret police, for example, take their orders directly from the Chinese. The trouble is we here in Zambia need their financial aid and many are afraid to stand up to them in case we lose their support." The governor was of another breed. In the course of our lunch conversation, he provided me with detailed information about what roads to take and where I might find some of the more obscure camps and work-sites. Grateful for the information and the meal, but now eager to get going, I excused myself and, back in the van, headed north out of Serenje. I spent the next four hours visiting as many railway work-sites as I could, distributing my combined delivery of red Chinese Gospels tucked in between English books.

By late afternoon the work gangs were packing up. Unable to distribute any more literature, I turned my attention to where I was going to sleep for the night. It had been a long, hot, although extremely satisfying day, but I was not keen to spend another night in the van. Chitambo, where the famous missionary David Livingstone carried on his medical work in the early 1800s, was only a few kilometers away. The mission station there was still well known for its medical services, so I decided to go and see if they could give me a bed for the night.

The soft, late afternoon sun reflected off the houses' west-facing windows as I drove into the Chitambo mission station compound. Parking the van in front of the semi-circle of brick houses, I chose a house at random as I did not know anyone here. A lean European man, his trousers meticulously creased and wearing a neatly ironed open-neck shirt, answered the door. I explained my plight. "I'm Dr. Durrie and I'm in charge here," he said, his clipped accent immediately betraying him as British.

"You are more than welcome to stay with us."

He ushered me into his tastefully furnished living room, and I sank thankfully into a comfortable chair, grateful for the cool breeze of the fan swirling from the ceiling above. I readily accepted the cool drink Dr. Durrie offered me. As he sat down in the chair beside me, our conversation quickly turned to my reasons for being here. I told him about my compassion for the Chinese working on the Tan–Zam railway project, and how I had been distributing our red-bound booklets to them all day. "That sounds like a great way of getting the Gospel to them," Dr. Durrie commented. "It's something we could do ourselves. There are a large number of Chinese assigned to this area." My mind started whirling. I had come seeking shelter. Maybe God had other purposes for my visit.

"Do you have any contact with them, or know where they are working?" I asked.

"No. My specialty is medicine. Our African pastor would know more. You could always talk to him." Dr. Durrie looked at his watch. "He should be home now. Come I'll introduce you to him. He lives on the other side of the compound." Dr. Durrie stood. After hours at the driver's seat, I was enjoying the comfort of an easy chair. But the chance to get more local information about the Chinese, and possibly find someone willing to distribute literature, was an opportunity too good to miss. I rose to my feet and followed Dr. Durrie.

As we stepped outside, dusk was fast approaching. Cicadas chorused in the long grass, and in the distance I could hear sounds of children laughing. The air was already cooling and the early evening's pink hues exuded an atmosphere of peace and tranquility. We were about halfway across the compound, heading towards the pastor's house, when a gray army truck roared into the missionary compound. Dust belching from its tires, it screeched to a halt beside my van and disgorged a dozen gun-toting African soldiers, all dressed in camouflage-combat uniforms. Accompanying them were three communist Chinese. Dr. Durrie and I stared in disbelief. "Hands up!" roared a burly-faced African officer, brandishing his gun in my face. My arms shot up automatically.

"Don't even think of running away!" the tough-faced officer sneered. Nothing was further from my thoughts. My heart raced. My muscles, already tense from my long day's drive, trembled from the sudden surge of adrenaline. Dr. Durrie, who had been pushed roughly to my left, stood by helplessly. Slowly the reality of my predicament filtered through my befuddled brain. I must have been followed. Someone had reported me!

"Where are your papers?" shouted the African commanding officer, pointing his gun at me. Too traumatized to speak, I pointed weakly in the direction of my white Volkswagen van. "Go, get them!" he snarled.

"Rudi, trust the Lord. I'm sure he'll get you out of this," I heard Dr. Durrie whisper behind me.

I appreciated his attempts to comfort me. But I was in real trouble; so big, I did not know if even God could get me out of it. In my wallet was a document declaring my status as a permanent resident of Rhodesia. Officially I was not even supposed to be in Zambia. The fact that I had taken a roundabout route through Botswana would only make my actions seem more suspicious. Also there was no record in my passport to indicate the months I had spent in Rhodesia. I had used a separate residence document for that. This paper of residence posed a very real danger. If the soldiers found it, they were certain to accuse me of spying for Rhodesia. Given their mood, they would probably shoot first and ask questions later.

Somehow I managed to persuade my legs to move. My hands shook uncontrollably as I tried to fit the key into the lock. I finally managed to get it open, and still trembling I picked up my wallet from the van. The soldiers were watching my every move. There was no way I could discard the incriminating paper of residence. *Lord, please get me out of this hopeless predicament*, I desperately prayed.

"Get on board," the soldier in battle fatigue ordered. My heart still beating wildly, I climbed onto the rear of the open army truck. From the grit and dust, I surmised it had been used to cart shingle for the Tan–Zam railway project. Clearing aside the gravel, I sat down. My fate was sealed. African soldiers piled in behind me. A Chinese driver, in his ill-fitting Maoist uniform, fired up the motor. But before we could take off, another truckload of African soldiers and Chinese officials came careening into the missionary compound. They screeched to a standstill beside us. One of the African soldiers yelled, "Wait! We need samples of everything this rascal has distributed!" The African beside me shoved me roughly off the truck. "Go and fetch them from your van!" I staggered slightly as my feet hit the ground, and gave an inward sigh of relief. Here was my chance to cover my tracks.

Going over to my van, I opened the back and began fumbling in one of the boxes of books I had stored there. I pretended to be searching for the samples the Chinese had demanded. In reality I opened my wallet and, keeping it hidden amongst the books, I rummaged through its contents to find the incriminating Rhodesian residence paper. Grabbing the wanted samples, I shut the van door and turned back towards the truck. Behind me safe-ly buried under a pile of literature was the Rhodesian residence paper. I breathed a little easier. Now my wallet contained only my Swiss passport that had absolutely no trace of my stay in Rhodesia.

A soldier pushed me back onto the truck. Dr. Durrie stood watching. There was nothing he could do. I cast one last, longing glance at him as I climbed on board and collapsed on the truck floor. Two of the African soldiers, their guns at the ready, sat beside me. The other four stood clinging to the side. The Chinese officials sat in the front and the truck shot forward. The soldiers clutched the sides firmly. Where were we going? What would they do to me?

15

Set Free

By now the sun had set. As we bumped along at a steady speed, the chilly night air swirled in the open truck, making me shiver. But it was more than physical cold; a dreaded chill of fear was settling into my bones. The Scriptures I had read that morning in my Daily Light flooded back into my mind. *The Lord is my light and my salvation—whom shall I fear? The Lord is the stronghold of my life—of whom shall I be afraid?* I clung to these promises like a drowning man grasping a rope. As I repeated them over and over to myself, a deep peace settled in my spirit. In my mind, however, my battle with fear continued. What would they do with me? Would I stand up under their grilling? Would God give me the right words to say?

In the dark it was impossible to tell where we were heading. Bouncing and jerking over the countless potholes, we must have driven for well over an hour before we turned up a side road. There lit by moonlight the barbed wire fence of a Chinese camp came into view. The wire mesh gate swung open as our truck approached. We drove through and came to a halt in front of four or five tin-roof barracks built African-style out of brown, mud bricks. I had often wondered what the inside of these camps looked like. Now at last I was seeing one, although not in a manner I would have desired.

Our entrance caused an immediate commotion. "Get him down!" a Chinese official ordered the African soldier next to me. He prodded me with his gun. I staggered. Dust flew as my feet hit

the dirt ground. I stood numbed by the hard ride and still somewhat traumatized by the unexpected turn of events. The Chinese
were yelling instructions at the African soldiers. Men were
scurrying in all directions. Africans and Chinese emerged from
their huts and stood staring at me. They were no doubt as confused as I was at what was going on. It was probably the first time
a white man had been brought into the camp, especially one
under armed guard.

After some 15 minutes of anxious waiting, the Chinese gave
instructions to the African soldiers, and I was marched along a
pathway into one of the barracks. A single, bare light bulb hung
from the ceiling. I was seated on a hard, wooden stool. Facing me,
behind a rough, wooden table, were five Africans all dressed in
civilian clothes. In front of them lay samples of the literature I had
been distributing, including the red Chinese Gospels of John. I
was aware that at least two of these men were the African special
police whom the district commissioner in Serenje had talked
about over lunch. The Chinese remained in the background,
moving in and out, whispering orders to the African soldiers. Just
as the governor had said, the Chinese were the ones pulling the
strings. My interrogators, the five stern Africans in civilian clothing in front of me, were mere puppets carrying out their orders.

The questions were fired at me like bullets from a gun, thick
and fast. "Where are you going?"

"Back to Tanzania and then to Kenya," I said truthfully.

"Where did you enter the country?"

"Botswana."

"When?"

"Three days ago, sir." They could have asked how long I had
been in Botswana. Had they known I had only been there two
hours, that could have opened a Pandora's box. Fortunately that
question remained unasked.

"Where did you get this literature?" the chief interrogator, one
of the African special police, asked, lifting up our imitation Mao
Gospel.

"I had it in the van. I brought it in with me." They did not ask
where it had been printed and I certainly did not tell them.

"This is illegal literature," the chief interrogator snapped, throwing the little red book on the table. "You smuggled it through."

"No, I did not. I declared it at the border."

"You're lying. You smuggled it in!" I pulled out the customs declaration form from my wallet.

"See, it's written here." How glad I was the Christian customs officer had made me include the Chinese booklets on my form. The chief interrogator snatched it from my hand and peered at it. He passed it to the others. They all looked at it closely. There was nothing they could say. It was written right at the bottom of the list in black and white, complete with the blue official stamp: *Chinese Gospels.*

"Huh!" the last African to look at the form snorted, throwing the paper in my direction.

They could not accuse me of smuggling so they tried another angle. "You're a spy," the chief interrogator said. "You're spying on the railroad."

"No, I'm not, sir." I was grateful that I had been able to remove the Rhodesian residence paper from my wallet. Had they known I was a Rhodesian resident, they would have real grounds for their accusations. As it was, they only knew me as a neutral Swiss. My only possible link with the hated white minority here in Africa was that I had been employed by them to help disrupt the railway project. They plugged this line for all it was worth. I kept assuring them I was a full-time missionary and my only purpose here in Zambia was to share the message of God's love, which of course was true.

"Who sent you?" one of my Africans interrogators asked sharply, trying to get me to confess my links with South African or Rhodesian white terrorists.

"God sent me," I said, suddenly overwhelmed by a deep sense of love for these men. "You are valuable to God and so are the Chinese. It's my duty as a Christian to get his word out to you. That's why I've been on the road handing out literature."

They laughed. "We don't need your God and we don't believe in him," one of them sneered.

They began repeating their questions, insisting I was lying and that my real crime was espionage. As I persistently but courteously rejected their accusations, they became increasingly angry and began shouting at me. The more emotional they got, the calmer I felt, and the more my compassion for them increased. God really had given me a love for my enemies.

Some Chinese brought in bowls of steaming hot noodles and placed them on the table in front of my five interrogators. They also offered me some, but I refused. How could I be sure my portion was not poisoned? Also, despite the amazing calm in my spirit, my stomach was in knots. I could not eat even if I had wanted to. I did, however, accept a bottle of Fanta from them. It was opened in front of me, so I knew it was safe. I asked my interrogators if I could pray over their food. They angrily refused but I went ahead anyway, thanking the Lord out loud for the food they were about to eat. It was one more way of declaring my faith and showing them I was not going to be intimidated.

The questioning relaxed as the men dug into their noodles; then it started again in earnest. They continued to accuse me of spying, abusing and ridiculing me and repeating their questions over and over, trying to trap me into contradicting myself. The more they questioned, the calmer I felt and the greater my love for them grew.

"I could be living a comfortable life in Switzerland," I told them. "After all, it's one of the richest nations in the world. But I have given up my career and the best years of my life to come here and share God's Word with you in Africa. I'm not doing this for personal gain. I've come because I love you. I'm concerned about your spiritual standing before God." They continued to brush aside my remarks, jeer, shout abuses and make fun of me.

I persistently responded with words of love telling them of God's great compassion for them and how he had sent Jesus to die on a cross so they could be saved. I became more and more bold in my witness. They might be my interrogators and I the accused; but like Jesus before Pilate, it was fast becoming obvious I had the upper hand. There was nothing they could say or do to rattle me.

Finally, after about an hour and a half, the chief interrogator had had enough. Clearly agitated by my quiet, persistent declaration of God's love for them, he could take it no longer.

Throwing up his hands, he pushed back his chair and shouted, "Stop that! Get on your feet!" What was coming now?

I was marched outside into the chill night air and ordered back into the truck. I was only wearing a light shirt and thin trousers, so I was thankful that this time I was allowed to squeeze into the front cabin between two African soldiers. Other soldiers climbed on the back. We drove out the camp gates and, as far as I could tell in the dark, headed south. After about an hour's drive, another Chinese work camp loomed into view. Illuminated by strong floodlights, they cast a foreboding shadow on the barbed wire fence. We drove inside. I was ordered off the truck and stood shivering in the cold night air, guarded by African gunmen. Chinese officials were going in and out of the buildings.

Suddenly out of nowhere a large German Shepherd dog lurched forward to attack me. I jumped. My heart raced as the dog's bared teeth came at me. Just in time the soldiers, laughing at my fearful reaction, called the dog off. It slunk into the darkness. Gasping for air at yet another unexpected attack, I looked around. My nerves were on edge. What was coming next? It struck me that as the only white person there, I had been the dog's solitary target. He had not bothered the Africans. Unlike the white Rhodesian and South African guard dogs, which are trained to attack African intruders, this dog had been specifically trained to sniff out whites. It brought home the reality of the animosity so many blacks, as well as Chinese, felt towards whites. I shivered with fresh concern at what might be coming next.

I must have stood by the truck with the African guards for around half an hour before the Chinese officials in baggy trousers emerged from the building. Without any explanation as to what was happening, the soldiers ordered me back into the truck. We headed out the camp and continued our journey south. The uncertainty, the accumulated tension of my long day's drive, together with the trauma of my arrest and interrogation was beginning to take its toll. It was getting late into the night and I was exhausted. But I was so on edge that even though I shut my eyes once or twice, I could not sleep. My mind was whirling. They had nothing they could pin on me. But in Africa, even as a foreigner, I could be thrown in prison and left to rot without a trial for years. Where were they taking me now?

It was only as houses came into view, and I recognized some landmarks, that I realized we were back in Serenje, the town where I had had lunch with Reverend Bulangano and met the district commissioner. We drove into the middle of town and stopped in front of the police headquarters. As we walked up the steps to the stone building, I was fully expecting to be led to a police cell. Instead, I was escorted into an office where a uniformed police official sat behind a polished, wooden desk.

I was directed to a hard-backed chair. My African guards retreated, and I was left alone in the room with a police officer. I could tell immediately from the smartness of his uniform and his authoritative manner that he was not a man to be fooled with. He was not just any policeman, but apparently a high official from Lusaka who happened to be in town and who had been especially brought in to review my case. I stiffened involuntarily. I would really have to be on my guard with this man. He picked up my passport and flicked through the pages. "So you are Swiss?"

"Yes. I'm on my way back to Kenya."

"The Chinese have accused you of spying?" he said, waiting for my response. There was none of the anger or emotion of my other African interrogators, just a polite, but firm, tone to his voice.

"I'm not a spy. I'm here in your country as a missionary. As part of my work, I have been distributing Christian literature to people I have met along the way."

The officer listened intently, saying nothing, but clearly summing me up. Unlike the Chinese-controlled African special police, I judged him to be a man who was open to reason. Suddenly it occurred to me how I could convince him of my innocence. "How could I be guilty of spying, sir, when right here in Serenje, I had lunch today with the district commissioner. We were both at the home of a Presbyterian minister, Reverend Bulangano, who has one of the largest churches in town. The governor even saw some of the Chinese Gospels and gave his approval."

The officer sat up with interest. "Could Reverend Bulangano verify this?" he asked.

"Yes, certainly," I replied. For the first time all night, I had a glimmer of hope. I had been so concerned when the reverend had shown the governor our red-bound Chinese Gospels. Now I could see God had his purpose in what I had viewed as an irresponsible act. I gave him the reverend's number. Picking up the phone on his desk, he immediately gave him a call. I could hear the phone ringing. It was after midnight and the reverend would be fast asleep. Finally I heard a faint and bleary voice at the other end of the phone.

"Hello. Bulangano speaking."

"Reverend Bulangano, we need you down here at the central police headquarters immediately," the officer ordered without further explanation. I could only imagine what the reverend must be thinking, getting such a call in the middle of the night. I sat there, my mind churning. Would Reverend Bulangano back up my story or would he turn tail and run scared in fear of his own safety? "He's on his way," the officer said, putting the phone back on the hook.

"So you say you are here as a missionary not a spy, Mr. Lack? What has been the center of your operation?" I tensed. This officer was not a man to be taken lightly. I needed to be careful. I explained about YWAM and our work in Kenya, Tanzania and the other African countries, but I carefully avoided mentioning Rhodesia. Any moment I expected him to ask how long I had been in Botswana or where I had spent the last few months. Instead, he went on to question me about the literature. I sat on the edge of my seat waiting for him to ask the dreaded question. "And where did you print this literature, Mr. Lack?" If he got even a hint that I had lived and worked in Rhodesia, I would be done for.

The questioning continued for about 20 minutes until Reverend Bulangano arrived, looking disheveled and clearly distressed by his unexplained midnight call. He stopped short at the door, his mouth agape, when he saw me sitting in front of the officer's desk. As far as he was concerned, I was many hundreds of kilometers away.

"Mr. Lack! What are you doing here?" he spluttered.

"You know this man?" the police officer asked calmly.

"Yes, he had lunch with me today," the reverend said, his eyes fixed on me and his head shaking. The puzzled look still on his face, he sat down on the upright chair the officer had pulled out for him.

"And was the district commissioner with you?" the officer asked. The reverend looked at him.

"Yes, he was my invited guest." He then reverted his gaze back to me. "Look, what's this all about? Why is Mr. Lack back here in Serenje?"

"He has been accused by the Chinese of spying and distributing literature to their workers." Reverend Bulangano gave a low whistle.

Turning to the official, he said firmly, "I can assure you, officer, Mr. Lack is not a spy. He is a missionary from Switzerland."

"Tell the police officer what we discussed over lunch," I said.

"Why I showed the governor the special Chinese Gospel you had produced and he thought it was a great idea."

"I see," the police officer replied, noncommittally. But I could see Reverend Bulangano's answer had cast a whole new light on my case. Turning to me, the police officer asked, "Did you declare this literature?"

"Yes, I have it here on my customs declaration," I said, pulling the form from my wallet and again thanking the Lord for the Christian customs officer who had made me add *Chinese Gospels* to my list.

The police officer pursed his lips as he read the stamped form. I could almost read what he was thinking. I had done everything legally. If I, as a foreign visitor to his country, was detained with no proven charges, it could spark an international incident. That would not go well for Zambia, especially as the nation's international relations were already strained to breaking point. "Mmmm." He handed the customs form back to me. "It looks as if our men might have over-reacted." Turning to the reverend, he thanked him for his help and apologized for pulling him out of bed so late at night.

Then looking at me, he said, "Well, Mr. Lack, I can't see we have any further need to detain you. I can only express my sincere regret on behalf of the police that you have been wrongfully accused and taken into custody. I am sincerely sorry for any unnecessary emotional distress this has caused you." From a wanted criminal facing a possible prison sentence, I became a person to be given every courtesy and care. "I will arrange for a car to take you back to where you came from," the police officer said.

Seeing I had been freed of all charges, Reverend Bulangano bade me goodbye and made a hasty retreat. The police officer called in two lower-ranking African policemen. "Get a car and take this gentleman back to the mission station at Chitambo." They clicked their heels and saluted smartly. "Yes, sir." Their respectful attitude indicated to me afresh the high position this police officer held.

A white, late model Peugeot pulled up in front of the police headquarters. Cordially shaking my hand and again apologizing for my wrongful arrest, the police officer opened the back door and ushered me in. I sat in comfort as the car purred along in the darkness towards the mission compound in Chitambo. What a contrast to the bumpy ride on the back of the shingle-covered army truck that had so rudely snatched me from the compound eight hours earlier.

Reflecting on the events of the night, which were now beginning to take on a nightmarish unreality, I marveled at the incredible way the Lord had gone ahead to provide my way of escape: the customs officer's insistence that I add *Chinese Gospels* to my declaration form; Reverend Bulangano's apparent blunder in showing the district commissioner our red-bound Chinese Gospel; my last-minute reprieve that allowed me to remove the incriminating Rhodesian resident paper from my wallet; and even my interrogators' failure to ask questions that would have revealed my connections with Rhodesia. How easily I could be sitting in a prison cell, instead of being driven back in luxury as a free man.

Thank you, Lord. Thank you for the privilege of allowing me to suffer just a little for you. But thank you too, for making a way of escape for me. I was reminded of Paul's words in 1 Corinthians 10:13: *God is faithful; he will not let you be tested beyond what you can bear. But when you are tempted, he will also provide a way out so that you can stand up under it.*

In contrast to my circuitous bumpy ride on the back of the army truck, it only took an hour to get back to the Chitambo mission compound. It was now early morning, not a suitable hour to rouse anyone. So crawling into my van, I climbed fully dressed into my sleeping bag and fell into a deep, exhausted sleep. At around 7am, rays of sun streaming through the window awakened me. My first thought was to give praise to God for my freedom; my second, was to let Dr. Durrie know I was okay.

His mouth opened in shock as he answered my early morning knock. "Rudi! You're back? What happened?" As I sat in his living room recounting the events of the night before, he was as thrilled as I was at the way God had come through for me. But he was also deeply disturbed. "I had never realized how hot an issue this was. If they can do this to you, they can do it to any of us. This nation boasts that it has religious freedom. We need to rise up and defend these rights or they could too easily be taken away."

After my harrowing night, I would have preferred to spend the day resting. But I was concerned the authorities might change their minds and come searching for me; I wanted to get out of the area as quickly as possible. So I refreshed myself, ate a quick breakfast and hit the road. I headed north towards Tanzania. I still had boxes of undelivered Chinese Gospels, and while I felt it wiser to refrain from distributing any more myself, I was as determined as ever to get them into the hands of people who would. Over the next few days, as I continued north through Zambia and then into Tanzania, I was able to "offload" my books into the hands of faithful Christians who were willing to take over where I had left off. It was comforting to know that while the Lord might be calling me out of the hands-on distribution, there were those who were willing to continue to take every opportunity they could to reach the communist Chinese while they still remained in Africa.

My last distribution drop-off was with Simon Malya in Temeke, Dar-es-Salaam. With the center of my activity moving to Salisbury, it had now been three years since we had seen one another. We had a wonderful time of mutual encouragement and renewing friendship. Like me, Simon had received his setbacks. Some churches had disappointingly let the Gospels gather dust on back shelves and failed to get the seed out. In other cases, churches had returned the red booklets because they were afraid of being caught and imprisoned. After my own recent brush with the authorities, I could appreciate in a new way their fear. I was doubly encouraged that in spite of this, Simon was prepared to continue to act as a distribution center for the Chinese Gospels. He would do this until later that year when the Tan–Zam railway project was completed and the Chinese returned to Mainland China.

Before leaving, Simon and I prayed together. Our request was the same as we had asked from the beginning: that just as God promised his Word would not return empty but achieve the purpose for which it was sent, so these Gospels would fall into the right hands. They would find root in good soil and produce fruit. The whole project of reaching the Chinese workers on the Tan–Zam railway project had been a venture of faith, one of sowing seed. Because it was a project initiated by God, we could only do our part and trust him to do his. Only eternity will reveal the fruit that resulted from the seed we and many others had scattered in faith.

There had been many involved. There was the original inspiration and practical financial support from Brother Andrew. Then there were the publishers, both at Kisumu and in Salisbury, who had printed the Gospels at very reasonable prices. We could never have continued without the generous donations from friends and churches back in Europe. Most important were the numerous individuals: those in Malya's church, the White Fathers, YWAM outreach teams and the many other churches and missionary organizations who had assisted in the practical footwork of distributing tens of thousands of red-bound Chinese Gospels. We were a team, each in our own way helping to cross those uncrossable borders and penetrate the barbed wire fencing of communist propaganda and anti-Christian prejudice.

It was only as I returned to Europe and began to share my adventures in Africa that I came to appreciate the importance of another crucial part of that team: the intercessors, those who picked up the burden in prayer. Constantly people would tell me how they had been praying for me, especially during my recent trip through Zambia. One close prayer warrior, a German lady, told how she had been praying by herself one day and had a vision of me surrounded by a ring of soldiers. Realizing I was in some kind of danger, she called her husband. Together they knelt in prayer and interceded on my behalf. They continued for several hours late into the night, until they sensed the burden lift and knew their prayers had broken through and I had been released without harm. They were greatly encouraged when they heard the details of my arrest and realized the part their prayers had played in paving the way for my freedom.

But while, like the apostles Paul and Peter, God had miraculously delivered me from prison, there was one young man who was not so fortunate. In July 1975, a few months after my trip through Zambia, I was back in Salisbury visiting the base and seeking to encourage the new leadership. I was in my old third-story office, tying up loose ends, when the phone rang. I picked it up and a familiar voice sounded down the line. It was the long-haired Californian and Mozambique team leader, Tom Bauer. "How are you, man?" I said, pushing my swivel chair away from the desk and swinging it round so I could look out the window.

"Rudi!" Tom's surprised voice sounded down the phone. "I thought you were back in Europe." I laughed.

"It's just a short visit, Tom. I'm here to sort out a few things and give some encouragement to the team. But what are you up to? How are things going there in Mozambique?"

"I'm not in Mozambique, Rudi. I left a few weeks ago." I thought I caught an edge to his voice.

"Oh?"

"With Independence Day coming up June 25, and the FRE-LIMO taking over, every white person, including missionaries, is fleeing the country."

"So where are you calling from?"

"Bulawayo." Tom's voice seemed unusually quiet.

"How's Salu?" Bulawayo was where we had first met. "Is he with you?" Tom's voice started to crack.

"No, he isn't, Rudi. He and Don are still in Mozambique."

"What's wrong, Tom?" I asked, catching the agitation in his voice. "Are they all right?"

"No," Tom replied quietly. "They have been arrested." I jerked my chair round to face the desk.

"They've what?" I did not want to believe what I had just heard.

"They are in prison," Tom repeated slowly. "Don was arrested July 3. Salu was taken a few days later."

"Oh no!" I moaned. Memories of my own close brush with the communist authorities loomed in my mind. I could only imagine what Salu and Don would be going through. "Do you know what the charges are?"

"As I understand, they haven't been officially accused of anything. But I'm sure it's because of our literature distribution. We knew time was running out and in recent days had really gone for it. We even tried handing out Gospels at the FRELIMO headquarters, but the armed guards wouldn't let us."

"That was a bit risky, wasn't it?"

"Yes, it was, and I tried to warn Salu and the others that it was time to get out, but they wouldn't and now...." Tom's voice trailed off as his sobs sounded down the line. I sat in stunned silence. I tried to visualize what the conditions would be like inside a Mozambique prison. Tom's broken voice sounded through his tears.

"If only I had been more insistent about them coming with me, Rudi."

"I am sure you did all you could, Tom," I said, seeking to reassure him.

"Pray for me, Rudi. I am going to see Salu's parents today to break the news to them. It's not going to be easy."

"I'll pray," I promised.

I put the phone down and, swiveling my chair back towards the window, stared out over the high-rise skyline. What was Salu doing right now? What was he thinking? Had his young faith in God been shattered? I had often challenged the students that if they were going to live 100 percent for God, there was a cost involved. Now I was experiencing some of that cost first-hand. My eyes watered as I thought of Salu languishing in a dank,

Mozambique prison cell. A tear trickled down my cheek. *Lord, you be his companion and a present help in his trouble*, I whispered. Sighing, I rose from my chair to go next door and share the news with the girls working in the literature and tape-duplication office.

A few days later, Tom arrived in Salisbury. I was shocked at his haggard appearance. His normal scrawny features were drawn. He looked as if he had not eaten a decent meal in days. "Let me get you something to eat," I suggested the moment I saw him. Taking a loaf of bread from the kitchen cupboard, I started making him a sandwich. We were both staying in YWAM's house. It was the middle of the day and the others were working at the city office, so Tom and I were alone. "How was it with Salu's parents?" I asked as I put his peanut butter and jelly sandwich on the table in front of him. Tom looked at me, a tear glistening in his eye.

"Salu told me about his village upbringing, Rudi. But it wasn't until I went to Shabani myself that I really appreciated the disadvantages he has had to overcome. When I saw how simply they live, with none of the amenities we take for granted, it made me almost ashamed to be white. I understood in a new way, why Salu had harbored such strong feelings against us." As he spoke, I could visualize the simple, thatched-roof, dirt-floor structure that was home for so many Africans, and I nodded.

"How did his parents take the news of his imprisonment?"

"Naturally they were devastated. I hated to be the bearer of such bad news." Tears welled in Tom's eyes. "If only I had made him come out with me, Rudi." He shook his head and stared across the room, his half-eaten sandwich left forgotten on the plate. I reached over from where I was sitting and placed my hand lightly on his shoulder.

"You mustn't take it personally, Tom," I said, tears welling in my own eyes. "You can't take the blame. I know Salu's only 20, but he's his own person. He made the choice to stay himself." Tom did not say anything. Staring vacantly at the kitchen table, he nodded.

"I guess you're right, Rudi. It doesn't make it any easier though."

"No, it doesn't," I said, drawing my chair next to his and putting my arm around his shoulder. He sighed and looked at me.

"One good thing, Rudi. Salu's parents let me pray for them. I tried to explain how God loved them and I asked the Holy Spirit to comfort them at this time. But I don't think they really understood."

"Probably not," I agreed. "No more than they understood Salu's radical change in lifestyle when he embraced Christianity."

"What can we do, Rudi?" Tom asked in a half whisper, tears rolling down his cheeks. "I told Salu's parents we would do everything we could to get him released. But as I left their small hut, I had such a heavy heart. I felt I was giving them false hope. Isn't there something we can do to get him out of that Mozambique jail?" I gave Tom's shoulder a squeeze.

"There's nothing we can do, Tom. We can only put him in God's hands."

Over the next few days, I racked my brains for someone I could turn to, some person with political clout or even the necessary interest to plead Salu's cause in circles that carried weight. But I could not think of anyone. I could have written letters, visited the police, contacted government officials and even made a personal visit to the local parliamentarian to rustle up support for Salu. But I knew it would not do any good. The Mozambique government was flexing its young communist muscles. They were not going to budge for anyone, especially for what they considered to be an insignificant black Rhodesian prisoner who held no political sway. All we could do as I had said to Tom was to intercede in prayer. The Lord alone was going to have to engineer Salu's release. When and how, I had no idea.

It was with a heavy heart a few days later that I boarded my plane and headed north for Europe. As we flew over Zambia, I strained through the window to see if by any chance I could glimpse the now completed Tan–Zam railway project. I reflected on the long hours that I had spent driving in the white VW, searching out Chinese work camps. The Chinese had now gone home, but my love for them had not abated. Although the Bamboo Curtain remained as resistant as ever, I was still hopeful that one day God would permit me to cross this impenetrable barrier and enter into Mainland China itself. *Oh well*, I sighed as the African continent slipped from view beneath a blanket of thick clouds and the plane winged its way towards Europe, *maybe it will happen one day.*

16

A Dream Fulfilled

OVER the years, I had read all I could about Mainland China. More than once I had visited the Chinese Embassy in Bern, Switzerland, in an effort to obtain a visitor's visa into the nation, but without success. Anywhere I had access to a Chinese Embassy, whether in Africa, Japan or even Laos, I checked to see if, just by chance, the rules of entry in that nation were less stringent. Always, I hit a blank wall. The door to Mainland China—as with Salu's prison cell—remained tightly barred and bolted.

It was not until mid-1976 when God took me to the uttermost part of the earth that there, in the small Pacific nation of New Zealand, I gained the first glimmer of a possible chink in the impenetrable armor of China's entry requirements. I was speaking at a Baptist church in the North Island town of Tauranga about my experiences with the Chinese in Africa, and exhorting the congregation on how they also could evangelize the Chinese. Since arriving in New Zealand, I had discovered there were many Chinese immigrants there. Chinese fishermen came in commercial vessels, while others came on trade missions and cultural exchange tours. As well, there were delegates at the Chinese Embassy. "As foreigners, we may not be permitted to set foot inside Mainland China, but God has his ways of bringing the Chinese to us," I challenged the congregation.

After the meeting, I was standing at the door, chatting with people as they left, when a middle-aged woman approached me. "I was interested in what you said about foreigners not being permitted to set foot inside Mainland China," she said. "I actually have a son Rodney who is in Peking." My ears pricked up.

"Really? How is that?"

"He's working with the New Zealand Embassy as a maintenance mechanic and chauffeur. I received a cassette tape from him just a few days ago in which he gives some vivid descriptions of life there. You'd be very welcome to listen to it if you wanted?" Did I want to? I was willing to devour any news about China. So I readily accepted this rare chance to hear from a foreigner actually residing there.

The lady dropped by with the tape the next day. Closeting myself in the bedroom of the house where I was staying, I eagerly pushed the start button on the borrowed cassette machine. The production was scratchy, but that did not worry me. I strained forward, anxious to hear whatever up-to-date information I could about China. While the tape was interesting, what particularly caused my heart to skip was a comment Rodney made in his introductory remarks. "Mother, when are you planning to come and see me? Remember how I told you that as diplomatic personnel, I'm permitted to invite anyone to stay with me here in Peking."

As I turned the tape off, my heart was racing. Maybe here was a crack in the closed door to China. I rang Rodney's mother, got his address and, without wasting any time, immediately wrote to him explaining who I was and asking if he would officially invite me to visit him. The letter was forwarded in a diplomatic bag safe from government surveillance.

I was back at the YWAM base in Lausanne, Switzerland, when I received a plain envelope graced with unfamiliar Chinese stamps. Inside, written on a single sheet of official New Zealand Embassy stationary, was a formal invitation from Rodney to visit him in Peking.

It was with triumph that I walked up the now familiar steps of the Chinese Embassy in Bern. When I explained my purpose to the Chinese clerk, I could see he was about to make his usual response that China was not open to visitors just now. But he stopped when I handed him Rodney's invitation. As he scanned it, his eyes opened and he cleared his throat. "So you have an official invitation to Peking, Mr. Lack." He no doubt had many questions he wanted to ask: for example, how did I have such high-level connections? But he made no comment although he did take great care to check and recheck to make sure the letter was authentic. But everything was legal. There was nothing he could do to block my application. It was just a matter of going through the formal process, and my entry visa would be granted.

As I sat at the dark mahogany table filling out the scads of official forms, often having to write the information in triplicate, I silently cheered. I was about to embark on what to all intents and purposes was an impossible journey. Hundreds of Chinese from Hong Kong and Macao were allowed to enter Mainland China daily to visit relatives, but in 1976 tourism was almost non-existent. Mainland China was still a nation tightly closed to anyone who was not Chinese.

I handed my completed forms to the embassy clerk. "Your application needs to be forwarded to Peking for approval," he said. I looked at him anxiously.

"How long will that take?" I was leaving for Canada in a couple of weeks' time to participate in YWAM's Montreal Olympic Games Outreach.

"Three or four weeks maybe," he said evasively.

"Will you need to retain my passport?"

"Yes, we will."

"That could be a problem," I said, telling him of my upcoming trip to Canada.

"That will be no difficulty, Mr. Lack," the clerk smiled obligingly. "We can arrange for the papers to be forwarded to you in Ottawa. The Chinese Embassy there can stamp your passport with the entry visa."

"Thank you," I replied. But I still had misgivings. My application could easily get misplaced. But as I could not leave Switzerland without a passport, I had no alternative. So agreeing with his plan, I gave him the details where the Chinese Embassy in Canada could contact me in Montreal.

We were halfway through the Games Outreach when I received notification from the Chinese that my visa had been approved. I made the hour's trip to the embassy in Ottawa, handed over my passport and had it officially stamped. As I walked away from the embassy, I flicked through its pages. There, taking up an entire page was the blue and red stamped visa. As I examined it, my heart missed a beat. Written in blue below some indecipherable Chinese were the words: DURATION OF STAY 30 DAYS. VALID UNTIL SEPTEMBER 30TH. It was already mid-August. To get the full value of my allotted month's stay in China, I would need to arrive September 1, less than two weeks away.

My most direct route was to fly into Tokyo and then take a flight on Japan Airlines into Peking. But while I had decided on this route, I still had not booked my ticket. One reason was the busyness of the Games Outreach. But the other was my own uncertainty. I had begun to suspect that in seeking to maximize my time in China, and get there at the earliest date possible, I might be running ahead of God. This was the most important assignment I had ever undertaken. I needed to be sure I was operating according to God's timetable. So, following the outreach in Montreal, while at a YWAM staff retreat in Wisconsin, just days before I was due to leave for China, I took time out to be alone with God and ask him what day I was to enter that communist enclave.

The summer mid-afternoon sun spread its warm glow through the magnificent upright Douglas firs of a nearby Wisconsin forest. Deep in meditation, I wandered along the needle-strewn path, reflecting yet again at the amazing way God had finally swung open this closed and seemingly locked and barred door. Everything within me wanted to rush ahead and go through it. It was with tremendous difficulty that I forced myself into idleness, and stilling my heart, asked the vital question, *When, God? When do you want me to go to China?* I did not have to wait long. Instantly, and as clearly as the birds singing in the branches above, a date dropped into my mind, *The 15*.

I was sorely tempted to argue with God. It did not make sense. If I left September 15, I would miss half the month allocated to me. But I had had enough experience of hearing that still small voice to know that when the Lord instructs, his reasons are often beyond our understanding. I had received my orders. There was no time to waste. Hastening back through the forest, I stopped at a nearby phone booth and, placing some coins in the slot, rang Japan Airlines. A cordial but formal voice answered. "How may I help?"

"I would like to book a flight from Tokyo to Peking September 15."

"I'm sorry, sir. There is no flight for that day." I had no doubt I had heard from God and that the airline assistant must be mistaken, so I asked her to recheck the schedule.

I fed more coins into the slot. I could hear paper rustling and then, after what seemed an eternity, the airline assistant came back to me. "I've checked, sir. But I'm sorry, there are definitely no flights on that date."

"But there must be," I protested. *The 15* had rung so clearly in my heart. I knew it was not my own thoughts echoing back at me.

"Could you please check again?" Although outwardly still courteous, I discerned an edge to her voice.

"I don't need to, sir. There are no flights on September 15." But I stood my ground.

"Could you please make absolutely sure?

"All right if you insist," she replied, her professional tone giving way to clear annoyance. "But I tell you, I have checked and rechecked and there are no flights."

I stood nervously twiddling the telephone cord and continuing to feed in coins. I hoped I would not run out of them. Was I being so pushy? Yet I was so sure I had heard from God. In the background, I could hear the airline assistant talking with someone. Eventually she returned and clearing her throat said, "Well, sir, I've managed to find a flight for you on September 15, but it's with Iran Air. They fly from Tokyo to Tehran but make a stopover in Peking." My heart leapt.

"That will be fine," I said. "Book me on it." Ecstatic, I put the phone down and could barely restrain myself from doing a little jig outside the phone booth. Yet again, Jesus had demonstrated that he was involved in this mission.

The next few weeks whizzed past as I readjusted my schedule and made all the necessary arrangements for my trail-blazing trip to China. As far as I was aware, I was setting a precedent.

There was no other Western tourist I knew who had attempted to make such a visit. Information on what I could expect inside China was sparse. I managed to locate some Chinese New Testaments. I also had some copies of our red-bound Chinese Gospels of John. As well, I had procured ample supplies of slide film and borrowed a 16mm movie camera. I wanted to get as full a record of my days behind the Iron Curtain as possible.

I chose 16mm in preference to 8mm as it gave a more professional production. On hearing of my proposed journey, several television networks had already asked for interviews on my return. Their interest only reiterated to me the rare privilege I was being given of entering Mainland China at this time. Above everything else in my preparations, I solicited prayer support. I knew God himself had miraculously opened this tiny diplomatic hole in the normally impenetrable Bamboo Curtain. But all my efforts could be wasted if I did not have ongoing prayer covering for the whole time I was there.

On September 8, just over a week before I was due to fly from Los Angeles and connect with my Iran Air flight to Peking, news broke of Chairman Mao Tse Tung's death. After months of speculation, it was confirmed that the ailing patriarch had passed from this life. I wondered again at the significance of my arrival date. Did God have a purpose in timing my entry to coincide with the time of Mao's death?

In the mid-afternoon of September 15, our plane hovered over the sprawling city of Peking and prepared to land. My heart soared. What would the next two weeks hold? I was the only Westerner to get off the plane. Nervous and very aware of the forbidden Scripture portions stashed in my bag, I approached the line of customs officials. Each was dressed in the same baggy, ill-fitting blue trousers, and each wore a black armband as a public show of mourning for Mao's death. Although I was coming as a diplomatic guest, I knew I could not expect any special treatment from these entry officials.

I placed my passport on the table together with my declaration form. One of the two unsmiling officials behind the table firmly stamped it from a red ink pad and then scanned my customs form. "16mm filming in China not permitted!" he said pointing to where I had listed my cameras and rolls of film. "8mm? *Yes*. 16mm? *No*". My heart sank. Why had I chosen to bring the heavier and more professional 16mm? I raised my shoulders and opened my hands.

"But I'm here on diplomatic business. I've come all the way from Europe." I hoped against hope he would relent. But his resolve only hardened.

"No 16mm film! Not allowed!" he said stonily. The last thing I wanted was to jeopardize my entry into China or give them any reason to suspect me of spying, so I agreed to let them seal the unused film. Working together, the two officials laboriously wrapped string around the aluminum cans of unprocessed film, and then secured the ends with an official lead seal.

"You present an unbroken seal when you exit," the official instructed, handing me the string-wrapped bundle. He also made a notation regarding the film in my passport.

"Yes," I said, and meekly put the incarcerated film into my bag. I was bitterly disappointed. But at least this hassle had a positive side-effect. It diverted their attention. The rest of my bags containing my undeclared Chinese Scriptures passed through without a hitch.

It was a relief to get through all the entry requirements and out to the arrival lounge where Rodney, the only European in a crowd of monotonous blue-attired Asians, was waiting to greet me. After so many years of hoping and praying, I had finally arrived in China.

As we hauled my bags into the diplomatic black limousine that the ambassador had kindly lent Rodney and then made our way through Peking's streets, an immediate kaleidoscope of impressions struck me. Everyone was dressed in the same drab, blue trousers and shirts and all, like the officials at the airport, wore a black armband. And everything it seemed, was transported by bike. Some cyclists carried grocery items: a few vegetables strung together and sometimes a scrawny chicken tied by the feet. Others ferried children and a few transported larger items such as a cane chair or table. And then there were the rickshaws, also operated by cycle and carrying their human passengers. I had never seen so many bicycles in all my life. Ours was one of the few cars on the road. It was hard to believe I was driving through the capital of a nation with over a fifth of the world's population.

I was also struck by the shabby, unkempt state of the buildings. The rows of drab, unpainted, concrete apartment blocks, each with washing hanging on poles out the windows, were all built of the same monotonous design. The only visual relief was the large propaganda posters pasted on huge billboards. Although I could not decipher the Chinese, their communist message of a communal lifestyle dedicated to serving the state was clear. And everywhere there were huge posters of a stern, policeman-like uniformed Chairman Mao, his pointed hand stretched out as if to direct the passing populace. The man himself might have died, but his dominating presence still prevailed. A few red-tiled buildings scattered along our route were evidence of a more prosperous pre-communist age.

Rodney parked the black limousine in front of the building where the New Zealand embassy staff was housed. Rodney's tenth-floor, four-roomed apartment was simply furnished, bachelor style, with cushion-covered cane chairs. This, Rodney explained, was luxury compared with the way most Peking residents lived. In this burgeoning over-populated city, a whole family of five or more often crammed into two rooms. Many of the apartment blocks had 12 or more floors and no elevators.

Although we were in embassy accommodation, there was still a good chance that the rooms were bugged. So after a simple supper of fish, Chinese noodles and vegetables that Rodney had cooked, we stepped outside onto the balcony. It commanded a spectacular view over the city and here we could talk more freely. A fine layer of red dust covered everything. As Rodney brushed clean two wrought-iron chairs, he explained that the dust blew in from the Gobi Desert. In his mid-twenties, Rodney was a likeable, soft-spoken, unassuming man. He did not strike me as the type to venture into this atheistic, communist jungle. I was not too surprised, therefore, to learn that he got his mechanic and chauffeur position almost by accident.

"I was in the army and had applied for an overseas post," he told me. "Mainland China was the last position I expected to be offered and I wasn't sure I wanted to accept."

"So why did you?"

"I sensed God had a purpose in bringing me here. But it's not been easy," he confided. "Although I speak some Mandarin, even in diplomatic circles it's hard to make friends. The same fear and suspicion that binds the Chinese also invades and stifles relationships within the foreign community."

"Well, I'm very grateful you're here," I encouraged. "I would never have made it into China without your formal invitation. If for no other reason, God has brought you here for me."

The next day Rodney was working, so I borrowed a cycle and, with my slide camera slung round my neck, joined the bike-riding crowds of Peking. I attempted to merge in with the populace. But that proved impossible. Not only did my white face and Western style of dress mark me out from the blue-trousered crowds, but my thin, angular face and pointed nose were in odd contrast to their more rounded features. Everywhere I stopped or tried to walk, I attracted attention. Westerners—and in China that was mainly embassy staff—were not in the habit of cycling, walking the streets, or eating at roadside stalls as I was doing. I was possibly the first European many had seen.

The moment I dismounted from my bike, hundreds would crowd around me to get a closer look at this strange-looking foreigner. But when I lifted up my camera to take a photo, the people quickly melted away in fear. They were concerned that I would capture them on film and somehow this would become incriminating evidence against them. As the Red Guard Revolution in the 1960s had demonstrated, committee officials only needed to get suspicious that someone was entertaining Western ideals and that poor, hapless person could land in prison or be thrown into a re-education camp.

Fortunately I had taken the precaution of bringing with me a special lens used by journalists in sensitive situations. While I appeared to be pointing my camera at a building or some other object, in fact my 45-degree lens was pointing directly at the curious Chinese onlookers. Without them being aware, I was able to capture on celluloid their open curious looks. I thought regretfully of my stack of unused, string-bound 16mm film. How

I would love to capture the same sights on movie film.

Rodney had use of the embassy car the following day; we took advantage of it to visit the Great Wall of China. Built long before the birth of Christ to keep out invaders from the north, this massive stone edifice is the only man-made structure that can be seen from outer space. As fascinating as it was to visit and actually walk on this wall which snakes its way like a huge python into deep ravines and over high mountain ranges, I was equally captivated by my first real glimpse of China's countryside. I had seen pictures of Chinese peasants in wide-brimmed hats working with simple hand implements in the paddy fields. To view them for myself, albeit at a distance, brought home to me how isolated Mainland China really had become.

Since his death ten days earlier, Mao Tse Tung's body had been laid out in state at Tiananmen Square. People had lined up for hours to file past. It was the closest view the majority had ever had of this larger-than-life leader who had dominated and manipulated their lives for more than 30 years. When we returned to Peking from our day trip to the Great Wall, there was a subdued, almost morbid, atmosphere in the city as final preparations were being made for Mao's funeral the next day. Black shrouds draped many of the buildings and the city's already teeming millions had swelled. Many thousands were continuing to pour into the city, and crowds were already gathering on the streets in the hope of getting a prime view of the next day's proceedings.

This was to be a domestic occasion. Only a few foreign journalists were invited and diplomatic personnel were politely advised to stay indoors. As emotions in the gathering anti-Western crowd peaked, our very lives could depend on obeying their advice. It made me realize afresh the significance of my being here at this time. I would not say God had orchestrated Mao's death for the time of my arrival. But as an all-seeing, all-knowing God, he knew the events that were to take place when he directed me to arrive on September 15. Had I come earlier, I would likely have been out of Peking and on a tour of the provinces. As it was, God had me right there for this historic occasion.

When we awoke the next morning, even more people had

gathered. Although Westerners were forbidden to venture onto the street, Rodney and I had an excellent view from his tenth-story balcony. From here, we could clearly see the columns of olive-green uniformed soldiers as they marched in seemingly endless procession below. Ten- and twelve-man wide, these columns filled most of the broad boulevard. Alongside was another seemingly endless column of open trucks filled with more soldiers. There was also a long line of buses ready to take civilians to Tiananmen Square, where the official funeral proceedings were to take place, and another two- and three-wide column of empty trucks returning after they had delivered their load of soldiers at the square.

Again I marveled at the privilege of being here at this historic time. I had one regret. There were hardly any foreign journalists to capture the event. The only record the world would have would be official Chinese propaganda film. I thought again of my string-bound, lead-sealed aluminum cans of unused 16mm film. If only I could release them and make my own recording of the event.

Then I had an idea. I dashed into my room, picked up the string bundle and closely examined it. Maybe, just maybe, I could ease the string back and release one of the cans. It was worth a try. The string was tightly wrapped and I needed to be extremely careful that I did not break the seal. A broken seal would spell disaster for my border exit. Taking great care and with Rodney's help, I painfully eased back the string and finally managed to release one of the cans through the web. With one gone, the string collapsed and the rest came away easily. I then looked nervously at the lead seal and breathed with relief. It remained unbroken.

My hands sweating, I loaded the film, slipped back out onto the balcony and, placing my camera on the tripod, started filming. While Rodney and some of the New Zealand embassy staff peered through their binoculars, I peered through the lens of my camera. I was capturing on film what the official communist media would deliberately choose to ignore: following the procession, milling crowds, lost and confused, were unsure where to go from here. Their great leader was gone and, up to this moment, no clear leadership had emerged to take his place. Corrupt and conniving as he had been, Mao Tse Tung had been their chairman for 30 years. They had followed in blind obedience —mostly out of fear—to the dictates of his anti-Christian regime. What lay ahead? None of us knew.

The next week Rodney and I embarked on a tour of the provinces. We were about to witness firsthand some of the underlying political turmoil that would have a profound effect on this nation's future when it surfaced. The communist authorities had carefully scrutinized our itinerary. We needed to obtain permits for every city or provincial area we planned to visit. This stipulation was not restricted to us as foreigners. Travel for anyone in China was difficult. No one could travel beyond their provincial area unless they had first obtained a permit.

As we no longer had the embassy car, we traveled by train. Tour guides carefully monitored our movements. At each destination, our 'guide' would meet us off the train, take us to our hotel and then meticulously review the next day's activities. Although he would put it to us as a suggestion, we really did not have any choice. The schedule had already been arranged for us. The authorities had assigned the communal farm, factory or kindergarten we were allowed to visit. These were showcase propaganda tours designed to impress us with China's progress under communism. But while they tried to convince us of their great accomplishments, the cover-up had gaping holes. In one factory, for instance, I examined a piece of equipment said to be "Chinese-made". Stamped on the side I recognized the brand name of a well-known German manufacturer!

Also, the people's faces did not match the ideals being presented to us. The workers looked unhappy. Their shoulders drooped and age lines were etched on the faces of many whom I suspected were only a little older than I was. The few shops we saw were pathetically devoid of what we in the West would consider vital necessities. Only a few electrical goods were on display and basic items such as stationery or shoes were of a very poor quality.

One of the approved cities on our itinerary was Nanking. We arrived there after yet another long, tiring train journey. Weary and stiff from a lack of exercise, we were looking forward to a hot bath and good night's sleep in our hotel. As usual, our tour guide was there to meet us.

"It is not possible to stay in Nanking," he said as he greeted us off the train. "You must go on to Shanghai."

"What?" Rodney and I chorused. The authorities had made it clear we must follow our itinerary to the letter. There could be no deviation.

"Why? We are supposed to be here in Nanking today," I said, pulling out my itinerary. "Look, we have our permit to stay."

"You can't stay. You must go to Shanghai," the tour guide insisted, but without explaining why. He picked up our suitcases and headed towards another train platform. We had no choice but to follow. Before we knew it, Rodney and I were bundled into a train and heading for Shanghai.

It was late into the night when we finally arrived. Exhausted by the long journey and still confused by the unexpected change of plans, we wearily climbed the stairs to our hotel room. Like the many others we had stayed at, it only offered the bare necessities: a bed, running water, which was often cold, and heaters, which usually did not work. But we were thankful just to have somewhere to rest. All I wanted was to flop onto the bed and sleep. Both Rodney and I, however, sensed that we were in the middle of some spiritual battle. So, abandoning any thought of rest, we knelt by our beds and began to intercede.

It would not be until some time later that we understood the significance of our prayers. At that very moment in the city of Nanking, but unknown to the rest of the world, a crucial political battle was in progress. The infamous Gang of Four, including Mao Tse Tung's widow, was struggling for supremacy in the Chinese government. Concerned that, as foreigners, we might somehow get wind of their internal domestic struggles, the officials had stepped in to stop us entering Nanking. Had the Gang of Four won their political battle, China today might well still be entrenched in Mao's type of policies. As it was, their power was toppled and the chairmanship handed on to Deng Shao Ping, who, while still retaining an official communist atheistic policy, would open the country to much closer communication and trade with the rest of the world.

But in 1976, the doors were still tightly closed. All we could do was pray for them to be opened. As we were shown around the city docks in Shanghai and saw the freighters being unloaded, God gave me faith to pray that one day Bibles would be offloaded from these ships. Little did I realize then that, in a few short years, Brother Andrew's Open Doors ministry would float a million Bibles into the country and that the Operations Mobilization ship, The Logos, would dock at this very port. Also, the Church would have official permission to print Bibles inside Mainland China.

Our faith venture right now was of a much smaller scope. We needed wisdom to disperse our few dozen Chinese New Testaments along with the handful of slim red-bound Gospels that I had smuggled into the country. It had been too dangerous to distribute these in Peking. They could be too easily traced. Even here in the interior, there was a risk we could be detected. So Rodney and I chose our hiding places carefully. We surreptitiously hid our books behind some darkly lit museum object during one of our educational tours or stuffed one behind a cupboard where maybe in six months' or a year's time a cleaning maid might stumble across it. We tried to place the literature where it would not be immediately discovered and therefore traced back to us. None of this was easy, because during the whole trip our movements were under close surveillance. The tour guide was our constant companion and even joined us for breakfast.

There were the few occasions, however, when we were able to escape. For example, one night in Shanghai when we were supposed to be tucked away safely in our hotel beds, we sneaked out unnoticed and headed for one of the city parks to distribute Scriptures. Going our different ways, Rodney and I made out we were on an evening stroll. In fact, we were both carrying bags stuffed with Scriptures. As I approached an empty park bench, I had to first check to make sure nobody was watching and then, as I passed, casually drop a book on the bench.

I thought my movements had gone unnoticed under the cover

of the dim lighting in the park when suddenly I felt a hand grab my shoulder. I jumped with fright. Turning round, I found myself face to face with an angry, middle-aged Chinese man dressed in his blue, baggy Mao uniform. He took hold of my shoulders and shook them violently, all the time yelling at me in Mandarin. I looked at him stunned. Finally he let my shoulders go, no doubt realizing from my perplexed expression that I could not understand a word of what he was saying. With a look of disgust on his face, he turned away, giving me one last angry shake of his fist as he went. I did not think he had seen any of my deliveries. What he was probably expressing was pent-up hatred arising from years of propaganda against Westerners. However, I was not about to take any risks; so after seeking Rodney out, we quickly retreated to the safety of our hotel room.

Rodney's week of vacation was drawing to a close. He needed to return to Peking. I still had a few more days of my allotted two weeks in China so, saying farewell to Rodney, I set out on my own for the interior, but still with a tour guide as my constant companion. My route took me through the spectacular mountain area of Gwelin.

Even though I had grown up in the beautiful, snow-capped mountains of Switzerland, I gasped in wonder at the sheer magnificence of the scenery and the tall, rounded peaks of the Gwelin mountains. I then took a motorized barge down the Gwelin River. Of the 200 or so people on board, I was the only Westerner. My official escort, confident that I could not venture off into any forbidden territory, slept most of the journey while I boldly recorded my trip on film. Although my guide saw me filming, he never said anything. Possibly he could not tell the difference between 8mm and 16mm. Maybe he was not even aware that filming with a 16mm camera was illegal in China.

During the trip, I was able to capture sights which few, if any, Westerners had seen before. We passed isolated villages where mechanical machinery was unknown and every farm activity, including harvesting and threshing, was done by hand implements. In this densely over-populated nation, human labor was cheap. When our barge got stuck on a sandbank as frequently happened, about half of the passengers, mostly men, would jump into the river and, straining all their weight against the rusting iron, shove until it refloated.

Perhaps the sight that moved me most was the one on the side of the river, where teams of men, harnessed together like horses, dragged a barge upstream. It tore at my heart to see human beings, whom God created in his image, treated with less respect than animals. How crucial it was for this great nation to receive a revelation of the dignity of man and the unique role God has for us as humans. But this could only happen as these people came to understand the message of the Gospel, and this would only be possible as the nation was saturated with the Word of God.

By this time in 1976, news had leaked out to China watchers in the West that despite Mao's rigid, atheistic education programs, an underground Church did exist. But just how extensive this was, no one had any idea. I had heard one amazing account of a demon-possessed village girl, who was such a hopeless case that she spent two years sitting on a chair embedded in concrete. Her parents, desperate for a solution, had sought help from every possible source, but to no avail. Then some Christians had plucked up courage to ask if they could pray for her. Through their intercessions, the evil power binding the girl had been broken and she was totally set free. As a result, the parents and the girl had been saved and many in that region had turned to Christ. Although I continued to look for some evidence of this hidden Church, nothing had surfaced. I had not seen even a hint that a vibrant, let alone growing, Church existed.

While in Peking,[10] Rodney and I had attended a Sunday morning service in what used to be the Bible Society house. A few Western university students, some diplomatic personnel and a scattering of elderly Chinese made up the sparse congregation. But this official church was merely a token showcase of religious tolerance. There were no young people, nor any sign of real spiritual life. I longed to make contact with Christians who had real faith in God; so in every town I visited, I kept my eyes peeled looking for any signs that might lead me to a church fellowship.

It was not until I got to Guangzhou—my final city before

[10] Today renamed Beijing.

crossing into Hong Kong—that I saw any external evidence of Christianity. I was with my tour guide viewing the city from a hill-top, vantage point when I caught sight of the twin spire of a church. I made a mental note of where it was and determined to find my way to it. But I had two problems. I had to shake off my tour guide and I had to somehow find my way through the maze of narrow streets without a map. Neither could I ask for directions. That would be too risky.

That afternoon I feigned tiredness. "I think I'll just put my feet up and have a rest," I said to my tour guide. He looked at me annoyed.

"But we have a factory visit arranged for you, Mr. Lack." I yawned.

"Yes, I know. But I've had a busy schedule and I need a break." He tried to push me. But I resisted. Finally, but very reluctantly, the guide agreed to cancel the afternoon's arrangements.

I did lie down on my bed, but only for a short time. Then I went down to the lobby, checked to see that my guide was nowhere in sight and then casually walked out through the entrance and into the street. I felt like an escaping prisoner. But as I quickly mingled with the passing crowds, I breathed a little easier. For the first time since being on tour I felt free. *Lord, show me the way to the church*, I prayed as I set off down the narrow street in what I had worked out was the general direction. At one point I was about to make a right turn when I sensed, *No. Keep walking straight ahead*. Only a few meters further on, I turned down an alleyway and there in front of me stood the twin-spire church.

I paused for a moment, awed at how God had led me through the maze of alleyways to the exact spot. Mounting the half-dozen stone steps up to the church, I tried the shut door. It swung open, so I walked through. Inside, the church was totally bare. All the pews had been removed and there were no furnishings. As I stood for a few seconds wondering what to do next, a Chinese man burst through the door, waving his hands in protest and yelling to me in Mandarin. I could not understand a word, but his message was clear. I had entered forbidden territory. Pushing me roughly, he shoved me out the door. I stumbled back, my heart heavy. Somehow I managed to retrace my steps to the hotel. I fell onto the bed and, through my tears, cried out in prayer, *Oh Lord, let there be a breakthrough.*

God had opened the way for me to embark on this amazing two-week trail-blazing venture; but to really see the Bamboo Curtain shredded, there needed to be concerted intercession. For that to happen, Christians had to be informed about how to pray. In my possession was a wonderful, graphic means of opening people's eyes: an up-to-date report recorded on 35mm slide as well as 16mm film. There was just one difficulty. I had to some-how get that film safely out of the country. My slide films were not illegal, but I did not want to take the risk of some over-zealous customs officer confiscating them.

The night before I left for Hong Kong, I carefully cut the end off my toothpaste tube and meticulously scrapped away the toothpaste. I then inserted into it some of my most precious films: Mao's funeral procession, close-up facial shots in Peking and my barge journey down the Gwelin River. I rolled the end and stashed the film-stuffed tube back into my toilet bag. The greater challenge was getting my used aluminum cans of 16mm film back into their lead-sealed string web. It took some manipulating but, by carefully teasing back the string, I eventually managed to ease the final can back into the web without breaking the seal. I examined the repackaged film. Looking at it, no one would guess the cans had ever been removed. But I still had to put it to the test. Would the customs officials suspect it had been tampered with?

Normally my greatest moment of tension comes when I enter a communist nation. Mainland China was the exception. I stiff-ened as I approached the baggy, blue-trousered customs officer, but tried to appear as casual as I could as I put the string-bound package of film on the table for his inspection. He looked at the notation in my passport. I took an involuntary breath as he cast his eyes towards the aluminum cans. Would he notice anything astray? He nodded curtly and then signaled me through. Hardly daring to believe that my exit had been so easy, I quickly grabbed the film and walked briskly through to the Hong Kong customs on the other side.

That precious film would prove invaluable as over the next few months, both in the States as well as in Europe, I was interviewed and my film was screened on a variety of television talk shows. I was also interviewed over radio and displayed my slides in numerous church meetings. Everywhere I went, I urged people to pray for the persecuted Church in China. As I traveled, I also solicited prayer for another victim of communist injustice: my Rhodesian friend Salu.

17
Breakthrough

It had been nearly 18 months since Salu's arrest in Mozambique. He had still not been officially charged with any crime. We were kept abreast of his situation through local Christians who visited him regularly. They met under closely scrutinized security in an open yard surrounded by a nine-foot wall that was topped with jagged glass. Thankfully they were able to take food to Salu to supplement his poor prison diet and also to smuggle out letters.

Although cell visits were strictly banned, a Christian group called Friends in the West, who encourage prayer and practical support for believers in prison, managed to take a clandestine photo of him looking out the bars of his prison window. That photo was circulated among the Church for prayer support. People even wore Vietnamese POW-style arm bracelets engraved with his name as a constant reminder of his plight. But despite our prayers, there was no apparent change in his situation. At least outwardly, there was no indication that God had answered or even heard the many prayers that were being offered for him.

Nine months earlier after 300 days in prison, the American missionary Don Milam and a Brazilian worker, who had also been arrested with Salu, had been released. This was due to political pressure from their embassies. But for black Rhodesian Salu, there was no such lobbying force. His prison cell remained firmly shut.

Now Salu was alone, without the spiritual support of his fellow Christians. I knew of the intense pressure put on blacks to join the resistance and fight for the freedom of their country, and I could only imagine the propaganda to which his communist captors would no doubt have subjected him. If Salu gave in and indicated his willingness to join the black terrorist movement against Ian Smith's white-minority government, he would no doubt be released instantly. That would be a real temptation. Now that he was alone without the support of his believing inmates, the pressure to give up his faith would be even greater. Recalling the strength of his past hatred towards whites, my intercessions for him intensified. *Lord, please don't let Salu lose faith. Help him resist the communist propaganda. Please set him free.*

In January 1977 I was back in Africa teaching at a YWAM Discipleship Training School (DTS) in South Africa. The DTS was introduced as a preparatory course to the SOE and eventually replaced it altogether. Although my ministry was focused more on Eastern Europe these days, it was always exciting to touch African soil again. The smells, sights and even the heat—although it was more tempered here in Johannesburg—brought back fond memories of my days trudging through African villages, sleeping on thin, lumpy mattresses and surviving on rice and vegetables. Meat was a rare treat on our limited YWAM budget.

The school in white-dominated South Africa was held at Halfway House in the same kind of comfortable facilities we had enjoyed at the Rest Haven Retreat Center. Often when I was not teaching, I would stuff a few tracts in my pocket and head for the poorer, black areas of town. Invariably on such excursions, my mind would reflect on Salu, whose situation remained unchanged. He could languish in prison for years. This had happened before to others. I often questioned the Lord. *Why?!* Salu was a young man in his early twenties and oozing with potential. Why had he not been released to fulfill his destiny? I did not receive an answer. The windows of heaven remained as firmly locked as Salu's prison cell. One comfort was to learn through reports and letters that over the months, rather than weakening, Salu's faith had remained strong and unwavering.

One afternoon, around the middle of my week's teaching at the Johannesburg school, I was sitting in a lounge, fellowshipping over a cup of coffee, when one of the local YWAM staff burst in. "Rudi, we've been looking for you." I looked up startled by his sudden entry.

"Yes?"

"Do you know Salu Daka?"

"He was one of my students in Rhodesia. Why?"

"The British Ambassador to Mozambique is on the phone. Something to do with a passport and getting Salu out of jail." I jumped up from my seat and, taking two steps at a time, bounded downstairs to the office and grabbed the phone.

"Lack, here," I said, gasping at my sudden exertion of energy. A distinguished English voice sounded down the phone.

"Are you acquainted with Salu Daka?"

"Yes. He's in prison," I answered still breathing heavily. "Has he been released?"

"No." My suddenly raised hopes dashed, I sunk into a nearby chair.

"But I think I can get him out," the ambassador continued.

"Yes?" My voice rose in expectation. "How?"

"In a move to gain more credibility internationally, FRELIMO is softening their policy on foreign prisoners. Already a number have been released."

"But not Salu?"

"Not yet. But I can arrange a temporary British passport for him. And that will be his ticket to freedom."

"How can you do that?" I asked puzzled. "Black Rhodesians are not issued British passports."

"I know." The ambassador went on to explain that the British Government, in an attempt to foster the black independent movement against Ian Smith's intransigent policies, had recently issued some temporary British passports to blacks. "I'm sure I can pull some strings and get one for Salu," he commented.

I wondered why a British Ambassador would be taking a personal interest in an unknown black Rhodesian prisoner. "Why are you doing this?" I asked.

"Salu and I were in the same Portuguese language class at university. We often chatted together. I liked him and I don't believe he is guilty of any criminal activity. Since I heard of his plight, I've been seeking to help but until now my hands have been tied." By now my heart was doing somersaults.

"That's wonderful. You are certainly an answer to many prayers."

"There's just one stumbling block," the ambassador added.

"Yes?" My heart sank. What was coming now?

"I'm sure I can arrange a temporary British passport which will get him out of prison. But with a British passport, he will need to fly out to Britain and Salu doesn't have money to pay for an air ticket."

"Oh, that's easy," I said with relief. "I can purchase that." Although that would exhaust my limited funds, I figured this was the least I could do for a dear friend who had been languishing in prison for 18 months.

"If you can arrange for a ticket in Salu's name to be sent to Maputo[11] airport, I'll go ahead and get a passport issued."

My heart beating crazily at the unexpected turn of events, I borrowed a car, drove immediately into town and raced into the airline office. There I booked a one-way ticket from Mozambique to London and arranged for Salu to collect it at the Maputo airport. The flight was via South Africa, which gave him a night's stopover in Johannesburg. As I walked out of the airline office, I still felt I was in a dream. Any minute I would be rudely awoken to reality.

But the reality hit some days later when on Monday evening, January 17, together with a friend from Open Doors ministry, I went to Johannesburg airport to greet Salu. It was almost with a sense of nervousness that I waited at the gates for him to come through. We had prayed for so long. Our hopes had been dashed so many times. It was still hard to believe that after two years—18 months of which Salu had been locked away in a prison cell—we were finally going to be reunited. I reflected on the tough, young man who had first approached me after the Bulawayo meeting. I thought of our shaky beginnings in the school. He had come right and gone through a test greater than any of us had endured. And he had passed with flying colors.

Wearing a smart green jacket, brown shirt and blue tie that

[11] New name for Lorenco Marques.

the ambassador had purchased for him during his first days of freedom in Mozambique, Salu looked like any other businessman as he walked through the door. But the strain of months in a dimly lit prison cell had taken its toll. Although only in his early twenties, there was early evidence of gray in his thinning hair. The prison diet had also had its effect. Salu was not the solid young man I had first met. After an emotional reunion of hugs, tears, laughter, prayers and thanksgiving, I picked up his battered, brown suitcase. We took him to the nearby Holiday Inn for a meal. Dazed by his sudden change of circumstances, he clearly felt out of place in such unfamiliar, luxurious surroundings.

But that night, as he shared my room with me at the YWAM base and we had further time to talk, details of his story emerged. As I had suspected, the pressure to throw his lot in with the black-resistance movement had been immense. The brutal inhuman treatment, sudden executions and suicides were just part of the emotional battle he had fought. Salu shared how on one occasion a fellow cell mate had become so depressed, he picked up the excrement-filled toilet bowl in the cell corner and dumped it on the head of a prison guard.

Then there was the continual pressure to conform to Marxist propaganda as they were forced to attend educational lectures. These, as Salu explained, were little more than slogan-yelling sessions in which the captors had them repeat over and over declarations such as: *Down with colonialism! Down with imperialism! Down with racism!* Many of the prisoners were white Portuguese doctors, teachers and successful businessmen whose only crime was that their capitalistic lifestyle did not fit FRELIMO's communist ideals. The white Portuguese would try to debate with their communist educators. But their resistance only caused their captors to lose their tempers. Screaming at them, they would threaten to send them back to Portugal in a coffin. "That wasn't idle talk, Rudi," Salu said, a tremble in his voice. "There was every chance they would carry out their threats."

The worst period of his 18-month imprisonment was the three months when a particularly cruel commandant called Karonga was in charge. An overweight, sadistic man, he fought with the FRELIMO in the guerrilla war that toppled the hated Portuguese colonialists.

My heart churned as I sat on my temporary mattress on the floor and listened as Salu described one especially gruesome incident that happened during Karonga's rule. A white Portuguese was caught fighting with another inmate, and was dragged bleeding into the classroom where Salu and his fellow prisoners sat. As they watched, the soldiers roped the poor man's arms behind his back and yanked them chest high. "He was in such pain, Rudi," Salu said, his voice quivering. "But that wasn't the worst. Karonga then ordered the soldiers to pour water and rub salt into his gaping wounds." Salu dropped to a whisper as he recalled the awful event. "As Karonga commenced his lecture, he was writhing in absolute agony on the floor. It was terrible. But none of us dared go to his aid." I sat in silence, picturing the scene. What Salu had gone through was even worse than I had imagined.

"Did you ever feel you couldn't keep going?" I asked.

"Yes, especially at the beginning, Rudi. The language of some of the inmates was pretty foul and I was in a room with a homosexual who kept trying to solicit me."

"Praise God, he protected you."

"I'm sure that was only through prayer. I knew people were praying. That meant a tremendous lot to me."

"And you had your Bible? Right?"

"That's what really kept me going, Rudi. Reading my Bible and having Don and the others with me, at least at the beginning."

"It must have been tough when they were released after nine months," I said.

"To be honest, Rudi, I think that was one the hardest moments of the whole 18 months." Tears swelled in Salu's eyes. I nodded with understanding. "When I was arrested, the police chief told me I would rot in prison for 40 years unless I changed my imperialistic ways. I tell you, when Don and the others left, I was sorely tempted to believe him he was right."

Getting up from my mattress on the floor, I went over to my bed, which Salu was using for the night, and embraced him.

We both wept. I loved this young man as a brother. Salu looked at me through his tears. "The day Don and the others left, I wrote just two words in my diary, Rudi: *Hard day!*" I gave his arm a squeeze.

"Praise God, you never lost your faith, Salu."

"It wasn't easy," Salu admitted. "There were days when everything seemed so black and hopeless, I wondered if it was worth carrying on."

"But you never gave in."

"I had God's promises in his Word, and although conditions were bad, I would often remember Jesus' sufferings. In comparison, mine were nothing." I felt humbled. Salu, the student, was now instructing me, the teacher. I realized how little I had really suffered for Christ.

When it came time the next day to see Salu off on his plane to England, it was hard to say goodbye. He waved as he turned to go through immigration. "See you." Putting on a brave face, I smiled and waved back. I had no doubt that in true YWAM tradition our paths would cross again. But it was with more that a little nostalgia that, a short while later, I also boarded a Boeing 747. Taking my window seat, I settled back for my return flight to Europe. Far below was the lush green of the African countryside.

I thought of the team still carrying on ministry in the downtown office in Salisbury. Then as the plane flew northward across Tanzania, I strained again through the window to see if by any chance I could glimpse the now completed Tan–Zam Railway. I thought of the long hours I had spent driving in the white VW van searching out Chinese work camps. I reflected on my own arrest. How easily I, like Salu, could also have ended up in a prison cell. But by now, January 1977, the Chinese workers had returned to Mainland China.

I thought back to my own thrilling two-week visit to China some months earlier. How I longed to go back. But a return trip was not in my immediate plans. God had other priorities, the most important being my upcoming marriage to Eliane Vuffray. A vivacious French Swiss nurse, Eliane had joined YWAM's ranks shortly after me. Our paths had frequently crossed, but it was not until the staff retreat in Wisconsin, immediately prior to my

China visit, that our friendship blossomed into romance. Eliane's French charm, along with her dedicated love for the Lord and passion for missions, had captured my Swiss German heart.

Loren Cunningham married us August 6, 1977, at Lausanne Cathedral. As we descended the altar steps, having said our vows, and started to proceed down the aisle, I looked over the 500 guests who filled the pews. There, witnessing our union, were many of our YWAM friends including Don, Deyon, Joe, Reona and Floyd. Standing out amongst the sea of predominantly white faces was Salu's dark, shining features. Memories stirred as I spotted him in the crowd, and we caught one another's eyes. My heart missed a beat and a tear formed in my eye. Since coming to Europe, Salu had continued his involvement with YWAM both in the United Kingdom and Switzerland. While we did not see a lot of each other, it was always a joy when our paths crossed. Soon he would also marry and return to Africa, where he would head up YWAM in the Cameroons.

Following our marriage, Eliane and I embarked on a year-long missions-related honeymoon that took us to 25 nations on every continent and where we slept in 67 different beds! There was one country, however, that we did not visit—one forbidden border that I still wanted to cross again: Mainland China.

In September 1976 I had wormed my way in through a tiny diplomatic hole in the Bamboo Curtain at what proved to be a strategic turning point in Mainland China's history. In the intervening years, that hole had expanded into an ever-widening gap. This, I firmly believe, was the result of many Christians' focused and informed prayer.

Under Deng Shao Ping's leadership, China's policy towards the West had slowly but surely changed. Realizing the need for foreign expertise and technology to bring China up to speed with the rest of the world, the Bamboo Curtain had gradually lifted to admit foreigners. There was a call for Western technicians to build factories and teachers to train Chinese students. Scientists, engineers as well as French and English teachers were in heavy demand. While missionaries were still officially banned, many Christians used these tent-making activities as a means of legitimately getting into the nation. New hotels were also erected and older ones modernized as an influx of tourists took advantage of China's new open-door policy. The Chinese Government tolerated this surge of curious "sight-seers" as they brought in much-needed income.

As the veil of secrecy lifted, details filtered through about a vast network of underground churches. Even during Mao Tse Tung's oppressive regime, these had evidently been functioning and expanding. Figures were hard to confirm, but it was estimated that between 50 million and 100 million people belonged to this non-conformist house-church network.

In mid-1980, while I was visiting Hong Kong, I decided to make an impromptu return trip to Mainland China. It had now been four years since my initial two-week visit. I no longer needed a diplomatic invitation. Instead I went into Hong Kong's China Travel Bureau and in less than an hour came out with my passport stamped with another blue and red entry visa. The next day I took the hydrofoil to Guangzhou. This time there was no tour guide tagging my every movement or a tightly monitored schedule that needed to be officially approved. Unlike my earlier trip, I was free to wander the streets of Guangzhou.

I was astounded at the changes that had taken place in just four intervening years. Color had been reintroduced into China. Gone were the monotonous, blue, baggy Mao uniforms. People were dressed in Western style, in varied colorful attire. While communist propaganda posters still dominated the landscape, the huge portraits of Mao had long been erased. Everywhere there was evidence of emerging capitalism. Set up along the roadside were privately operated stalls displaying a variety of household items and electrical equipment that before had been unprocurable.

Sunday morning, I decided to seek out the twin-spire church. As I mounted the stone steps and walked through the door, instead of a bare, unfurnished interior, I was greeted by smiling faces of Chinese believers who openly stretched out their hands to welcome me, a European. What a contrast to the rough, brutal treatment I had last received when I came through the doors of this church!

Although persecution still remains and we continue to hear of Christians being imprisoned, persecuted and even executed for their faith, and although Bibles are still a forbidden item on China's official customs list, my heart that morning was filled with joy as I looked around that church. God had answered my prayer and those of many others. There really had been a major breakthrough!

Epilogue:
Today's Challenges

TODAY, barriers to preaching the Gospel are very different from those I encountered in the mid-1970s. The fall of the Iron Curtain has allowed unprecedented freedom not only to distribute Christian literature and preach the Gospel within the former Soviet Union and other Eastern European countries, but also to do it over public television. No longer do we need to smuggle Bibles into Russia. These days, I am placing orders for tons of Bibles to be printed on local presses within that nation. In fact the very pages of this book have been printed there. Recently I organized a container filled with Christian literature to be shipped on the Trans Siberian railroad.

When the Russian ice hockey team came to play in the Swiss capital of Bern, I did not have to stealthily place Gospel portions on the stadium seats as I did when the Chinese football team visited Africa. The hockey players left loaded with armfuls of Bibles which I had personally presented to them and which they readily received. Twenty years ago, I stood in Red Square in Moscow for a May Day parade, holding a bundle of clandestine Bibles I had smuggled in. Communist posters, arrogantly blaspheming God and promoting anti-Christian ideals, plastered the walls. Not long ago, I stood in that same spot. Strung across one of the streets leading into Red Square was a banner which boldly declared, *Jesus is risen!* Yes, he truly is risen in Russia today.

Under communist rule in Eastern Europe, foreigners were often prohibited from preaching. Frequently when I spoke in a church, I did it secretly using the same veiled greetings I used when addressing the congregation in Sofia, Bulgaria. A short while ago, we preached openly to hundreds gathered in the central square of the Polish city, Lublin, and were able to use a public address system to more effectively broadcast our message. We had already packed away our gear and were sitting in the van ready to return to our hotel when a woman came running and urgently tapped on the window. "Tell me, what I have to do to accept Christ into my heart?" she asked. In the past, such open response would have been unthinkable. That night a television camera crew visited us at our hotel. They wanted us to give a repeat Gospel presentation in the square that they would film and air on Poland's nationwide television!

Recently I strolled down the streets of Almaty, capital of the former Soviet state of Kazakhstan, with a local pastor. As we walked, he pointed to a stadium where a few months earlier he had conducted an evangelistic campaign attended by around 50,000. He also operates a Bible school with 500 students. I had the privilege, through our ministry of GLIFA,[12] of supplying not only these students, but also the local Christian bookstore, with a container load of suitable Russian-language teaching books. These days we no longer have to smuggle small quantities of Bibles hidden in vehicles, but are sending in millions of pieces of literature in truckloads and containers. Whereas 20 years ago we carefully covered our tracks and met contacts in the dark, today I have declared the Gospel openly on nationwide television in Eastern Europe.

Zanzibar, the spice island where I sweated through the night to secretly distribute bags of Christian literature, still exudes the same aroma of cloves. The paint continues to peel off the buildings, but spiritually the island has been transformed. These days enthusiastic Christians are openly evangelizing, and we have been able to supply literature to the Christian bookstore. On a return visit to the island, I received an invitation to preach a series of meetings in the same cathedral where the priest had so scornfully thrown our literature on the pew, and from where Simon Malya and I had slunk quietly away,

[12] Good Literature For All.

deliberately keeping our identities undisclosed.

Doors that were once tightly closed to the Gospel have miraculously opened, and we have had opportunity to preach Christ in nations where 30 years ago we would not have dreamed it was possible. During our first SOE in Salisbury, when the South African student Logi told me he believed God had shown him he would visit Ethiopia, I did not believe him. I knew that humanly speaking there was no way such a vision could be fulfilled. Following the school, Logi went on to become a successful businessman. His love for missions, however, never dimmed. In the course of his business, he visited a number of countries; but because of South Africa's apartheid policy, the doors of Ethiopia remained tightly closed. Then Nelson Mandela took over the reins, and for the first time countries began opening their doors, to South Africa including Ethiopia.

A short while ago Logi visited Ethiopia on a business trip. While he was in his hotel room, he had an unusual encounter. He was visited by an angel who reminded him that this was more than a business trip. It was a fulfillment of a 30-year-old promise that some day he, as a South African, would break through the seemingly impenetrable political barrier and visit what for him had been a forbidden nation. Today, we are witnessing man's barriers to the preaching of the Gospel tumble. Communist headquarters have been turned into Bible schools and the doors of countries, where it was forbidden to even utter the name of Christ, have swung wide open.

But many of the old barriers still remain. Islam is on the march with increasing force around the world, and the Muslim resistance to the Gospel is as strong as ever. In Afghanistan, the extreme fundamental Taliban have not only veiled their women and confined them to their homes, but have also blacked out windows to prevent them from any visual contact with the outside world.

In contrast, there are Muslim countries where the Gospel is breaking through. In Morocco, the *Jesus Film* was recently shown to the Berber people. It was the first film to be translated into one of their languages. The movie was shown in mosques. It was so well received that, as a result of public pressure, it was aired on national television. Such a remarkable breakthrough now needs to be consolidated with an effective follow-up program of personal evangelism. Where are those who are willing to make the sacrifices necessary to see these people won for Christ?

Recently I traveled on the famous Karakoram highway in Pakistan to the highest border post on our planet, on the boundary between Pakistan and China. My purpose was to visit the Uighur[13] people in China—a Muslim minority numbering several million. Here Bibles are still forbidden. As I walked through the streets of the capital city, Urumchi, and looked into the faces of these unreached Muslims, I could not help but wonder: where are the daring young people of today who are willing to take the risks to bring such people the spiritual sustenance they so desperately need? Indeed, YWAMers have gone into this almost inaccessible region even as the Third Millennium approaches.

While many of the old barriers remain, new and different obstacles have also been erected to prevent the penetration of God's word. Typical of some of the challenges confronting today's crop of YWAMers is the outreach into the slums of Brazil. Most Christians in Brazil are afraid to enter these dens of iniquity where communities of between 10,000 and 100,000 people live in an atmosphere of murder, rape, drug trafficking and frequent gun battles. On completing his YWAM DTS[14] in Rio de Janeiro, however, Brazilian-born Pedro headed for the favella[15] of Borel with a backpack and a goal to start the Favella Ministries for YWAM. Although the barriers to the success of his mission were great, Pedro persevered and today the YWAM ministry in Borel has become an integral part of community life.

Recently a group of Borel YWAMers were visiting a church outside the slum. They told the congregation about the health clinic they operate. They explained their involvement with the youth and how they teach them art and crafts as an alternative source of income from crime and drug trafficking. The people listened enthralled. They were excited to learn how these young people were having the opportunity to influence children of the next generation through their preschool program. Here for the

---

[13] Pronounced Weegar.   [14] Discipleship Training School.
[15] Favella, Brazilian for slum.

first time, children of the favella were being presented with an alternative lifestyle and given a chance to break out of the inevitable cycle of drug trafficking and murder. Following their presentation, the congregation enthusiastically prayed for the team and asked God's blessing on their work.

After the service, a member graciously drove the team back in the church van. But instead of taking them up to the YWAM base, the driver dropped them at the bottom of the hill on the outskirts of Borel. He barely gave them time to shut the door before, stomping his foot on the accelerator, he beat a hasty retreat. It was only a two-minute drive to the Borel headquarters from where he had dropped them off. But it was one past prostitutes and rifle-toting drug traffickers and one which he, like many others, was unwilling to brave, particularly at night.

How many of us are like the members of that Brazilian congregation? We listen enthralled as we hear testimonies of how others have braved the rigors of opposition and broken through man's erected barriers to the Gospel, but we are reluctant to step out ourselves.

No matter how strong their atheistic resistance, eventually every civilization, nation and community will yield, and there will be representatives from every people group around God's throne. But for this to be accomplished, we need to be willing to persist in our penetration of the Gospel. At the time we first began to intercede for Albania, its national leaders were boasting that they led the only truly atheistic nation in the world. Not long ago in the Albanian capital of Tirana, I attended a public screening of the *Jesus Film*. In the next few days, a team of us were taken by helicopter into a number of isolated hamlets. There, along with several tons of food and clothing, we distributed thousands of pieces of Christian literature. In every village, the inhabitants warmly welcomed us and eagerly accepted everything we had to give them, including our Bibles and tracts. That Sunday, we attended a church service in Tirana that was packed with people eager to hear God's Word. What a contrast to the trip Reona made to this nation where the gift of a single Gospel nearly caused her execution.

Regardless of the nature of the obstacle, be it spiritual, political or social, the same principle remains true today as in the past. We need to trust God, be obedient and answer his call. If necessary, we need to be willing to forego our own freedom even if it means laying down our lives.

In the aftermath of the Cold War, we live in a world where the pools of ethnic turmoil and strife are being stirred as never before. There are places where refugees are fleeing for their lives in the dead of winter, leaving homes to be looted and destroyed by enemy soldiers. They have no place to go, no village to return to and neighboring nations are reluctant to take them in. They need our help. It may be dangerous. But today as never before, we have opportunity to reach out to these desperate people with a two-handed Gospel. Right now, trailblazers are needed to trek into limited-access nations with medical and school supplies, clothing and food, along with the spiritual sustenance of the Scriptures. Pioneers are required to teach English as a second language in countries where missionaries are still not welcome. Businessmen are needed to meet financial needs, while skilled technicians, engineers, scientists, builders and farm experts all have a place where they can serve. Nations in turmoil are God's opportunity for evangelism.

Despite the wonderful move of God we are witnessing, over half the world still has not heard the Gospel. Those nations where Islam, Hinduism and Buddhism still dominate, present a formidable barrier to the penetration of the Gospel. There are many frontiers of resistance to be broken. But while the challenge is real, the task of breaking through is not impossible

When I joined YWAM in the early 1970s, there were barely a dozen of us. The chances of us significantly impacting world evangelization seemed impossible. Today, YWAM has over 10,000 full-time staff, and every year over 15,000 students are being trained in over 100 schools. There are also tens of thousands participating in short-term outreaches.

Through my own ministry GLIFA, I have seen 200 tons of Christian literature transported in container loads to book-starved nations around the world. These books have impacted the lives of millions. The task is not easy. Every time we attempt to ship literature, we sense Satan's onslaught. We face customs restrictions, pilfering and dishonesty, and there is the constant need for funds. But where God has called us to a task, he always gives us the ability to perform it. All he is looking for are willing volunteers, ordinary people like you and me who are prepared to be the answer to our own prayers. *Lord, send laborers into the field; and here I am, Lord, send me.*

As I have attempted to demonstrate throughout the pages of this book, there is no barrier too lofty to keep God's Word out. The opposition will vary. It may be laws that governments have passed. It may be walls of tradition that have been erected by the fearful, and consolidated through religious habit. As we discovered in Uganda, the opposition may be demonically inspired. Resistance may be the result of hearts hardened through centuries of social and cultural conditioning. But if we are faithful to obey God's direction in our lives, no barrier, no matter how resistant or seemingly impassable, can withstand us. As Paul declared when writing to the Corinthians, God has given us *divine power to demolish strongholds, arguments and every pretension that sets itself up against the knowledge of God.*[16] With this in mind, we can push forward with confidence knowing that nothing can withstand our attempts to take God's Good News of salvation into every nook and cranny of this world. We have the ability to invade every people group, to overthrow every false religion and to cross every social or intellectual barrier. It may take time to achieve and require great persistence on our part. But if we push forward and do not give up, the task will be accomplished. There will be a breakthrough!

[16] 2 Corinthians 10:4,5.

For information on GLIFA (Good Literature For All), write to:

GLIFA
3704–Krattigen
Switzerland

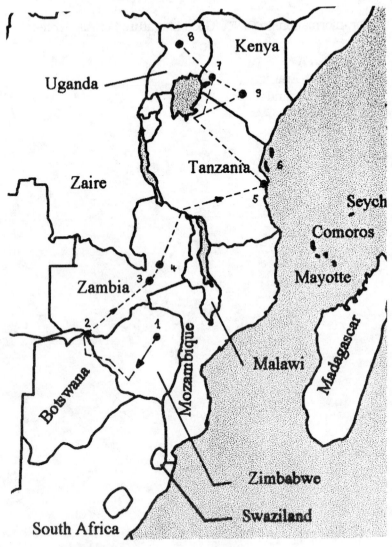

1 Harare/Salisbury	4 Chitambo	7 Kisumu
2 River Zambezi	5 Dar es Salaam	8 Soroti
3 Serenje	6 Zanzibar	9 Nairobi